The Aftermath of Feminism

The Aftermath of Feminism

Gender, Culture and Social Change

Angela McRobbie

Los Angeles • London • New Delhi • Singapore • Washington DC

First published 2009

Apart from any fair dealing for the purposes of research or
private study, or criticism or review, as permitted under the
Copyright, Designs and Patents Act, 1988, this publication
may be reproduced, stored or transmitted in any form, or
by any means, only with the prior permission in writing of
the publishers, or in the case of reprographic reproduction, in
accordance with the terms of licences issued by the Copyright
Licensing Agency. Enquiries concerning reproduction outside
those terms should be sent to the publishers.

SAGE Publications Ltd
1 Oliver's Yard
55 City Road
London EC1Y 1SP

SAGE Publications Inc.
2455 Teller Road
Thousand Oaks, California 91320

SAGE Publications India Pvt Ltd
B 1/I 1 Mohan Cooperative Industrial Area
Mathura Road
New Delhi 110 044

SAGE Publications Asia-Pacific Pte Ltd
3 Church Street
#10-04 Samsung Hub
Singapore 049483

British Library Cataloguing in Publication data

A catalogue record for this book is available
from the British Library

ISBN 978-0-7619-7061-3
ISBN 978-0-7619-7062-0

Library of Congress Control Number: 2008920955

Typeset by C&M Digitals (P) Ltd., Chennai, India
Printed and bound by CPI Group (UK) Ltd, Croydon, CR0 4YY
Printed on paper from sustainable resources

FSC
www.fsc.org
MIX
Paper from
responsible sources
FSC® C013604

CONTENTS

ACKNOWLEDGEMENTS

There are many people who have helped me complete this book, and I would like to start by thanking those who have invited me to present early versions of the work, and who have then, along with others present at these lectures, provided me with such stimulating feedback. These includes Sarah Banet-Weiser at the University of Southern California, Toby Miller at University of California Riverside, Ros Gill formely at the London School of Economics (ESRC New Femininities Programme), Sabine Hark at the Technische Universität, Berlin, Margie Wetherell and Tony Bennett both at the Open University (ESRC Identities Programme, and CRESC Project), Roisin Flood at Essex University, and Lidia Curti, Iain Chambers and Tiziana Terranova at the Universita Di Napoli 'L'Orientale'. I would also like to offer warmest thanks to my colleagues at Goldsmiths, University of London, especially those who have patiently read drafts and given me their time with great generosity, these are Mariam Fraser, Irit Rogoff, Lisa Adkins, Sara Ahmed, Lisa Blackman, Janet Harbord, Nick Couldry, Joanna Zylinska and Natalie Fenton. For intellectual friendship and support I am also grateful to Sarah Thornton, Denise Riley, Paul Gilroy, Vron Ware, Sean Nixon, Paul Du Gay, Mo White, Leslie W. Rabine, Judith Halberstam, Lawrence Grossberg, Charlotte Brunsdon, Lucy Bland, Monika Savier in Spoleto, and Marion Von Osten in Berlin. I would also like to thank Stuart Hall and Judith Butler for their wonderful body of writing which always inspires me.

INTRODUCTION: IN EXCHANGE FOR FEMINISM

This book examines a social and cultural landscape which could be called post-feminist if, by that term, one means a situation which is marked by a new kind of anti-feminist sentiment which is different from simply being a question of backlash against the seeming gains made by feminist activities and campaigns in an earlier period, i.e. the 1970s and 1980s. I argue that something quite unexpected has happened. Elements of feminism have been taken into account, and have been absolutely incorporated into political and institutional life. Drawing on a vocabulary that includes words like 'empowerment' and 'choice', these elements are then converted into a much more individualistic discourse, and they are deployed in this new guise, particularly in media and popular culture, but also by agencies of the state, as a kind of substitute for feminism. These new and seemingly 'modern' ideas about women and especially young women are then disseminated more aggressively, so as to ensure that a new women's movement will not re-emerge. 'Feminism' is instrumentalised, it is brought forward and claimed by Western governments, as a signal to the rest of the world that this is a key part of what freedom now means. Freedom is revitalised and brought up-to-date with this *faux*-feminism. The boundaries between the West and the rest can, as a result, be more specifically coded in terms of gender, and the granting of sexual freedoms. If this sounds like a conspiracy thesis, then one of the tasks I must set myself in this book is to demonstrate how this takes place at ground level, and how the consent and participation of young women is sought, and seemingly secured, in a multiplicity of ways that defy the notion of a centralised power in charge of the demise of feminism, in such a way that it will never again rise from the ashes. Granted, at one level, this is done through active vilification and negation conducted mostly at the cultural level, which makes feminism quite unpalatable to younger women (the words repulsive or disgusting are often used). A kind of hideous spectre of what feminism once was is conjured up, a monstrous ugliness which would send shudders of horror down the spines of young women today, as a kind of deterrent. But this is only one side of the equation, and the abandonment of feminism, for the sake of what Judith Butler would call intelligibility as a woman, is amply rewarded with the promise of freedom and independence, most apparent through wage-earning capacity, which also functions symbolically, as a mark of respectability, citizenship and entitlement. There is a kind of exchange, and also a process of displacement and substitution going on here. The young woman is offered a notional form of equality, concretised in education and employment, and through participation in consumer culture and civil society, in place of what a reinvented feminist politics might have to offer. If this seems fanciful, or even excessively vague, it is clearly my task in this book to make a coherent case for this as a kind of settlement, as Stuart Hall might call it, or as a new form of sexual contract. Another simple way of putting this is to say that women constitute half of the world's population and their subordination and experience of inequality, though changed, remains unequivocal and substantial. The idea of a global, through highly differentiated feminist politics would indeed be a considerable challenge to the current global and still patriarchal system of economic power and domination. Self-declared feminists have always been small in number, but their principles and ideas and beliefs and commitments have flowed out into and across the everyday world of women and girls in different countries across the world. It has been clear that this is, or was, a self-organised politics, taking place from the ground up, a kind of disputatious and contentious force, especially in matters of sexuality and family life, and this small force for change nevertheless has had enormous potential to create disruption and to bring about change. At the same time what feminism actually means varies, literally, from one self-declared feminist to the next, but this does not reduce its field of potential influence, quite the opposite. So it is this potential which I argue is the source of anxiety, concern and pre-emptive action, on the part of those bodies and institutions and organisations which do not wish to see established power and gender hierarchies undermined. I argue in this book that for this potential to be re-awakened and realised, we must understand fully the forces which are opposed to such a realisation, especially since they now take the guise of modern and enlightened 'gender aware' forms of governmentality.

This book also marks some changes in my own writing, and there is an element of self-critique. Some years ago I subscribed to a way of thinking which was influenced by the work of de Certeau, which sought to give value and meaning to the subversive strategies, the ways of 'making do' which ordinary, often seriously disadvantaged people took part in, and which became, as a result, vernacular features of resistance and opposition, visible within and across the landscapes of everyday life (de Certeau 1984). However, when it transpired that this kind of argument could so easily be rolled out, in a 'cultural populist' vein, and end up being a defence of women's capacities to turn around or subvert the world of consumer culture in which they were invested, for possibly subversive purposes, many alarm bells began to ring. When feminist cultural studies pursued this pathway, a concern to understand dynamics of power and constraint gave way to celebratory connections with the ordinary women, or indeed girls, who created their own, now seemingly autonomous pleasures and rituals of enjoyable femininity from the goods made available by consumer culture (e.g. television programmes like *Sex and the City*). If this could be done with what capitalism made available, then there seemed to be no real reason to challenge the principles upon which capitalism was based. Just how oppositional were these seemingly subversive practices? How far did they reach? What value did they deliver to women in the context of the relations of power and powerlessness within which they still found themselves inscribed? How did they articulate with other activities beyond the interface with popular culture? My rising discomfort encompassed a number of issues. Does capitalism actually give women more or less what they want, if indeed it provides them with such cheap and available narrative pleasures, in the form of popular entertainment, which also now incorporate something like a feminist agenda in their plots and story lines? What need might there be for a feminist politics at all, if women could simply subvert the meanings of the goods and the values of the dominant cultural world around them? Would this mean a suspension of the critique of capitalism, that has always been such a defining feature of the tradition of socialist–feminist scholarship? This work in media and cultural studies was also far removed from the earlier feminist psychoanalytically-inspired work, like that of Cora Kaplan which, for example, examined in depth the complexity of being a feminist reader troubled and intrigued by the fact that she found great pleasure in a conservative genre of popular romances, such as *The Thorn Birds* (Kaplan 1986). By the turn of the century some of the strands in feminist media and cultural studies which were optimistic about the power of popular feminism ran into difficulties when this gave way, to something more aggressive, the mainstreaming of pornography, for example. While many feminists, including myself, were never part of the pro-censorship and anti-pornography campaigning back in the 1970s and 1980s, there was nevertheless disquiet on my own part when confronted with new issues such as the trend for pole-dancing being promoted as yet another form of women's empowerment. It is not as though some puritanical streak buried inside myself surfaces in reaction to this kind of phenomenon, it is simply noticeable how little serious scholarly debate there is about what widespread participation in sex entertainment by women means for the now out-of-date feminist perspectives on pornography and the sex industry (McRobbie 2008).

Through the 1990s there seemed to be no longer a theory of sexual power in contemporary feminist media and cultural studies. Little attention was being paid to the complex ways in which women were being increasingly invited, by the forces of consumer culture that were now thoroughly tuned into, and able to adopt a feminist voice, to pursue new freedoms including sexual pleasure, as a kind of entitlement that was now being granted. Was it the case that some sort of rapprochement with capitalism had taken place, with the demise of socialism, and with the development of what was called for a short time, 'third way' politics? Or had the appetite for critique somehow faded? I did not find a rehearsal of such a political shift inside feminist media and cultural studies from the early 1990s onwards. And if a conversation was taking place about how to align a new left-feminist social democratic politics in relation to changes in global political culture, it was not happening, as far as I could see, within this particular feminist academic field. For more forceful and socially engaged critique, one increasingly had to look to debates about feminism and the micropolitics of becoming, in the work of feminist philosophers like Rosi Braidotti and Claire Colebrook, or to postcolonial feminist theory (Spivak and Ahmed) or to the psycho-social examination of gender and power found in Butler's writing. Meanwhile queer theory, of course, pushed ahead during this time, producing marvellously rich work, as did the new Deleuzian-influenced sociology of the body. (But in some ways, with the exception of writers such as Gayatri Chakravorty Spivak, Judith Butler and Wendy Brown, whose work I draw on in this book, the whole question of leftwing politics and the impact its current state of crisis, or indeed its demise, has had for feminism, was left to the side.) Feminist media studies had never fully engaged with psychoanalysis and this remained, in my mind, a deficit. It had promised however, by means of the interest in audiences and reception, to develop a full-blown cultural and media anthropology of how women participated in everyday life, but somehow the energy for this as an undertaking seemed to dissipate. Instead attention to everyday life was replaced by a proliferation of fan-based studies. In the light of what seemed like a fading away of feminist cultural studies, several feminist scholars took flight and de-camped to the fields of television and film studies, often embarking on important historical work in what was then to become a thriving area of new scholarship. It is only very recently that there has been a more forceful and critical engagement with the world of women's media and feminine genres, connecting anti-feminist elements with the resurgent values of neo-liberal political culture (see the work of Gill 2006).

Perhaps at this point I need to write myself into this narrative, since so much of the contents of this current book marks a revision of some of my own old ways, and points in the direction of an analysis of new constellations of gender power. I should address some of my misjudgements, for example, writing about women's and girls' magazines in the 1990s, I attributed too much hope in the capacity of the world of women's magazines, to take up and maintain a commitment to feminist issues, encapsulating a kind of popular feminism. I was over-enthusiastic about the impact the recruitment of feminist-influenced graduates might have on the editorial policies of young women's magazines, and I did not fully engage with the way in which the battle for circulation figures could see an editor sacked for displeasing a company with a lucrative advertising contract. Nor did I take into account the need for magazines to be constantly re-inventing themselves, which of course means that a strong feminist voice might well only last for as long as a couple of fashion seasons and then be discarded in favour of a new counter-trend. I found myself acknowledging, rather than confronting, the generic features of the magazine format, which seemed to be set in stone, the centrality of the fashion-and-beauty complex, for example, the dominant heterosexuality, the hermetically sealed world of feminine escapist pleasures, and in this respect I was perhaps myself complicit, without abandoning a feminist perspective, in accommodating to the genre itself, and reducing the level and intensity of critique, in favour of a kind of compromise position which aimed at having the staple contents co-exist with a strong but nevertheless popular feminist voice. (Doubtless this position on my own part was connected with my encouragement to students who were keen to find work in this world. Now I can see that this interface with the magazine industry and these forms of feminist 'knowledge transfer' need to be better understood, and subjected to scholarly scrutiny within a critical culture industry perspective). In actuality the idea of feminist content disappeared and was replaced by aggressive individualism, by a hedonistic female phallicism in the field of sexuality, and by obsession with consumer culture which in this current book I see as playing a vital role in the undoing of feminism. It is arguably the case that the self-definition as decisively post-feminist gave to the world of young women's magazines a new lease of life, as though they became unburdened through this transition.

It is perhaps relevant to note at this point also, that I was also over-optimistic about the election of the New Labour government in 1997, and in my assumption that Tony Blair would support women's issues and would engage with feminists involved in policy issues and in campaigning. In the early days of the New Labour government I even briefly held out some hope for the so-called third way agenda, never imagining that this government would prove to be hostile to feminists, and that it would in effect seek to reverse, or undo feminism, substituting for it the promise of seemingly more modern freedoms, along with ideas like the work-life balance, while at the same time introducing a kind of swaggering, resurgent patriarchalism, the political equivalent of the world of the lads' mags, where women had little choice but to fall into line, or risk the Siberia of feminism (McRobbie 2000a).

Feminist retrieval and renewal

There is some work of retrieval in the chapters that follow. In particular I look back to the feminist psychoanalytical writing on film and on the fashion image of the 1980s and I seek to reinstate its importance in understanding the mechanisms of identification and desire which come into play in the processes of consuming images. This body of work seems to have been lost from current discussion, and its absence marks a weakness in some of the most interesting work about how, for example, young girls look at images of themselves and of models and celebrities in magazines. Recent Deleuzian work rejects the rigidities of desire formulated within Freudian psychoanalysis, but just by referring back to the writing of, for example, Leslie Rabine or Diana Fuss, we can see how invaluable it was for understanding the technologies at play in the composition of images which sought to mobilise both the unleashing and the containment of female desire (Fuss 1994, Rabine 1994).

The chapters that follow introduce a number of concepts which are developed in the course of the analysis which combines elements of feminist sociology with cultural studies in an attempt to map out the field of post-feminist popular and political culture, primarily but not exclusively within a UK framework. These chapters are presented as suggestive in relation to the terrain they examine, they are not based on specific fieldwork undertaken, they are neither empirical nor ethnographic. Instead they survey changes in film, television, popular culture and the world of women's magazines. They also engage with recent writing by various scholars working in this area, and in particular they draw on Judith Butler's books and essays, translating them into a sociological vocabulary that in turn can be applied to concrete social and cultural phenomena. In an earlier response to Butler's short book *Antigone's Claim* (2000a) I presented some reflections on a 'double entanglement' which referred to the way in which there was in regard to sexuality and family life, both a liberalisation on the part of the state through the granting of specific family and kinship rights and entitlements to gays and lesbians, and also a neo-liberalisation in this same terrain of sexuality, with a more punitive response being shown to those who live outside the economic unit of the two parent family (McRobbie 2003). Likewise there was the way in which feminism had achieved the status of common sense, while it was also reviled, almost hated. In this book I continue to develop these ideas, and introduce concepts designed to provide a 'complexification of backlash' through this idea of 'double entanglement'. These concepts include the 'spaces of attention' which I use to examine the spotlight effect of power, or in Deleuzian parlance the luminosities which bring young women forward, as individualised subjects, and which attribute to these young women, a range of capacities such that they can be understood as agents of change. This also marks the field of 'feminism undone'. There is a re-drafting of gender hierarchies, I claim, which has repercussions for questions of social class and race and ethnicity. The coming forward of young black or Asian women, along these individualised pathways, entails the granting of unusual, if not exceptional, and exemplary status, while elsewhere within the field of luminosities, where anti-racism is also undone, there is also a kind of 'nostalgia for whiteness' and indeed a process of cultural re-colonisation. White women in the UK increasingly live out their class positions, to re-phrase Stuart Hall, through the modality of gender and femininity. They have also become more autonomously feminised (and glamourised) in their class identity, no longer taking this status or adhering to it, from their position as wives of men, or as daughters of fathers. Black and Asian women also find themselves caught up and inscribed within this re-drafting process. They live their class identity through the modality of race as Hall argued, but their femininity also increasingly comes forward as a key factor in the more meritocratic society, such that the intersection of gender and ethnicity finds new social meaning and significance. I also refer, not to a new women's movement, but to the opposite, to a 'movement of women'. This is a key aspect of the new forms of gender power that have emerged and that seek to manage the requirements of the new global economy and the availability of a femininised workforce through producing and overseeing changes for women, young women in particular.

In Chapter 3 I provide a number of concepts for understanding post-feminist femininity, what in Foucauldian language we might refer to as technologies, each of which are made available to young women as part of a process of substitution and displacement, and each of which also appears to offer possibilities of freedom and change in the status and identity of young women today. These are first, the 'post-feminist masquerade', second, the figuration of the 'working girl', third, the 'phallic girl' and fourth, the 'global girl'. I argue these emerge as new constraining forms of gender power which operate through the granting of capacity to young women. Later in the book I draw on Bourdieu's notion of symbolic violence to examine the changing dynamics of class, race and gender which are played out through the genre of make-over television programmes, arguing that here too there is an enforced 'movement of women' for the sake of recognition and cultural citizenship. In the final chapter I continue to reflect on the movement of women through processes of educational migration, as young women from across the world flow to cities like London and to institutions of higher education to increase their qualifications. So diverse are these globalised biographies that they refute the possibility of immediate sociological understanding, while also raising a whole series of new questions about female individualisation, the new international division of labour, the role of well-educated young women and the economic rationale which underpins this form of female migration

(Beck and Beck-Gernscheim 2001). Spivak, for example, would surely see this as a capitalist mobilisation of 'global girls' in the service of the now multi-cultural corporations, and at the expense of the impoverished people who remain at the point of departure, who also lose a class of possible radical teachers, educators, doctors and others, who are lured into a kind of migration-trap (Spivak 2002). We can see then a re-configuration of young womanhood emerging through these different assemblages, indeed we might think of them as sharing a kind of kinship or sisterhood, they are part of the same extended family, all four figures interconnect with each other, the immaculately groomed young woman in masquerade, the sexy adventurous phallic girl, the (hard) working girl and her 'pleasing' global counterpart.

The chapters in this book examine what we might mean by 'complexification of backlash'. In Chapter 1 I trace a double movement which was taking place concurrently in the early 1990s, both inside the feminist academy and outside in the world of popular culture. In the academy, for good theoretical reasons, feminism dismantles itself, by asking questions about foundationalism and universalism, and about representational claims. It queries for example the processes by which feminists speak on behalf of other women. Who are these other women who are the subjects of such representational claims? What hierarchies underpin certain feminist agendas? At the same time in popular culture there is also an undoing or dismantling of feminism, not in favour of re-traditionalisation, women are not being pushed back into the home, but instead there is a process which says feminism is no longer needed, it is now common sense, and as such it is something young women can do without. I use the film Bridget Jones's Diary to develop the argument about feminism taken into account. Feminism has a ghostly existence in the film, Bridget has it to thank for, it has given her, to paraphrase Ulrich Beck, 'a life of her own', yet she is not sure that this is what she wants, i.e. to be single and childless in her early thirties, even though she pokes fun at the narrow world of the 'smug marrieds'. The prominence of wedding culture, apart from contributing to the expansion of consumer culture, rides on this tidal wave of celebratory post-feminism, as though to say, 'thank goodness, girls can be girls again, that time of dourness and censoriousness is over, and who can really object to something as light-hearted and innocuous as a 'hen party'? Who would dare to challenge the consensus that prevails in relation to the empowerment of women manifest in the ladies' night at the local pub featuring male strippers performing the 'full monty'? And since gay men and lesbians are also now invited to take part in wedding culture, there is, it seems, even less reason to inquire as to what might also be entailed in these rituals of enjoyment.

In Chapter 2 I trace a line of connection between the forces of the new right which from the start of the 1970s, mobilised against the women's movement through various actions and strategies, many of which were documented by feminists including Judith Stacey and Susan Faludi in the US and Bea Campbell in the UK, and the more recent practices which operate through incorporation and instrumentalisation. I make use of Hall's theory of articulation but put this into reverse gear, and through the idea of disarticulation I show how cross-border solidarities, for example, between black and white feminist and anti-racist struggles, between single mothers and lesbians and gay men also living outside the fold of the nuclear family, are eroded, and how feminism's 'chains of equivalence' are broken down. Disarticulation is a defining feature of the process of undoing. Feminism's wider intersections with anti-racism, with gay and lesbian politics, are written out of the kind of history which surfaces even in serious journalism, and the feminism which is then vilified and thrown backwards into a previous era, is a truncated and sclerotic anti-male and censorious version of a movement which was much more diverse and open-minded. I argue that this denigration is also increasingly directed to anti-racist and multi-cultural politics of the same period, they too are reduced to cliches of 'political correctness' and their demise is seen to usher in a new period of more enlightened and modern community politics, where righteous anger and self-organisation are replaced by a politics of role models or mentoring or assimilation and integration or through cultural leadership programmes. Black politics *per se* fades and new racialising pathologies become visible, including a 'nostalgia for whiteness'.

In Chapter 3 I disentangle some of the new technologies of young womanhood, emphasising a movement of coming forward while feminism fades away. I also stress the spectacular dimension of this visibility, or luminosity, as government and its willing helpers, the fashion-and-beauty complex take young women by the hand, and lead them towards a modern kind of freedom. There is a great deal of drama in this process of coming forward, young women are endowed with capacity and are as a result expected to pursue specific life pathways which require participation in the workforce, which in turn permits full immersion in consumer culture. This new sexual contract rests on economic and cultural activity, and consumer citizenship at the expense of a newly defined feminist politics.

In Chapter 4 I focus more directly on feminine pathology and on its prominence, indeed its normalisation, in contemporary culture. Young woman are increasingly 'made up' in accordance with a horizon of expectation within which various disorders become naturalised, and even seen as the high price of freedom. I argue that these illegible rages and pathologies come close to confronting the limits of Butler's heterosexual matrix, but they are acted upon and constrained within this grid of sexual normativity. Better to be still recognisably positioned as an, albeit, ill anorexic girl within a properly oedipal family, than to be interrogating and breaking out of such psycho-social arrangements. In Chapter Five I examine the 'movement of women' which is undertaken within the genre of make-over television programmes. What I argue is that there is a specific entanglement of class and gender relations underpinning these programmes, the desirable outcome of which is a more glamourised and individualised feminine subjectivity. The woman who is made-over embodies the values of the new, aspirational lower middle-class, in which she has a more autonomously feminine identity.

In the final chapter I engage critically with some of those strands in contemporary feminism which are affirmative and optimistic about the progress that has been made. These include 'gender mainstreaming', third wave feminism, and I also find some sociological grounds for being cautious in regard to Rosi Braidotti's philosophy of feminist affirmation. I end the book by reflecting on my own feminist classroom, a space where one might imagine a strong case for feminist affirmation could be made. But reality is always more unpredictable. It is a challenge and also a privilege to be teaching in an environment which is now populated by young women (and young men) from literally all over the world. This process of what appears to be educational migration, since so many of these young women hope to find jobs in London or else in some other global city, raises many questions about young women's role in the new international division of labour, and about what is entailed in this movement, about the strains on family and kinship, on the seeming postponement of marriage, and the postponement of having children. These young women also engage with the kinds of feminist issues that are the subject of this book, directly and indirectly. They are both inside and outside of them. And it is as though the forces which propel them to find a way of moving from, let us say, Korea, or Taiwan or Albania or Indonesia to London, and in so doing avoid or put on hold, some of the expectations and constraints otherwise imposed on them, produces an openness to debates about power and sexuality, gender and desire. Lastly I should emphasise that despite the many references to films and television, magazines and popular culture, this book is fundamentally sociological. It is concerned to dissect the management of social change and the forms of gender power which operate within an illusion of positivity and progress while locking young women into 'new–old' dependences and anxieties.

1

POST-FEMINISM AND POPULAR CULTURE: BRIDGET JONES AND THE NEW GENDER REGIME

Introduction: complexification of backlash?

This chapter presents a series of possible conceptual frames for engaging with what, in this book, I refer to as post-feminism. Broadly I envisage this as a process by which feminist gains of the 1970s and 1980s are actively and relentlessly undermined. (What exactly is meant by the words 'feminist gains' is examined throughout the book.) I propose that through an array of machinations, elements of contemporary popular culture are perniciously effective in regard to this undoing of feminism, while simultaneously appearing to be engaging in a well-informed and even well-intended response to feminism. I then propose that this undoing, which can be perceived in the broad cultural field, is compounded, unexpectedly perhaps, in those sociological theories, including the work of Giddens and Beck, which address themselves to aspects of gender and social change, but as though feminist thought and years of women's struggles had no role to play in these transformations (and this is returned to in Chapter 2 and briefly in Chapter 3). It is also suggested in the pages that follow, that by means of the tropes of freedom and choice which are now inextricably connected with the category of young women, feminism is decisively aged and made to seem redundant. Feminism is cast into the shadows, where at best it can expect to have some afterlife, where it might be regarded ambivalently by those young women who must, in more public venues, stake a distance from it, for the sake of social and sexual recognition. I propose here a complexification of the backlash thesis (which, again, will be examined in more detail in the chapter that follows).

Faludi refers to a concerted, conservative response to challenge the achievements of feminism (Faludi 1992). Her work is important because, like that of Stacey and others, it charts anti-feminist interventions that are coterminous with feminism more or less as it happens (Stacey 1985/1986).

My argument is rather different, which is that post-feminism positively draws on and invokes feminism as that which can be taken into account, to suggest that equality is achieved, in order to install a whole repertoire of new meanings which emphasise that it is no longer needed, it is a spent force. This was very apparent in the (UK) *Independent* newspaper column *Bridget Jones's Diary*,[1] then in the fantastically successful book and the films which followed. The infectious girlishness of Bridget Jones produces a generational logic which is distinctly post-feminist. Despite feminism, Bridget wants to pursue dreams of romance, find a suitable husband, get married and have children. What she fears most is ending up as a 'spinster'. Bridget is a girl who is 'once again' reassuringly feminine. She is not particularly career-minded, even though she knows she should be. She makes schoolgirl errors in her publishing house, not knowing that the literary critic F. R. Leavis is long dead. She delivers an incoherent speech at a book launch, her head seems to be full of frivolous thoughts, though she is clever and witty in her own feminine way. But most of all she is desperate to find the right man. The film celebrates a kind of scatterbrain and endearing femininity, as though it is something that has been lost. Thank goodness, the film seems to be saying, that old-fashioned femininity can be retrieved. Post-feminism in this context seems to mean gently chiding the feminist past, while also retrieving and reinstating some palatable elements, in this case sexual freedom, the right to drink, smoke, have fun in the city, and be economically independent.[2]

Broadly I am arguing that for feminism to be 'taken into account' it has to be understood as having already passed away. The pushing away which underpins the passing away is very much the subject of this book. This is a movement detectable across popular culture, a site where 'power ... is remade at various junctures within everyday life, (constituting) our tenuous sense of common sense' (Butler, Laclau and Zizek 2000: 14). Some fleeting comments in Judith Butler's short book *Antigone's Claim* suggest to me that post-feminism can be explored through what I would describe as a 'double entanglement' (Butler 2000a). This comprises the co-existence of neo-conservative values in relation to gender, sexuality and family life (for example George Bush supporting the campaign to encourage chastity among young people, and in March 2004 declaring that civilisation itself depends on traditional marriage), with processes of liberalisation in regard to choice and diversity in domestic, sexual and kinship relations (for example gay couples now able to adopt, foster or have their own children by whatever means, and in the UK at least, full rights to civil partnerships). It also encompasses the existence of feminism as at some level transformed into a form of Gramscian common sense, while also fiercely repudiated, indeed almost hated (McRobbie 2003). The 'taken into accountness' permits all the more thorough dismantling of feminist politics and the discrediting of the occasionally voiced need for its renewal.

Feminism dismantling itself

The impact of this double entanglement which is manifest in popular and political culture, coincides however, with feminism in the academy finding it necessary to dismantle itself. For the sake of periodisation we could say that 1990 marks a turning point, the moment of definitive self-critique in feminist theory. At this time the representational claims of second wave feminism come to be fully interrogated by post-colonialist feminists like Spivak, Trinh and Mohanty among others, and by feminist theorists like Butler and Haraway who inaugurate the radical de-naturalising of the post-feminist body (Mohanty 1988, Spivak 1988, Trinh 1989, Butler 1990, Haraway 1991). Under the prevailing influence of Foucault, there is a shift away from feminist interest in centralised power blocks, eg the State, patriarchy, law, to more dispersed sites, events and instances of power conceptualised as flows and specific convergences and consolidations of talk, discourse, attentions. The body and also the subject come to represent a focal point for feminist interest, nowhere more so than in the work of Butler. The concept of subjectivity and the means by which cultural forms and interpellations (or dominant social processes) call women into being, produce them as subjects while ostensibly merely describing them as such, inevitably means that it is a problematic 'she', rather than an unproblematic 'we', which is indicative of a turn to what we might describe as the new feminist politics of the body (Butler 1990, 1993). In feminist cultural studies the early 1990s also marks a moment of feminist reflexivity. In her article 'Pedagogies of the Feminine' Brunsdon queried the (hitherto assumed) use value to feminist media scholarship of the binary opposition between femininity and feminism, or as she put it, the extent to which the 'housewife' or 'ordinary woman' was conceived of as the assumed subject of attention for feminism (Brunsdon 1991). Looking back we can see how heavily utilised this dualism was, and also how particular it was to gender arrangements for largely white and relatively affluent (i.e. housewifely) heterosexual women. While at the time both categories had a kind of transparency, by the late 1980s these came under scrutiny. Not only was there a homogenising force on both sides of the equation, but it also became apparent that this binary permitted a certain kind of useful, feminist, self-definition to emerge, particularly in media and cultural studies where there was an interest in the intersections of media with everyday life, through conceptualisations of the audience. In this case the audience was understood to comprise housewives who would be studied empathetically by feminists. The concept of the housewife in effect facilitated a certain mode of feminist inquiry, but we were at the time inattentive to the partial and exclusive nature of this couplet.

The year 1990 also marked the moment at which the concept of popular feminism found expression. Andrea Stuart considered the wider circulation of feminist values across the landscape of popular culture, in particular magazines where quite suddenly issues which had been central to the formation of the women's movement like domestic violence, equal pay, and workplace harassment, were now addressed to a vast readership (Stuart 1990). The wider dissemination of feminist issues was also a key concern in my own writing at this time, in particular the intersection of these new representations with the daily lives of young women who, as subjects (called into being) of this now popular feminism, might then be expected to embody more emboldened (though also of course failed) identities. This gave rise to the idea of feminist success. It suggested that forms of popular mass media like magazines were in fact more open to change than had previously been thought, and this in turn gave rise to a brief tide of optimism. What could have an impact inside the academy in terms of the feminist curriculum could also have some impact beyond the academy, indeed in the commercial world. Of course no sooner is the word success written than it is queried. How could this be gauged? What might be the criteria for judging degrees of feminist success?

Female success

Admittedly there is some extravagance in my claim for feminist success. It might be more accurate to remark on the keen interest across the quality and popular media, (themselves wishing to increase their female readers and audiences) in ideas of female success. As feminist values are indeed taken on board within a range of institutions, including law, education, to an extent medicine, likewise employment and the media, high profile or newsworthy achievements of women and girls in these sectors shows the institutions to be modern and abreast with social change. This is the context then within which feminism is acknowledged and this is what I mean by feminism taken into account. The kind of feminism which is taken into account in this context is liberal, equal opportunities feminism, where elsewhere what is invoked more negatively is the radical feminism concerned with social criticism rather than with progress or improvement in the position of women in an otherwise more or less unaltered social order. But across the boundaries of different forms of feminism, the idea of feminist success has, so far, only been described sporadically (for accounts of girls' achievement in education see Arnot et al 1999 and also Harris 2004). Within media and cultural studies both Brunsdon and myself have each considered how with feminism as part of the academic curriculum, (ie canonised), then it is not surprising that it might also be countered, that is feminism must face up to the consequences of its own claims to representation and power, and not be so surprised when young women students decline the invitation to identify as a 'we' with their feminist teachers and scholars (Brunsdon 1991, McRobbie 1999a). This interface between the feminist academy and the student body has also been discussed in US feminist journals, particularly in regard to the decline of women's studies, and this is a subject I return to in the concluding chapter of this book. Back in the early 1990s (and following Butler) I saw this sense of contestation on the part of young women, and what I would call their distance from feminism as one of potential, where a lively dialogue about how feminism might develop would commence (Butler 1992, McRobbie 1994). Indeed it appeared to be in the very nature of feminism that it gave rise to dis-identification as a kind requirement for its existence. But it seems now, that this space of distance from feminism and those utterances of force-ful non-identity with feminism have consolidated into something closer to repudiation rather than ambivalence, and it is this vehemently denunciatory stance which is manifest across the field of popular gender debate. This is the cultural space of post- feminism.

In this context it requires both imagination and hopefulness to argue that the active, sustained and repetitive repudiation or repression of feminism also marks its (still fearful) presence or even longevity (as afterlife). What I mean by this is that there are different kinds of repudiation and different investments in such a stance. The more gentle denunciations of feminism co-exist however with the shrill championing of young women as a metaphor for social change on the pages of the right wing press in the UK, in particular the *Daily Mail*.[3] This anti-feminist endorsement of female individualisation is embodied in the figure of the ambitious 'TV blonde' (McRobbie 1999b). These so-called 'A1' girls are glamorous high-achievers destined for Oxford or Cambridge and are usually pictured clutching A-level examination certificates. We might say these are ideal girls, subjects *par excellence*, and also subjects of excellence. Nor are these notions of female success exclusive to the changing representations of young women in the countries of the affluent West (Spivak 1999). Young women are a good investment, they can be trusted with micro-credit, they are the privileged subjects of social change. But the terms of these great expectations on the part of governments are that young women must do without more autonomous feminist politics. What is consistent is the displacement of fem-inism as a political movement. It is this displacement which is reflected in Butler's sorrowful account of Antigone's life after death. Her shadowy, lonely existence, suggests a modality of feminist effectivity as spectral; she has to be cast out, indeed entombed, for social organisation to once again become intelligible (Butler 2000a).

Unpopular feminism

The media has become the key site for defining codes of sexual conduct. It casts judgement and establishes the rules of play. Across these many channels of communication feminism is routinely disparaged. Why is feminism so hated? Why do young women recoil in horror at the very idea of the feminist? To count as a girl today appears to require this kind of ritualistic denunciation, which in turn suggests that one strategy in the disempowering of feminism includes it being historicised and generationalised and thus easily rendered out of date. It would be far too simplistic to trace a pattern in media from popular feminism (or 'prime-time' feminism including TV programmes like *LA Law*) in the early 1990s, to niche feminism (BBC Radio 4, *Woman's Hour*, and the Women's Page of the *Guardian* newspaper), in the mid-1990s, and then to overtly unpopular feminism (from 2000 onwards), as though these charted a chronological 'great moving right show', as Stuart Hall once put it in another context (Hall 1989).

We would need a more developed conceptual schema to account for the simultaneous feminisation of popular media with this accumulation of ambivalent, fearful responses. We would certainly need to signal the seeming enfranchisement of women in the West, of all ages as audiences, active consumers of media and the many products it promotes, and by virtue of education, earning power and consumer identity, a sizeable block of target market. We would also need to be able to theorise female achievement predicated not on feminism, but on 'female individualism', on success which seems to based on the invitation to young women by various governments that they might now consider themselves free to compete in education and in work as privileged subjects of the new meritocracy. Is this then the New Deal for New Labour's modern young women; female individualisation and the new meritocracy at the expense of feminist politics?

There are various sites within popular culture where this work of undoing feminism with some subtlety becomes visible (see also Brunsdon 1991). The Wonderbra advertisement showing the model Eva Herzigova looking down admiringly at her cleavage, enhanced by the lacy pyrotechnics of the Wonderbra, was through the mid-1990s positioned in major high street locations in the UK on full size billboards. The composition of the image had such a textbook 'sexist ad' dimension (the 'male gaze' is invited and encouraged by the gaze of the model herself to look towards her breasts) that one could be forgiven for supposing some ironic familiarity with both cultural studies and with feminist critiques of advertising (Williamson 1978). It was, in a sense, taking feminism into account by showing it to be a thing of the past, by provocatively 'enacting sexism' while at the same time playing with those debates in film theory about women as the object of the gaze (Mulvey 1975/1989) and with female desire (Coward 1984, De Lauretis 1988). The picture is in *noirish* black and white and refers explicitly through its captions (from 'Hello Boys' to 'Or Are You Just Pleased To See Me?') to Hollywood and the famous lines of the actress Mae West. Here is an advertisement which plays back to its viewers well known aspects of feminist media studies, film theory and semiotics. Indeed, it almost offers (albeit crudely) the viewer or passing driver Laura Mulvey's theory of women as object of the gaze, projected as cityscape within the frame of the billboard. Also mobilised in this advertisement is the familiarity of the term political correctness, the efficacy of which resides in its warranting and unleashing such energetic reactions against the seemingly tyrannical regime of feminist puritanism. Everyone and especially young people can give a sigh of relief. Thank goodness, the image seems to suggest, it is permissable, once again, to enjoy looking at the bodies of beautiful women. At the same time, the advertisement also hopes to provoke feminist condemnation as a means of generating publicity. Thus generational differences are also produced, the younger female viewer, along with her male counterparts, educated in irony and visually literate, is not made angry by such a repertoire. She appreciates its layers of meaning, she gets the joke.

When in a TV advertisement (1998/9) supermodel Claudia Schiffer takes off her clothes as she descends a flight of stairs in a luxury mansion on her way out of the door towards her new Citreon car, a similar rhetoric is at work. This advert appears to suggest that yes, this is a self-consciously sexist ad. Feminist critiques of it are deliberately evoked. Feminism is taken into account, but only to be shown to be no longer necessary. Why? Because it now seems that there is no exploitation here, there is nothing remotely naïve about this striptease. She seems to be doing it out of choice, and for her own enjoyment. The image works on the basis of its audience knowing Claudia Schiffer to be one of the world's most famous and highly paid supermodels. Once again the shadow of disapproval is evoked (the striptease as site of female exploitation) only instantly to be dismissed as belonging to the past, to a time when feminists used to object to such imagery. To make such an objection nowadays would run the risk of ridicule. Objection is pre-empted with irony. In each of these cases a spectre of feminism is invoked so that it might be undone. For male viewers tradition is restored or as Beck puts it there is 'constructed certitude', while for the girls what is proposed is a movement beyond feminism, to a more comfortable zone where women are now free to choose for themselves (Beck 1992).

Feminism undone?

If we turn attention to some of the participatory dynamics in leisure and everyday life which see young women endorse (or else refuse to condemn) the ironic normalisation of pornography, where they indicate their approval of and desire to be pin-up girls for the centrefolds of the soft porn so-called lads' mags, where it is not at all unusual to pass young women in the street wearing T-shirts bearing phrases such as 'Porn Queen' or 'Pay To Touch' across the breasts, where in the UK at least young women quite happily attend lap-dancing clubs (perhaps as a test of their sophistication and 'cool'), and where *Cosmopolitan* magazine considers how empowering it is for young women to 'flash ' their breasts in public, we are witness to a hyper-culture of commercial sexuality, one aspect of which is the repudiation of a feminism which is invoked only to be summarily dismissed (see also Gill 2003, 2006). As a mark of a post-feminist identity, young women journalists refuse to condemn the enormous growth of lap-dancing clubs. They know of the existence of the feminist critiques and debates (or at least this is my claim) through their education, since as Shelley Budgeon describes in her study, most girls these days are 'gender aware' (Budgeon 2001). Thus the new female subject is, despite her freedom, called upon to be silent, to withhold critique in order to count as a modern sophisticated girl. Indeed this withholding of critique is a condition of her freedom. There is quietude and complicity in the manners of generationally specific notions of cool, and more precisely, an uncritical relation to dominant commercially produced sexual representations which actively invoke hostility to assumed feminist positions from the past, in order to endorse a new regime of sexual meanings based on female consent, equality, participation and pleasure.

Female individualisation

By using the term female individualisation I am drawing on the concept of individualisation which is discussed at length by sociologists including Giddens (1991), Beck (1992), Beck and Beck-Gernscheim (2001) as well as Zygmunt Bauman (2000, 2001). This work is to be distinguished from the more directly Foucauldian version found in the work of Nikolas Rose (1999a, 1999b). Although there is some shared ground between these authors, insofar as they all reflect on the expectations that individuals now avidly self-monitor and that there appears to be greater capacity on the part of individuals to plan 'a life of one's own', there are also divergences. Beck and Giddens are less concerned with the way in which power works in this new friendly guise as personal advisor, and instead emphasise the enlargement of freedom and choice, while in contrast Rose sees these modes of self government as marking out 'the shaping of being', and thus the 'inculcation of a form of life' (Rose 1999a). Bauman bewails the sheer unviability of naked individualisation as the resources of sociality (and welfare) are stripped away, leaving the individual to self-blame when success eludes him or her. (It is also possible to draw a political line between these authors, with Bauman and Rose to the left, and Giddens and Beck 'beyond left and right'.) My emphasis here is on the work of Giddens and Beck, for the very reason that it appears to speak directly to the post-feminist generation. In their writing there are only distant echoes (if that) of the feminist struggles that were required to produce the new-found freedoms of young women in the West. There is no trace whatsoever of the battles fought, of the power struggles embarked upon, or of the enduring inequities which still mark out the relations between men and women. All of this is airbrushed out of existence on the basis that, as they claim, 'emancipatory politics' has given way instead to life politics (or in Beck's terms the sub-politics of single interest groups). Both Giddens and Beck provide a sociological account of the dynamics of social change understood as 'reflexive modernisation'. The earlier period of modernisation (first modernity) created a welfare state and a set of institutions (e.g. education) which allowed people in the second modernity to become more independent and able, for example, to earn their own living. Young women are, as a result, now dis-embedded from communities where gender roles were fixed. And, as the old structures of social class fade away, and lose their grip in the context of late or second modernity, individuals are increasingly called upon to invent their own structures. They must do this internally and individualistically, so that self-monitoring practices (the diary, the life-plan, the career pathway) replace reliance on set ways and structured pathways. Self-help guides, personal advisors, lifestyle coaches and gurus and all sorts of self-improvement TV programmes provide the cultural means by which individualisation operates as a social process. As the overwhelming force of structure fades, so also, it is claimed, does the capacity for agency increase.

Individuals must now choose the kind of life they want to live. Girls must have a life-plan. They must become more reflexive in regard to every aspect of their lives, from making the right choice in marriage, to taking responsibility for their own working lives and not being dependent on a job for life or on the stable and reliable operations of a large scale bureaucracy, which in the past would have allocated its employees specific, and possibly unchanging, roles. Beck and Giddens each place a different inflection in their accounts of reflexive modernisation, but overall these arguments appear to fit directly with the kinds of scenarios and dilemmas facing the young women characters in the narratives of contemporary popular culture. There is an evasion in this writing of social and sexual divides, and of the continuing prejudice and discrimination experienced by black and Asian women. Beck and Giddens are quite inattentive to the regulative dimensions of the popular discourses of personal choice and self improvement. Choice is surely, within lifestyle culture, a modality of constraint. The individual is compelled to be the kind of subject who can make the right choices. By these means new lines and demarcations are drawn between those subjects who are judged responsive to the regime of personal responsibility, and those who fail miserably. Neither Giddens nor Beck mount a substantial critique of these power relations which work so effectively at the level of embodiment. They have no grasp that these are productive of new realms of injury and injustice.

Bridget Jones

The film *Bridget Jones's Diary* (a world-wide success) draws together many of these sociological themes. In her early 30s, living and working in London, Bridget is a free agent, single and childless and able to enjoy herself in pubs, bars and restaurants. She is the product of modernity in that she has bene-fited from those institutions (education) which have loosened the ties of tradition and community for women, making it possible for them to be dis-embedded and to re-locate to the city to earn an independent living with-out shame or danger. However this also gives rise to new anxieties. There is the fear of loneliness, the stigma of remaining single and the risks and uncer-tainties of not finding the right partner to be a father to children. In the film, the opening sequence shows Bridget in her pyjamas worrying about being alone and on the shelf. The soundtrack is *All By Myself* by Jamie McNeal and the audience laughs along with her in this moment self-doubt. We immedi-ately know that what she is thinking is 'what will it be like if I never find the right man, if I never get married?' Bridget portrays the whole spectrum of attributes associated with the self-monitoring subject, she confides in her friends, she keeps a diary, she endlessly reflects on her fluctuating weight, noting her calorie intake, she plans, plots and has projects. She is also deeply uncertain as to what the future holds for her. Despite the choices she has, there are also any number of risks of which she is regularly reminded. The risk that she might let the right man slip from under her nose, so she must always be on the lookout, prioritising this over success in the workplace. The risk that not catching a man at the right time might mean she misses the chance of having children (her biological clock is ticking). There is also the risk that, without a partner she will be isolated, marginalised from the world of happy couples.

With the burden of self-management so apparent, Bridget fantasises about very traditional forms of happiness and fulfilment. Flirting with her boss during office hours, Bridget imagines herself in a white wedding dress surrounded by bridesmaids, and the audience laughs loudly because they, like Bridget, know that this is not how young women these days are meant to think. Feminism has intervened to constrain these kinds of con-ventional desires. But it is surely a relief to escape this censorious politics and freely enjoy that which has been disapproved of, and this is what the film not only allows but absolutely encourages and enjoys. Feminism was anti-marriage and this can now to be shown to be a great mistake. Feminism is invoked, in order to be relegated to the past. But this is not simply a return to the past, there are, of course, quite dramatic differ-ences between the various female characters of current popular culture from *Bridget Jones* to the girls in *Sex and the City* and to *Ally McBeal*, and those found in girls' and women's magazines from a pre-feminist era.

These new young women are confident enough to declare their anxieties about possible failure in regard to finding a husband, they avoid any aggressive or overtly traditional men, and they brazenly enjoy their sexuality, without fear of the sexual double standard. In addition they are more than capable of earning their own living, and the degree of suffering or shame they anticipate in the absence of finding a husband is countered by sexual self confidence.

With such light entertainment as this, suffused with irony and dedicated to re-inventing highly successful women's genres of film and TV, an argument about feminism being so repudiated might seem heavy handed. Indeed *Bridget Jones's Diary* is exemplary as a women's genre film, re-invented to bring back romance in a specifically post-feminist context. Neither it, nor *Ally McBeal* nor *Sex and the City* are rabid anti-feminist tracts, instead they have taken feminism into account and implicitly or explicitly ask the question, 'what now?' There is a strong sense in all three that young women somehow want to reclaim their femininity, without stating exactly why it has been taken away from them. These young woman want to be girlish and enjoy all sorts of traditional feminine pleasures without apology, although again, quite why they might feel they have to apologise is left hanging in the air. But it seems we the audience, like they the characters, are meant to know the answer to this question because it is so obvious. Feminism, it seems, robbed women of their most treasured pleasures, i.e. romance, gossip and obsessive concerns about how to catch a husband, indeed as I write this I am reminded of being right back there in the land of *Jackie* magazine, where I myself implicitly scolded readers for falling into these traps, especially the fantasies of romance and marriage (McRobbie 1977/2000b). It is as though this is the vengeance of the younger generation who had to put up with being chided by feminist teachers and academics at university for wanting the wrong things. (This well-educated female demographic is factored into the *Bridget Jones's Diary* narrative, littered as it is with references to Germaine Greer, Jane Austen, Salman Rushdie, post-modernism and literary theory.) The post-feminist moment of *Bridget Jones's Diary* also coincides with the new popularity once again, massively promoted by consumer culture, of weddings, including gay and lesbian weddings and all the paraphernalia that goes with them. The cultural references and the humour in this particular 'rom-com' are up-to-the-moment. Girls now get so drunk they tumble out of taxis, they have sex when they feel like it, without always being prepared with the best underwear and so on. But, as we know, relations of power are indeed made and re-made within texts of enjoyment and rituals of relaxation and abandonment. These young women's genres are vital to the construction of a new gender regime, based on the double entanglement which I have described. They endorse wholeheartedly what Rose calls 'this ethic of freedom', and young women have come to the fore as the pre-eminent subjects of this new ethic. These popular texts normalise post-feminist gender anxieties so as to re-regulate young women by means of the language of personal choice. Despite all of this planning and diary keeping even 'well regulated liberty' can backfire (the source of comic effect), and this in turn gives rise to demarcated pathologies (leaving it to late to have a baby, failing to find a good catch, etc.) which carefully define the parameters of what constitutes livable lives for young women without the occasion of re-invented feminism.

Bridget Jones's Diary celebrates the return of romance in a soft rather than hard post-feminist framing. Bridget is endearingly plump and reminiscent of any number of literary predecessors, but most obviously Jane Austen's Elizabeth Bennett. She is self-mocking, self-disparaging, and her witty observations of the social life around her create a warmth and an audience who is almost immediately on her side, as she negotiates the codes of contemporary sexual relationships. Although she constantly defines herself as a failure, and even plays dumb, messing up the chances that come her way to shine at work, and saying the wrong thing in public places, she is also aware of every wrong step she takes, scolding herself along the way. Much of the comic effect evolves around her daily attempts to become the sort of woman who she thinks will be the kind of woman men want to marry, hence the crucial romantic moment in the film is when Mark Darcy says he likes her just the way she is. There is of course poignancy here, since who does not want to be liked for just who one is, whoever that may be? *Bridget Jones's Diary* speaks then to female desire, and in a wholly commercialised way, to the desire for some kind of gender justice, or fairness, in the world of sex and relationships. Here too the ghost of feminism is hovering. Bridget deserves to get what she wants. The audience is wholly on her side. She ought to be able to find the right man, for the reason that she has negotiated that tricky path which requires being independent, earning her own living, standing up for herself against demeaning comments, remaining funny and good humoured throughout, without being angry or too critical of men, without foregoing her femininity, her desires for love and motherhood, her sense of humour and her appealing vulnerability.

Notes

1 *Bridget Jones's Diary* appeared first as a newspaper column in the UK newspaper the *Independent* in 1996. its author Helen Fielding then published the diaries as a book, and the film, *Bridget Jones's Diary* directed by Sharon McGuire, opened in 2001. The sequel *Bridget Jones: The Edge of Reason* directed by Beebron Kidron opened in November 2004.

2 There are several moments in the film where 'feminist issues', i.e. workplace harassment, sex discrimination and equal pay, are invoked only to be wittily abandoned as Bridget self-consciously sleeps with the boss, and then later takes a job which requires her to be obviously sexy.

3 The newspaper the *Daily Mail* has the highest volume of female readers in the UK. Its post-feminist stance is unambiguous, it frequently commissions recanting feminist journalists and writers to blame feminism for women's contemporary complaints, e.g. the famous novelist Fay Weldon wrote a piece called 'Look What We Have Done' (23 November 2003: 12–13) arguing that all feminists created was 'a new generation of women for whom sex is utterly joyless and hollow.' See also the following chapter.

2

FEMINISM UNDONE? THE CULTURAL POLITICS OF DISARTICULATION

Disarticulating feminism

We left off, at the end of the last chapter, with Bridget Jones aged 32 but adamantly girlish, or perhaps by necessity girlish, insofar as it is these qualities of girlishness which are required in the pursuit of a husband. The audiences laughs at her mishaps as though she was a rather immature 18 year old, and while the qualities of girlishness are not in themselves inherently harmful or dangerous to womanhood, they nevertheless play a kind of boundary-marking function, leaving seriousness, angry humour, and being perhaps old for one's age rather than by necessity youthful at 32, in some other undesignated space. Within the field of popular culture this becomes dominant, women must be young women. Kylie Minogue at 38 years old must act, every time she steps over her own doorstep, like a giggling teenager. To make a point like this, takes us right back in time to early and rather crude feminism, which reflected on what was required for women to be taken seriously. It is as though every feature of media and contemporary popular culture insofar as it engages with femininity somehow reverses and displaces those arguments made by feminists in the early 1970s.

In this chapter I attempt to explain the idea of 'feminism undone'. I will introduce the term disarticulation to understand how some of the institutional gains made by feminism over a period of 30 years are now being eroded. This is happening, within the context of UK political culture, in the name of modernisation. Modernisation in turn functions through a remit which is apparently advantageous to women, especially young women, to the extent that it can even stand as a substitute for feminism, a kind of *faux* feminism. This process of undoing, taking place most visibly in the privileged site of culture, connects with and is part of the breaking up of what Stuart Hall has many times referred to as the post-war social welfare settlement (Hall 1989, 2003). In this chapter, and the one that follows, I focus on how this breaking up has accelerated (especially from the mid-1990s) and how young women are now targeted as having a special role to play in this dismantling and modernisation process.

The idea of disarticulation serves two purposes. It gives depth to the notion of anti-feminist backlash, while also marking out a continuity with and extension of Stuart Hall's writing, over the years, on the politics of articulation. Hall has drawn on the work of Laclau and Mouffe whose theory of hegemony and socialist strategy in the mid-1980s marked a new moment in radical democratic thought (Laclau and Mouffe 1985). He took from their work the idea of articulation as a process where various progressive social movements (trade unionism, feminism, anti-racism, gay and lesbian rights), might forge connections and alliances with each other, and in so doing would also be constantly modifying their own political identities and their 'horizons of intelligibility'. Predicated on a post-structuralist and psychoanalytic understanding of identity as never transparent, never fulfilled or authentic, and never wholly corresponding with the structural categories of class, race or sex, they argued that lived social identities were always formed from a range of unstable and historically contingent elements. These inevitably intersected with each other, never existing in a pure form. When subordination is understood primarily in terms of one or other of these subject positions, for example gender, and when a social movement for change emerges from the collective understanding of that subject position, e.g. as women's oppression, there is the strong possibility that these always, already, open-ended identities will draw from the historical experience of other neighbouring struggles (e.g. the Civil Rights movement, or the working-class movement) and enter into what Mouffe and Laclau refer to as a chain of equivalence.

In the UK the women's movement in the late 1960s and through the 1970s, was strongly influenced by the history of socialist struggles, much more so than in the US. It drew on some of the repertoire of class struggle, but also modified this through challenging its productivism, its patriarchalism and the over-determination of class, with the effect that sexuality, race and ethnicity were always to be subsumed within the overarching logic of class. For Laclau and Mouffe chains of equivalence are constituted out of these kinds of intersections and cross-over radical solidarities, without any one being fundamentally privileged over the others. In the UK these intersections have shaped the field of feminist scholarship and also women's and gender studies courses. Chains of equivalence have provided a theoretical basis for understanding how radical democratic pluralist politics might conceivably become more expansive, as a post-socialist strategy for the radical left, in which no single struggle takes precedence over the others. I will argue here that it is also this kind of politics which is now being actively disarticulated. In regard to feminism I aim to demonstrate, in the pages that follow, how disarticulation is the objective of a new kind of regime of gender power, which functions to foreclose on the possibility or likelihood of various expansive intersections and inter-generational feminist transmissions. Articulations are therefore reversed, broken off, and the idea of a new feminist political imaginary becomes increasingly inconceivable. In social and cultural life there is instead a process of unpicking the seams of connection, forcing apart and dispersing subordinate social groups who might have possibly found some common cause. This in turn makes unlikely the forging of alliances, affiliations or connections. The appeal to young women in the West, that they are the fortunate beneficiaries of Western sexual freedoms, now actively pitches them against gender arrangements in other cultures where female sexuality is subjected to different modes of surveillance and control. In a post-feminist frame, the only logic of affiliation with women living in other, non-Western cultures, is to see them as victims. Past alliances also appear to be irretrievably broken, and inter-generational connections become unappetising. Of course within feminism alliances were invariably fraught and fragile, as much characterised by open conflict and argument, as by shows of unity. But the cutting off process which I will examine here, not only disarms what may still exist of feminism, but also interrupts whatever chances there may be for feminism to speak again to a wider constituency of women. Instead there is an over-supply of post-feminist substitutes from within the new hyper-visible feminine consumer culture.

There is a double movement, disarticulation and displacement, accompanied by replacement and substitution. What is being disarticulated is a field of sexual politics which was (as was shown in the previous chapter) by necessity endlessly dismantling itself, but in so doing was also widening its field of effectivity. By disarticulation I mean a force which devalues, or negates and makes unthinkable the very basis of coming-together (even if to take part in disputatious encounters), on the assumption widely promoted that there is no longer any need for such actions. I perceive this process of disarticulation as occurring across a wide range of social and cultural spaces. Through the repudiation of unstable sexual identities and same-sex desires, there is an aggressive dismantling of the sensibilities which would lead young women, for example, to share a common voice with each other, across the boundaries of heterosexuality and homosexuality.[1] Disarticulation also operates through the widespread dissemination of values which typecast feminism as having been fuelled by anger and hostility to men. This is now understood as embittered, unfeminine and repugnant. Young women are discouraged from becoming involved politically in areas like sex work or the pornography industry for fear of offending men, and being branded a feminist. This results in the stifling of dissent, debate and solidarity among young women, about, for example, the existence of differential access to sexual freedoms and to protection in regard to these freedoms.[2]

Disarticulation works then as a kind of dispersal strategy. It defuses the like-lihood of cross-border solidarity. Often it appears to be pre-emptive, knowing and informed. There is a sense or a threat that feminism could be re-awoken, and that it was, in the past, a force to be reckoned with. A hysterical and mon-strous version of feminism therefore informs the political practice of disarticu-lation as that which is somehow known about, and must be efficiently dealt with, before it has the chance to be rekindled by a younger generation. This gives rise to new forms of gender power which, I will argue, are most embed-ded within the field of popular culture. The sphere of leisure and consumer culture is dominated by the vocabulary of personal choice, and is the primary site for hedonism, fantasy, personal gratification, and entertainment. While there is nothing new in the casting of this sphere as replete with disciplinary techniques in the guise of self-management and personal choice, it is my inten-tion in this chapter to trace some of these processes of post-feminist disarticu-lation which are conducted inside popular culture.

The cultural forms which function according to this logic of substitution are also spectral re-workings of their feminist predecessors, now transplanted into a popular domain. They promote a highly conservative mode of femi-nine 'empowerment', the hallmark of which is the active connecting-up of young woman with notions of change, the right to work, and with new free-doms, particularly sexual freedoms. This conservatism entails a set of limits being inserted within these discourses of freedom. 'Our' young women are encouraged to conceive of themselves are grateful subjects of modern states and cultures which permit such freedoms unlike repressive or fundamental-ist regimes. This in turn suggests a specific mode of encountering and under-standing other less fortunate women, who have no access to Western freedoms, or who at best might be encouraged to aim for such possibilities. Of course this discourse of Western enlightened values in regard to sexual-ity, defined in contrast with seemingly less advanced countries of the world, has long been a theme in women's magazine journalism (especially *Marie Claire*), but in the last decade, and particularly since 2001, this disarticula-tion process is much more visible, and more sustained. In an uncanny way this kind of media reportage on women who are deemed to be less fortu-nate both mimics and distorts discussions within feminism and anti-racism around difference. It disarticulates possible affiliations which would be based on Western feminist post-colonialist critique of how Western sexual freedoms are strategically deployed so as to support notions of civilisation and superiority, and by preventing such a possibility, it displaces possible solidarities, with a re-instated hierarchy of civilisation and modernity, and a discourse which celebrates the freedoms of fashion-conscious 'thong-wearing' Western girls in contrast to those young women who, for example, wear the veil. This is again a kind of pre-emptive disarticulation, foiling an exchange or a banding together, before it might ever happen. Modern young women are therefore being threatened by the rise of Islam, and this becomes a repeated theme in newspapers like the *Daily Mail*. When there is an address to young British black or Asian women within this new popular culture now imbued with celebratory pro-Western values, it is again to discourage empathy and affinity in favour of the desire for assimilation and success within the terms set by the feminine consumer culture (i.e. career success, glamour and sexuality).[3] Or to put this another way, everything that might be learnt from feminist post-colonialist theory within an academic context, which could indeed form the basis for a politics of affiliation predicated on cultural difference, and on a shared critique of the neo-imperialism which now instrumentalises female equality, often in the form of a kind of symbolic violence, is reversed, undone and to be unlearnt and dismantled within popular culture or within the new feminine 'public sphere' dominated by consumer culture.

The social processes referred to so far, can be understood within the frame of transformation and modernisation embarked upon by the New Labour government since it came to office in 1997. In the US such changes have taken place within the seemingly inexorable rise of neo-liberalism. The politics and economics of US neo-liberalism have recently been subjected to critical scrutiny by feminist scholars Wendy Brown (2005) and Lisa Duggan (2003). In *The Twilight of Equality* Duggan provides a highly persuasive account of the unfolding logic of neo-liberalism in the US in the last 30 years, with particular reference to the dismantling of feminist and anti-racist politics. Although my focus here is more specifically on the UK context and the field of popular culture as a privileged terrain for the implementation of these new forms of gender power, Duggan's wide-ranging and historical analysis is extremely helpful. She argues that a key mechanism for the implementation of these aggressive policies, which establish a ground-plan for the eradication of welfare, is the defining of economic policies as somehow neutral, a matter of pure expertise and technique. This permits a sense of mastery, authority and confidence which is somehow unquestionable, and unassailable while in effect the deployment of economic policies is anything but neutral and, as she shows, they are completely designed to intervene in areas which have long been associated with feminism, ie sexuality, race and ethnicity, family and culture. (As I show in the next chapter, the seeming neutrality, in the guise of technological expertise in the field of economics in the UK, on the part of the New Labour government, is combined with a rhetoric of confidence and capacity, which extends into the social field, where young women are frequently congratulated for their recent successes in education, and their ambition in the world of work.) In addition these economic policies are aimed at countering and undermining what Duggan calls the left-progressive cultures of the 1960s and 1970s with their focus on downward re-distribution of resources. This challenge to left social welfare policies was implemented in the 1980s, but gained ground and accelerated through the 1990s.

Duggan offers one salient case study which illuminates the backlash against feminism. This episode, which relied on extensive media coverage, involved a right-wing woman, Candace de Russy, on the board of trustees of the State University of New York making objections to the contents of a feminist and lesbian conference; eventually forcing the resignation of the Vice-President of SUNY and more generally establishing a climate of dissatisfaction with the apparent misuse of public funds, which in turn gave legitimacy for the 'shrinking of public institutions', in this case the university, with its 'irrelevant' feminist curriculum. Duggan argues that a key feature of neo-liberalism is the implanting of market cultures across everyday life, the relentless pursuit of welfare reform, and the encouragement of forms of consumer citizenship which are beneficial only to those who are already privileged. Undoing the anti-hierarchical struggles of the social movements is also a priority within the discourses of neo-liberalism. And an attack on disadvantaged social groups is, she suggests, masked by the prevailing and apparently non-racist and non-sexist language of self-esteem, empowerment and personal responsibility. (In the UK these terms are combined with the ethos of the 'new meritocracy'.) The reduction in spending on social provision intensifies the difficulties faced by low qualified and low paid women who are forced to make private child-care arrangements, and then forced into long and unsociable hours, without the provision of youth clubs, and social facilities for their children. Overall these seemingly neutral economic policies are, suggests Duggan, designed to shrink spending in public education, social services and the arts. They also seek to dismantle old alliances across the spectrum of left, feminism and anti-racist movements through adapting some features of identity politics to the purposes of the neo-liberal cultural agenda. The scene was set for this as, under attack in the 1980s, elements within these progressive social movements found themselves fragmented and evolving into single issue groups, often as a way of ensuring survival and access to some public funds. Duggan describes the neo-liberal endorsement of 'equality feminism' and 'gay normality'. She understands this recognition as part of a mainstreaming process undertaken within a 'third way rhetoric'. This in turn sees a further disarticulation of leftist movements characterised as 'irresponsible or anachronistic', and their replacement by neo-liberal versions of equality, diversity and tolerance. Duggan emphasises that in supporting the autonomy of sexual and multicultural politics, left social movements were not to blame for this tapping into and appropriation of identity politics. She argues against Wendy Brown for criticising identitarian strands within victim-oriented feminism for becoming sites of wounds and injuries, and also (in my mind more justifiably) she argues forcefully against Todd Gitlin for his call for a (nostalgic) return to old (new) left values, without the seeming excesses and vanities of those movements which have been dubbed 'merely cultural' (and thus indelibly linked with cultural studies and all of its failings), as though this merely cultural status marked out a dilution and weakening of something that would otherwise be strong and resilient. Instead Duggan positions her argument alongside that of Butler, who is showing that the 'distinction is a kind of *ruse* of capitalist liberal discourse – a ruse that obscures the intricate imbrication of race, gender, sex and class in the institutions of capitalist modernity' (Duggan 2003: 83).

Duggan's analysis is useful in that it helps to establish the critical framework for the analysis here which focuses on cultural processes of undoing. While that which is being undone, is, and possibly always was, fragile and seemingly torn apart by internal conflict, it did nevertheless constitute a terrain of radical political articulations, comprising groups who perceived inequities and oppressions across the boundaries of sex, race and class, none of which were self-standing. In the pages that follow my attention is focused primarily, though not exclusively, on the cultural sphere as a key site for disarticulation. I examine how the 'backlash against feminism' has been understood by the feminist academic Judith Stacey, and by the journalist Susan Faludi (Stacey 1985/1986, Faludi 1992). I then comment briefly on the nostalgia for whiteness and for white femininity, as an undoing of multi-culturalism and black feminism. In the final section of this chapter I engage critically with the sociological writing of Giddens, Beck and Lash, showing how these authors in their analysis of epochal social transformations, presume a post-feminist era, and how in doing so they invalidate the idea of renewed feminist struggle and provide a counter-analysis to the politics of post-structuralist feminism in the academy. I then turn to the work of Mouffe and Laclau once again, and also to that of Judith Butler for the insight they provide in understanding the disarticulating logic of neo-liberal culture and its consequences for feminism.

Early post-feminists

The recent work of Duggan, taken together with Stacey and Faludi, reminds us that the concerted attempts to undermine and immobilise the women's movement have in fact been virtually coterminous with feminism. All three writers are primarily concerned with American feminism, although Faludi does draw on some British material. And while this US focus is clearly a limiting factor, the detailed attention paid to the growth of the new right and Moral Majority, and the attacks on feminism from within these movements, raises some vital questions. If these processes of continuously undermining the egalitarian convictions of feminists have indeed been in motion since the late 1970s, then how might we differentiate between this longstanding hostile activity and the practices of disarticulation in evidence today, and in my case, in the UK? This is a question that I will be attempting to answer in the chapters that follow. But first let us look at Stacey's seminal article published first in 1985 and titled 'The New Conservative Feminism', and then subsequently in a collection edited by Ann Oakley and Juliet Mitchell in 1986 and called 'Are Feminists Afraid to Leave The Home?' (Stacey 1985/1986). Stacey herself was part of a team of feminist scholars who as early as 1978 commented on the backlash against feminism in the US. Following this, the word 'post-feminism' was then used in a journalistic piece in the *New York Times* in 1982 as a means of marking out a new kind of politics which was vaguely feminist, in a pro-woman sense, but repudiating the angry strident tones associated with feminism per se.[4] This idea of holding onto some mild, and media-friendly version of feminism, has been a consistent feature of the post-feminist backlash, and it becomes more emphatic as it evolves into a substitute for feminism. What Stacey shows is how, from the start of second wave feminism, there has been a constant flow of anti-feminist discourse and activism emanating from a resurgent new right in the US. She also reminds us how feminism has been forcefully rejected by many women, as well as by men. And the unacceptable nature of feminism to this wide constituency, is then consolidated with the collapse of the left and the decline of liberalism, in the US.

Alongside this wave of anti-feminist sentiment, are those responses by recanting feminists including Friedan and Greer, both of whom write in a journalistic vein, but also, for example, the feminist scholar Jean Bethke Elshtain who introduces a kind of conservative pro-family feminism, predicated on a retreat from the critique of sexual difference and of male dominance of the public sphere, in favour of an under-theorised re-valuing of the home (as haven in a bureaucratic world), heterosexual love, mothering and the domestic environment. It has to be said that the rather eccentric recanting by both Friedan and Greer was, even then, to most UK feminists, unsurprising, including Greer's sentimental elevation of the extended family, arranged marriages and her celebration of female power in the household. Friedan seemed to regret her earlier writing, and now emphasised pro-family values as well as a kind of appeasement with men. What these more popular former feminist writers are all saying is that 'actually we got it wrong', or 'feminism did not work, it was too anti-men, too pro-lesbian and far too anti-family' and 'this not only alienated ordinary women, it also rebounded on feminists themselves, by isolating them from family life and cutting them off from the pleasures of having children and from the meaningful community which emerges around motherhood'. Stacey herself fully confronts the centrality of the family at the heart of feminist politics, implying, if not fully developing, a sense that the radical undermining of gender inequities in the heterosexual family was more difficult, and perhaps an unrealistic goal. Stacey contextualises these anti-feminist positions, first through the biographical history of leading feminists like Greer and Friedan, which saw them put off having their own children, and also finding themselves later in life single, and without the stability of a loving partnership, and second, in regard to the needs of children and the way in which feminism in the 1970s and early 1980s emphasised an anti-family position and the collective care of children. Stacey wonders what it might mean to re-think feminism taking more fully into account parenting. She is cognisant of the argument by black feminists whose pro-family stance is based on both the family as a semi-private zone, indoors from the racism of the street, and also a space of female strength especially in single mother households. Nevertheless the drift of the post-feminist backlash is to repudiate feminist experimentalism in regard to alternative family structures, and to retreat from the challenge to male domination. Overall this results in a kind of defensively sentimental celebration of femininity, especially when it is connected with maternity, a sense in which lesbianism went too far in its various critiques of male power, and that this image of feminism only made the movement deeply unpopular and indeed unpalatable to so-called ordinary women. Stacey remarks on the loss of momentum subsequently within the field of sexual politics, the cleavage between lesbians and heterosexual women with the latter, she suggests, made to feel their desires as somehow faulty, and on the fragmentation inside the feminist academy also increasingly apparent. Overall Stacey argues that conservative pro-family feminism has managed to re-define the landscape of feminist debate so that it is defensive, maybe even helpless and this now poses an urgent challenge to those who retain a commitment to the multifaceted struggle for gender justice.

In fact the very word gender is anathema to those who endorse these kinds of conservative feminist positions, since what is being argued for is a return to the full endorsement of sexual difference, and in particular to the social value of maternity. Over 20 years since the article by Stacey first appeared, its achievement is that it combines an engagement with the power of the new right to reclaim some feminist-influenced version of modern womanhood, with an account of those elements inside feminism which were also part of this undoing, notably in the form of recantation. This article pre-dates the emergence of queer politics and its appeal to a younger generation of women, not just on the basis of sexual desire, but also because of the decreasing relevance of maternal feminism for the young women who are either delaying maternity or deciding against it altogether (McRobbie 2005: 75–77). Stacey's article only fleetingly acknowledges the impact of black feminism and post-colonial feminist theory, which means that its focus is towards white, middle-class American women and their repudiation of feminism. This raises the question of how different feminisms have had an impact in other locations. In the US in the mid-1980s there was a flowering of black feminism and also the rise of the Chicana women's movement, and in Europe socialist-feminism continued to have some existence until the early 1990s when it transformed itself into either a politics of gender mainstreaming or, in the academy, and under the influence of post-structuralist and post-colonialist theory, into a post-Marxist radical politics of gender, 'race' and difference.

Susan Faludi's bestseller *Backlash: The Undeclared War Against Women* was published to great acclaim in 1992. Faludi follows in the tradition of feminist journalists who have, in many ways, shaped the character of feminism outside the large social institutions and have also created for feminism what Nancy Fraser has called a feminist counter-public sphere (Fraser 1997). Like Stacey, Faludi's focus is primarily on white America, and she also traces the growth of the new right and its sustained attack on feminist principles. Faludi shows how the media, throughout this period, sought out, and made extensive use of what were later found to be inaccurate statistics or social surveys with doubtful methodologies, or else with skewered and unreliable interpretations. At every opportunity it seemed journalists or campaigners who were keen to attack feminism looked to young and not yet established academics, particularly social scientists at top-rated universities like Yale, who were willing to risk their academic reputations for national and international media coverage, presumably for the pay-off which this might bring. Faludi tracks how often these academics themselves later blamed the media for misrepresenting their research findings, or else they agreed they were pressured to publish the results of what was work in progress and so on. But still this kind of material was consistently deployed to suggest that (heterosexual) women over the age of 30 had little chance of finding a partner, that there was an epidemic of infertility, that feminism was to blame for any number of illnesses and female complaints, that no-fault divorces resulted in impoverishment for women, and that 'mommy tracking' in the workplace, with little or no chance for advance or promotion, was a preferred option for working mothers. A key term here is 'trends' and the power such phenomena have to shift the field of cultural values to one of fear and anxiety, on the part of young women especially. The disregard for accuracy in the reporting of these trends also reveals the way in which academia was, and is, used as a source of validation and expertise, so that reporting on facts relevant to the lives of women is then subsumed into the field of entertainment, lifestyle and popular culture. The drama of a headline, backed up by data from Ivy League universities, becomes an effective tool in the success of lifestyle journalism. Ideas like the shortage of men, or the epidemic of infertility, or women's desire to return to the home, all become popular idioms and new forms of common sense. Faludi shows how many of those women who have been foremost proponents of new traditionalism and the return to the home and to domesticity, especially those working for new right campaigns, are themselves high achieving working mothers, many of whose partners are willing to take a back seat to allow their wives to promote the cause of traditional family values. And as Faludi points out, because these women are championing the cause their husbands are wholeheartedly in favour of, presumably more effectively than they, this contradiction is overlooked, indeed irrelevant, since the limiting of opportunities for poor women to better their lives and gain equality alongside their male counterparts, corresponds entirely with new right agenda of reinstating social hierarchies and eradicating welfare and social security in favour of self-help, and personal responsibility.

The women who are employed as actresses and producers in the making of programmes like the soft focus post-feminist TV sitcom *thirtysomething*, report to Faludi that they felt uncomfortable with the values being promulgated in the series, since they themselves were juggling childcare with the need to earn a living. Nevertheless the decisions about the script were inevitably out of their hands, all they could do was try on occasion to modify the storyline evolving round their own characters.[5] And likewise the making of the film *Fatal Attraction*, which many feminists saw as inaugurating a moment in popular culture which saw the demonisation of the single woman and the defence of the nuclear family, involved a dramatic shift from the original script which was, as Faludi discovers, much less antagonistic to the character of Alex played by Glenn Close. Thus popular culture, including women's magazines, the fashion and beauty industries, as well as women's genres of film and television programmes, come to function as the primary disseminators of the new traditionalism. Faludi pays a good deal of attention to the idea of 'cocooning' and the appeal it seems to hold for female consumers of lifestyle magazines. This is also played out in the 1986 film *Baby Boom* with Diane Keaton playing the woman who steps off the fast track in the city and finds maternal bliss, romantic love and the opportunity to become an entrepreneur of healthy baby food in the countryside.

In Chapter 5 I will return to the fantasies of home and hearth peddled in UK TV cooking programmes and summed up in the figure of Nigella Lawson who is promoted as a 'domestic goddess' (Brunsdon 2005). I would like to suggest here however that we must pay more attention to the fantasy dimension in this kind of comforting scenario. Faludi is perhaps too quick to read off from this kind of popular culture a sense in which these phenomena operate simply as part of the whole backlash against feminism. But we need to ask, 'why this kind of fantasy?' What are women viewers longing for or dreaming about, when they find themselves hooked into the soft focus images of happy families gathered round the table to enjoy a Sunday lunch cooked by a glamorous looking and unstressed mother? Judith Stacey does recognise the need for a psychoanalytic approach to understanding the deeper appeal of fantasies about the domestic sphere, maternity and good housekeeping, while Faludi, in contrast, adopts a more one-dimensional account of a war of attrition against feminist ideas and the possible threat they pose to the social and sexual hierarchy. Faludi recognises the way in which anti-feminist values are presented as sophisticated and knowing in the postmodern sense. She describes the way in which young cultural producers typecast feminism as out of date and 'uncool', and how they take risks, or are seen as taboo-breaking, for daring to represent women, once again, in demeaning ways, but whose get-out clause is provided by the use of irony, as though to say, 'we don't really mean it'. Overall Faludi provides a wide-ranging account of how American culture and politics organised itself through the 1980s to disparage, ridicule, disavow and pre-emptively disarm the critical force embodied in the women's movement as it gained some ground from the late 1960s onwards. In the chapters that follow I will pursue many of these issues, but in particular I will ask, how does the nature of the response, what I refer to as the cultural politics of disarticulation, change in the light of what seems to be an irreversible shift into the labour market on the part of younger women? How are these processes of undoing played out in the context of British society? How does what Stacey calls pro-family conservative feminism transmogrify into a governmentally orchestrated 'new sexual contract' to young women?

Single women and sexual danger

The film *Fatal Attraction* (dir. A Lyne 1987) has been widely recognised as instrumental in setting in motion a reaction, within popular culture, against predatory, sexually emancipated, possibly mentally unbalanced, single women who are also economically independent, live in cities, and pose a threat to the lives of men and women who have chosen what Faludi and others refer to as the new traditionalism, i.e. the country-living nuclear family with a profes-sional male breadwinner and a wife and mother who is apparently his equal, but who has chosen to stay at home. Of course the film itself is primarily enter-tainment, a hybrid of thriller and story of sex in the city, and its success surely lay in its creation of a new kind of villain, a monstrous woman who uses her sexual power to wreak havoc in the life of a man who is morally decent (despite being open to an affair), a hard working, loving father and husband.[6] So successful has it been, that its narrative, as well as its key dramatic elements (what came to be known as the famous 'bunny boiler' episode)[7] have entered into popular discourse re-surfacing intertextually in other forms of popular cul-ture including the film *Bridget Jones's Diary* and the TV series *Sex and the City*. Because Alex played by Glenn Close became a kind of evil, insane, hate figure (a contemporary witch) she also entered the popular imagination of younger women as someone they must avoid ever becoming in their pursuit of inde-pendence alongside love, sex, marriage and motherhood.

For the purposes of this discussion, what is imperative in the film's narrative is that the figure of Alex disrupts the moral economy of the new traditionalism, she threatens its viability. She challenges the sexual privileges which in the past have accrued to white middle-class males who have played the role of breadwinner and loving father. Whether this entails simply the occasional affair, or else a long-term mistress, such entanglements have been an unstated premise, a reality underpinning the longevity of the modern nuclear family. Lifelong monogamy has invariably clashed with male desire, and within a context where the husband and father is also the financial provider, infidelity has been semi-institutionalised, involving various arrangements, and also, of course, often resulting in divorce. What the film *Fatal Attraction* suggests is that this kind of double life fuelled by sexual desire on the one hand, and a loving, faithful wife on the other, is destabilised with the advent of a new kind of sexually voracious and possibly mentally ill, single woman who, as mistress, will no longer abide by the rules. There is a seemingly equal and respectful partnership between man and wife, but now, the submissive mistress is no more, instead she has been transformed, through the spread of feminist values, into a demanding, and then demented, and life-threatening figure of pure evil. The fact that the film, when it was first shown in US cinemas, gave rise to shouts from men in the audience to 'kill the bitch', also suggests the extent to which male privilege in sexuality has been eroded, and how this is a source of anger and aggression. The double standard has been exposed and overruled. If women emerge as subjects of sexual desire, and if this is also understood, thanks to feminism, as a kind of entitlement, then men must beware. Most specifically they need to check their desire before embarking on sexual adventures involving seemingly empowered and possibly interesting and financially independent women who might even become pregnant to satisfy their own maternal longings. Extra-marital sex must now become a matter of caution, consideration and calculation.

This film gave vent to a kind of male fury which had perhaps been simmering underneath throughout the years of feminist struggle. *Fatal Attraction* gave legitimacy to male grievance. The innocence of a one night stand or a fling, in effect the innocence of male desire, finds itself destroyed because women no longer abide by the rules, they can no longer be relied upon to be passive, grateful recipients of male sexual passion. *Fatal Attraction* brings into being a cultural sensibility which allows men to feel they have been wronged by women, or that they might find themselves wronged by women. From now on they must be on their guard, they must defend themselves against a kind of violent sexual exploitation by women. This idea provides a justificatory framework for the growth of more unapologetically aggressive masculine values in campaigning organisations like *Fathers 4 Justice* and also in the world of men's magazines from the late 1980s. It provides the basis for a resurgent sexism, a re-instatement of female objectification, for example, but with a pervasive sense of irony, as though to ameliorate offence and avoid accusations of sexism. The film *Fatal Attraction* seemed to suggest that men might now rightfully harbour antagonistic feelings to women who are somehow too confident, too independent, too capable themselves of sexually exploiting men. As a huge success in the box offices, bringing in $100m in the first four months of its release, *Fatal Attraction* unleashed male anger, and contributed to the cultural politics of backlash, as Faludi shows. Its three characters comprise a triangle of figures each of whom becomes central to the demonisation of feminism, Dan the husband, despite his infidelity, is fundamentally committed to wife and home, and is quickly exonerated from succumbing to sexual temptation. His wife in turn embodies exactly the qualities of accomplished, middle-class femininity extolled by Elshtain in her defence of pro-family conservative femininity, while Alex is unhinged in her bitterness, her voracious sexual desire and her single status. The implication to male viewers is that if they wish to have casual sex, and no-strings attached encounters, then they should stay single, and this in turn becomes a recurrent feature within the women's magazines and other women's genres about the difficulties young women now face in finding someone who will commit to marriage and parenthood. Overall the film legitimates male grievances and establishes a narrative framework for justifying anger if not outright aggression.

Sex wars in the American university

Fatal Attraction was, of course, a major Hollywood blockbuster aimed at a mass popular audience. The 1992 play by David Mamet, *Oleanna*, had a similar kind of impact among a more middle class theatre-going audience. It too reportedly aroused anger and outrage in the stalls. It became known as a highly controversial play about what can happen when feminism is taken too far. Here too the erosion of white male privilege is addressed in dramatic form. Following on from the famous Anita Hill and Clarence Thomas case the previous year,[8] the play was seen as confronting the corrosive power of what came to be known as political correctness. This term, like that of backlash, has immediate relevance to my concern here with how disarticulation operates in culture. There is, inevitably, underpinning the charge of political correctness, some sense in which quite reasonable and acceptable ideas like gender equality, ideas which most people would now find acceptable, have been somehow distorted, taken too far, abused and turned into something monstrous, dogmatic and authoritarian. The rhetorical power of the charge is to legitimate some return to normality, so that common sense prevails, and this in turn sews the seeds of doubt about various forms of radicalism. It devalues the women's movement and the anti-racist movement as sites of extremism, attractive only to angry and dangerous kinds of people. The term political correctness is a tool not just of the new right, and in the UK, of the

Conservatives, but also of those politically in the centre, and indeed in New Labour, as it re-positioned itself from the mid-1990s. The play *Oleanna* fuels this critique of political correctness within a university setting.[9] Its two characters have depth and complexity lacking in the cartoonish characters in *Fatal Attraction*. John, a lecturer whose help is sought by Carol, one of the students in his class, has, like Dan in *Fatal Attraction*, the force of moral good on his side, despite his visible flaws. He is infuriatingly pedantic, he inhabits his role as pedagogue with almost absurd intellectual vanity, he loves the authority, the performance, the patriarchal role. Throughout the encounters between the fragile, unconfident, young woman who tries to explain to him how she doesn't understand his language and his conceptual vocabulary, John takes a number of phone calls from his wife regarding the details of a new house they are buying. These calls serve to establish the background of a loving home, and his role as breadwinner and father as well as husband. If in the first act the audience is irritated by the pompous way in which he seems to enjoy running intellectual circles round his inarticulate female student, disavowing some of the principles of education which his office would expect him to uphold (with a kind of *faux* radicalism), by the second act it is she who begins to show herself as dangerous, damaged, manipulative and sinister.

The moral centre of gravity is consistently on the side of the humanistic, caring, if overbearing John. Indeed his probing of the intellectual basis of his own knowledge and his judgements, and his critical analysis of pedagogy and academic procedures and the way in which he opens out to the student in his office, contribute to the play's defence of academic freedoms against the rigidity and dogma which Carol seems increasingly to be influenced by, through her references to her 'group'. The dramatic climax of the play comes at the moment in which she tells John that she has made a complaint against him, claiming that his actions, including what the audience has seen to be of a non-sexual nature, constitute rape. John's tenure is refused, he cannot go ahead with his house purchase, and the implication is that his life is destroyed when, eventually provoked, he hits out in fury. The character of Carol gains self-confidence in the course of these encounters, though this seems to come as much from the sinister group of feminists who she is reporting back to, as it does from the intellectual exchanges with John. Every so often throughout the play, she displays what the audience are intended to recognise as warning signs. At no point does she declare any emotional interest in or attraction to John, but her interest in his domestic life is too keen, and he falls into this trap by referring to his wife and son with masculine pride. Carol is over-attentive to his words, and she provides an enraptured audience to his intellectual posturings. John, like Dan in *Fatal Attraction*, is seen by the audience as too innocent, he is being set up by a young woman who is more manipulative than her girlish, and rather prim persona suggests. *Oleanna* (the title of the play is taken from a 19th century Norwegian experiment in utopian living) describes a kind of disenchantment with the idea of gender equality, it marks out the terrain of liberal disappointment, there is nothing which is inherently aggressive or obnoxious in the masculinity of John and the implication is that he has been wronged by a version of feminism, which has somehow gone too far and robbed him of his wellbeing, his rightful place as a man in the world, and eventually his livelihood.

In this instance the politics of disarticulation is at work inside the feminist academy, where the finger is pointed by the playwright at the feminists and the women's groups who are malevolent and dogmatic. The play is self-consciously clever, and entails a good deal of word-play and indeed just the kind of high-charged critical exchanges which the university system prides itself on encouraging, and it is by this means that it very effectively drives a wedge between those who defend liberal values, and academic freedom, and those who are militants and extremists and who are the driving force for change, and who challenge the relatively innocuous patriarchal authority and the everyday pomposity of the male professoriat. Any reasonable person would be sympathetic with John's outrage, and would find explicable his eventual resorting to violence, against this unfair accusation. And likewise any sympathy the audience might have had for Carol quickly dissipates as she begins to show signs of some kind of brainwashing by her group, and as she retains an unhealthy interest in the personal life of her tutor. She ticks him off for calling his wife 'baby' on the phone, which enrages him. On the other hand, this term of endearment seems to be intentionally deployed to annoy her. Both characters by this stage know what is at stake in the invoking of the domestic idyll, something which he has, and she might well never have, because of her strident feminist beliefs.

The play challenges the liberal assumptions of the audience, encouraging it to rid itself of any sympathies for feminism, which is now revealed for its rigid, aggressive and dangerous agenda. More specifically it brings to public attention, the existence of the feminist academy. The liberal university is being undermined from within, and the play seeks to expose the way in which militant feminism has established itself inside higher education. The play vilifies academic feminism and implies that feminist activity on campus is organised by extremists and men-haters. The powerful impact of the play is then to create a chasm of misunderstanding and antagonism between feminist students, and those who are outside of the academy, even those with otherwise liberal sympathies. The play contributes to a cultural politics of disarticulation, by demonising feminism inside the academy and by foreclosing on the impact which academic feminism might otherwise have in the outside world. The play also sets the scene for the further attacks on women's studies as fuelled by hatred of men, and it contributes directly to the various acrimonious debates inside the US universities and also in the public world which came to be known as the 'culture wars' (Gitlin 1995).

Post-feminism as daughter's revenge

The first scenes of Fay Weldon's novel *Big Women*, adapted into a four part series for UK Channel 4 in 1999, include a women's consciousness-raising group held in a large and comfortable middle-class London house in 1971. Four attractive and fashionable young women are spellbound by the words of one of their group who is academic-looking (serious, plain and bespectacled) and is delivering a lengthy lecture on Marxism and women's oppression. The narrative follows the setting up of a feminist publishing house (*Medusa*, based on the real-life *Virago*), the conflicts within the group and the inevitability of hierarchy (including the dominating influence of the confident and charismatic Layla, played by the actress Daniella Nardini), the emotional entanglements and contradictions accruing from free love and open relationships, and the tragedy of a more conventional woman Zoe, who is in a violent marriage and who commits suicide leaving behind a young son and a daughter. In the third episode of the series the daughter of Zoe, Saffron, has grown up into a confident blonde and sharp-suited, women's magazine editor. She is every inch the post-feminist ruthlessly individualistic young woman with no time for emotional solidarity with her female counterparts. However she is also avenging the death of her mother and ends up being the breadwinner and supporting her now alcoholic father as well as her brother. The drama charts the historical moment of 1970s middle-class feminism with its independent publishing ventures, and the decline of that idealism with the Thatcher years, and, more specifically, the displacement of feminism by the women's magazine market which has by now taken on board some of those values. The drama of *Big Women* in effect parallels the argument in this book. There is none of the aggressive vilification of feminism seen in both *Fatal Attraction* and in *Oleanna*, indeed there is some fondness and good humour in Weldon's recollections of 1970s feminist activity. However the chronological narrative, the flashbacks, the retro-style of the sequences set in the 1970s and 1980s, in contrast to the sharpness of final scenes which include footage from the 1997 election and the New Labour victory, ensure that feminism is understood to be firmly in the past. Its moments of warmth and solidarity are somehow non-transmissable, and its successors are confident, materialist, post-feminist young women like Saffron.

Indeed the decline of feminism is offset with the rise of a style of consumer-led capitalism which now incorporates women's issues, which in fact 'mainstreams' many of the concerns which were previously associated with more separatist feminism. The last two episodes of *Big Women* are scattered with words and phrases like 'backlash against feminism' and 'mainstreaming women's issues' as the characters battle it out against each other, when it becomes clear that their independent publishing ventures are increasingly unviable, and as they themselves begin to see how old-fashioned and out-of-date their books, as well as their ideas, now appear. Weldon also emphasises the continuity between ruthless individualism within feminism then (in the figure of Layla), and the compromises she was willing to make to see through her dreams into fruition (sleeping with an investor to get the funding for the publishing house), and Saffron now, her post-feminist counterpart. The point here is not simplistically that good old feminist collectivity gives way to bad new female individualism, but that, there were, back then, as many hidden hierarchies and compromises made in the feminist co-operative, as in the more transparently and hence, honestly, competitive world of glossy 1980s capitalism, which now is willing to incorporate women's concerns. Layla is the real role model for Saffron, domineering, arrogant, and self-seeking. Feminism is both historicised by Weldon and revised as a kind of political opportunism, a way for strong or big women to make their way in the world at a time when that was less possible than it is now. Despite the many references among the characters to socialist as well as feminist ideals, Weldon's ideas about feminism are firmly rooted within the liberal feminist notion of striving for equality, and the ethos of female empowerment (the soundtrack for the scene which shows Saffron striding into her women's magazine office is by the Spice Girls). Earning one's own living, and being financially successful replace what Weldon shows to have been paper-thin idealism. Within the genre of popular TV drama, Weldon creates a version of feminist history which, despite the flashes of warmth, casts a shadow over its political integrity and its genuine solidarity with women across social boundaries. The academic feminist character, Alice, who delivered lengthy feminist lectures to the group back in the 1970s has become a new age eccentric hippy, living alone in a caravan, while the idealist Steffi, in contrast to her long-term bestfriend Layla, is a broken and bitter lesbian who is incapable of moving with the times and accepting the inevitability of gender mainstreaming and the selective incorporation of feminist values into the commercial world of female dominated consumer culture.

Rolling back on anti-racism

Although I have used the phrase 'young women' with great frequency in the course of this discussion, this category is itself always and invariably cut across by relations of race, ethnicity, social class and sexual identity. In the film, the play and the TV series examined above, all of the protagonists are white. If we fast-forward to the field of contemporary media and popular culture, dominant feminine-whiteness becomes an invisible means of rolling back on anti-racism, indeed a key element of this can be seen at work in the idea of a nostalgia for whiteness. Just as there is a seemingly liberal relaxation of some dynamics of everyday life, with feminism taken into account as a kind of common sense, so too there is the need for a re-securing of the boundaries of required femininity, required that is for cultural viability as a modern girl. What has been undone is the possibility of feminism remaining in circulation as an accessible political imaginary, a means of collectivising what have now otherwise become merely privatised and individualised experiences. We can see similar processes at work in the celebration of black and Asian women's entrepreneurial success, and the self-definition of Britain as a diverse society which will not tolerate the kind of racism displayed by people in the media like Jade Goody (a minor celebrity who was a housemate in the reality TV show *Big Brother* and who subjected her fellow contestant Shilpa Shetty to aggressively racist bullying, similar to what happens in school playgrounds up and down the country) and yet which refuses the relevance of the political vocabularies of critical multi-culturalism as now old-fashioned, in favour of new models of assimilation. With this exclusion of angry politics of race, a green light is given which permits a return to whiteness as the norm, it becomes once again totally de-ethnicised (Ware 1992, Dyer 1997). There is a nostalgia for whiteness in the dramatic 1940s Hollywood-star look of Dita Von Teese, the Burlesque star, just as there is in the recent *Vogue* Prada fashion advertisements, a kind of looking back to periods of time 'undisturbed' by the need to take race and the politics of mul-ticulturalism into account. Where in the past whiteness was assumed, a norm without ethnicity, a norm against which everything else was different, so that only non-whiteness was equated with race or ethnicity, this new 'powder puff' whiteness emerges as more emphatically untouched by the requirement of white to register itself as ethnic.

The celebration of whiteness, is also visible within the world of the down-market celebrity magazines where the blonde hair and white skin associated with the style of the 'footballers' wives', is rarely interrupted by the pres-ence of a black or Asian young woman. And the more upmarket world of *Vogue* magazine, in the last few years, has been celebrating the white beauty of the new generation of East European and Russian models. There is a subtle provocation factor in all of these genres, as though to suggest that they are ebulliently refuting the now old-fashioned, or no longer relevant multi-culturalist demands or anti-discriminatory requirements for equal representation, indeed for simple visiblity, by adopting the style for flagrant anti-political correctness. This can be understood as a rolling back on anti-racism, through the nostalgic resumption, on the part of the media and popular culture, of how it used to be. Little effort is made to respond to the needs of black or Asian consumers, instead and in accordance with the new assimilationist policies endorsed by the present government, ethnic minor-ity women are encouraged to abandon multi-cultural difference and find ways of identifying with the majority. And if they choose not to, or prefer their own black or Asian magazines, then that too is a personal choice, one which again suggests a re-consolidation of boundaries, a firming up of the divisions between white and black culture. Lola Young has described the way in which inside black women's magazines like *Pride* there is a new concern with 'achieving upward social mobility' through abandoning strong marks of racial authenticity in hairstyles and dress (Young 2000); the 'aspirational Black woman' cuts herself off from her too-black counterparts, the woman for example who wears 'round-the-way-girl braids, big dangly earrings, and 10-inch red talons, which set me back two centuries' (Blackwood and Adebola 1997, quoted by Young 2000: 422). At the same time there is anger and resentment against light-skinned black girls who have 'always been favoured over us. They walk up and down with "superiority" stamped on their foreheads, thinking they …..can have any man they want' (Blackwood and Adebola quoted by Young 2000: 423). Young acknowledges how black women's magazines are renouncing old-fashioned feminist solidarity in favour of the re-instatement of familiar 'colonial-induced racial self-hatred'.

To sum up, what is disarticulated in these magazines and in forms of popular sexual entertainment like Burlesque is the relevance of feminist and anti-racist critique. Consumers are described as informed, discerning, nowadays empowered and hence able to make their own choices, and this particularly applies to women. This rhetoric of the confident female consumer forecloses on the re-emergence of feminism in favour of apathy and de-politicisation. The world of popular culture including sex entertainment no longer needs to pay any attention whatsoever to those who are concerned with sexual or racial discrimination since they have been silenced or disempowered. The re-colonising mechanism in contemporary popular culture re-instates racial hierarchies within the field of femininity by invoking, across the visual field, a norm of nostalgic whiteness.[10]

Re-traditionalisation as feminist undoing

In Chapter 1 I referred to both the figure of Bridget Jones and to the sociologist Anthony Giddens. In some ways the character of Bridget Jones, her lifestyle and habits, so closely corresponded with Anthony Giddens's sociological analysis of social transformations in late modernity, and the production of new kinds of selves, that he could have almost written the column, the book and then the film-script himself. Here I want to pursue the significance of Giddens and Beck in the process of feminist disarticulation. Giddens, following the pioneering work of Ulrich Beck and his concept of 'risk society', provided an account of processes of dis-embedding, of individualisation, of the growth of the self-monitoring subject, and of the decline of community, tradition, and social embeddedness (Beck, 1992, Giddens 1991). The argument shared by Beck and Giddens is that the new second modernity brings into being kinds of people whose lives are no longer wholly determined by roles ascribed to them by the older or traditional structures of class, race and sex. Some of the historical features of first modernity, such as the social institutions of education and the growth of the welfare state, produce these very conditions which permit in generations to come, a loosening up of dependency and an increasing social fluidity. In the second modernity, and with the changes in the economy which produce a shift to post-Fordist forms of production, individuals are required to become more reflexive, to reflect on the various rules and constraints and the structural factors which impinge upon them, as a necessary mechanism for self-realisation, and also to become self-reflexive, to monitor and evaluate themselves, to plan their life biographies, to regularly assess the opportunities available to them, since, from now on, no one or no institution will bear that kind of responsibility. The sociological writing of Giddens, Beck and also Scott Lash in the last quarter of the twentieth century, examined the deeper changes and transformations in affluent Western countries, and these theories in turn began to have an impact in wider cultural and political life (Beck et al. 1994). Anthony Giddens became a senior advisor to the New Labour government in 1997 and was widely acclaimed for being the architect of the third way, a political strategy which he had already rehearsed in his sociological writing; Ulrich Beck was his colleague and he too found a role in developing the *Neue Mitte* in Germany under the Schroeder government. The ideas of these two leading figures also found a popular readership in newspapers like The *Independent* and The *Guardian* and also magazines like the *New Statesman*. In the acknowledgements section of her novel, *Bridget Jones's Diary*, the author Helen Fielding thanks her editor Charles Leadbeater for encouraging her to write the original column (upon which the novel was based) about her own generation of young women heading towards 30. Charles Leadbeater, like Giddens, was one of the most influential ideas persons for the Blair government.[11] My question is, do Giddens, Beck and Lash, in their accounts of reflexive modernisation as a process which marks out a political shift away from the distinctiveness of the left and the right, also pave the way sociologically for the undoing of feminism? Can their work be seen as part of this process for the reason that they attribute feminism as belonging to a left radicalism, whose emancipatory politics, which Giddens describes as being a product of the dis-embedding possibilities created by the big social institutions of the welfare regimes, have now been superceded by what he calls life politics? That is to say, in arguing for a move beyond conventional left politics, do these authors also contribute to the inauguration, within sociology, of a social theory which regards feminism as overtaken by the appearance of new female subjects for whom there is no longer any need for a women's movement? What do these sociologists have to say about women? Is it the case that gender studies, and feminist theory, of the type which informs a good deal of the thinking in this book, are at odds with this sociology of reflexive modernisation? In effect is this sociology a counter to and undermining of the kind of Marxist-influenced feminist cultural studies perspectives which became so established in the arts, humanities and social sciences from the early 1980s onwards?

Ulrich Beck and Elizabeth Beck-Gernscheim, in effect, acknowledge the surpassing of feminism, in their analysis of 'Individualization and Women' (Beck and Beck-Gernscheim 2001). Where it would not be accurate to suggest that the role of the women's movement is wholly written out of this sociology, in favour of these large structural and epochal shifts which somehow produce conditions for freedom and choice becoming available to women, it is the case that the instrumental role of feminism in actively struggling for equality in education, in law, in family life and in political culture, is overlooked. It is implied that the changes which have occurred for women have come about in some kind of pain-free transition. Capitalism has produced the need for, and the possibility of, womens's liberation. There is, it seems a smooth handover of power, from the big social institutions of the welfare regime, which find themselves replacing the old support mechanisms which once bound people together, to, in this case, the young women who are then charged with the responsibility of self-organisation, and of playing an active role in creating the kind of individualised structures which will secure and service their own dis-embedded careers and pathways. If Giddens points to the role of therapeutic self-help culture as the new forms of individualised guidance now available to facilitate these practices of self-responsibility, Beck and Beck-Gernscheim argue that choices are opened up to young women primarily through the expansion of education, 'thus as women were increasingly released from direct ties to family, the female biography underwent an "individualization boost" and connected with this what functionalist theory calls a shift from "ascribed" to "acquired" roles' (Beck and Beck-Gernscheim 2001: 55). In their account they concede that patterns of gender inequality still exist, and they express wariness about narratives of progress. Nevertheless 'qualitative changes have led to fairer treatment and entitlement than in the past' (ibid 58). And they argue that these new 'normal biographies' are able to display the characteristics of reflexivity by 'react(ing) back upon the structures of society as a whole' (ibid 76). That is to say, reflexive young women are in possession now of degrees of agency which allow them to have an impact on the society in which they live. Despite concluding their chapter with a roll-call of what the women's movement still wishes to change or influence, the analysis they provide seems to suggest that Western society was somehow predisposed to allow women to become more equal. There is no hint that patriarchal structures and other forms of power have regulated women's lives, and continue to do so in a multiplicity of ways. Given that they envisage social transformation as almost benign, and at the very least, improving the lives of women, it is not surprising that in their account of the second modernity with its self-reflexive subjects, there is a similar inattention to coercion and constraint in favour of choice and the construction by women now of individualised biographies.

In short if the struggles of the women's movement, and in particular the writings by Marxist-feminists about how social class and ethnicity invariably intersected with inequalities of gender and sexuality, have no place in the sociology of the Becks, it is hardly surprising that in this transformed world of greater gender fairness, the urgent need for new forms of feminist analysis is either missing, or else is subsumed under rather banal references to the fact that the work of the women's movement will surely continue. Since the social theory of Ulrich Beck has been immensely influential in contemporary sociology, we might surmise that this emphasis on the good that has taken place, has contributed to an occlusion of concern with the re-instatement of gender inequality and with the existence of new forms of gender regulation, in favour of a post-feminist gender settlement organised around choice and consent. The thinking of Beck and Beck-Gernscheim (and Anthony Giddens) is contrary to and quite at odds with the arguments being presented here. What they provide is a new variant of sociological functionalism, of grand social theory, which is predicated on a majestic grasping of the big picture, a social totality, which unfolds according to developments in technology, communications, and knowledge production, (overtaking the structures of first modernity) and which produces new possibilities for human agency, including in this case possibilities for women (the beneficiaries of the second modernity). This kind of sociology is a direct challenge to the Marxist and neo-Marxist approaches which were so influential in sociology and cultural studies, and which were informed by historical materialism, by dialectics, and of course by understanding social change as the product of the contradictions of capital and class.

The argument by Beck, Beck-Gernscheim and by Giddens that freedoms have been won, and that women have more agency and more choice totally ignores the continued existence of gender hierarchies and the perhaps more subtle ways in which these are constantly being reproduced. Lisa Adkins takes all of these figures to task in a way which is relevant to this discussion about undoing feminism (Adkins 2002). I would like to take Adkins' feminist critique of second modernity theory further, and suggest that what she pinpoints as one of its outcomes, that is re-traditionalisation, is in fact a feature of resurgent patriarchalism, in the guise of the seemingly benign power of unfolding social transformation. And because Beck and Giddens each stake out a political, as well as an intellectual investment, in this new period of reflexive modernity, I want to argue that their sociology contributes to the eclipsing of feminism as a valid force for social and political change. What is more I would even suggest that, with different inflections, their sociology overall provides a rationale for the rise of neo-liberalism and the shift to the right of centre in democratic politics.[12] Both writers have reasons to disavow the time of the new left (and its affiliated social movements), they are not overtly hostile to feminism, or antagonistic to the feminist academy. But the power of this new sociology is to move things on, in a kind of roll-forward motion, to suggest that what is now relevant, is this particular vocabulary of reflexive modernity and with it of individualised agency. Within this overarching field of social change, women, by definition, and across the boundaries of class and race, are now able to make choices, and to play an active role in their own life-biographies, which in itself is to say that there is no longer any need for the kinds of combative, or angry styles of political organisation, associated with feminism.

Adkins argues that there is insufficient attention in the work of these three writers to the consequences of reflexive modernisation in the economy and in the realm of work, for women. While the capacity for reflexivity increases with the de-stabilisation of the determining structures of the old social order, and this provides women with more possibilities for choice and agency (although we might inquire as to which women, in which locations), Adkins proposes that so-called de-traditionalisation and individualisation in fact produce patterns of gender re-traditionalisation or what I would call the re-instatement of gender hierarchies through new subtle forms of resurgent patriarchal power. Disembedding from old institutions (for example those of a bureaucratic workplace which still has in place anti-discriminatory legislation) can mean working in an environment where, as Scott Lash himself points out, there is a kind of return to older pre-modern family-based units. Not surprisingly Adkins takes Lash up on this point to remind him that this invariably means a return to the norms of the patriarchal household, with the husband in this case able to benefit from the new reflexivity of the network sociality of the new economy on the grounds that his wife, as his business partner, is able to step in and work long or unsociable hours in a way that would never be expected of her if she was an employee of a local council, for example. Feminist practices which are now possibly embedded in what remains of the social institutions are undone or disarticulated in this more flexible economy. At least Lash notes that women are 'reflexivity losers', leaving Adkins to suggests that women possibly fare better in the old style structures of class and gender segregated Fordist forms of employment. Lash also suggests that the new economy may well push women downwards into a new lower class status along with migrants and other low qualified persons. But instead of this giving grounds for more critical analysis, as to how the gains of the left and of feminism in the workplace are being eroded and made irrelevant, Beck, Giddens and Lash all overlook this downside and with it the re-introduction of traditional pre-feminist gender norms, as somehow expendable or perhaps relatively insignificant. What Adkins sees as re-traditionalisation I would want to take further and see as a determined overturning of feminist gains, a resurgent patriarchal attempt to undo the achievements of the women's movement in these spheres of work and home. Adkins agrees that there are 'new forms of social domination' at play in these 'post-occupational socialities', where I would argue that there is a kind of sociological complicity taking place in this work by Beck, Giddens and Lash, insofar as it fails entirely to reflect on the way in which these processes, which seem somehow inevitable or inexorable and which seem to free up people, and give them more choices, are in fact new and more complex ways of ensuring that masculine domination is re-instated, and at the same time protected from the possibility of a new feminism, in sociology as well as in public life.

'The end of a radical sexual culture' (Butler 2004)

There is also, in this sociological field, a consolidation of the disciplinary boundaries of sociology in contrast to the deconstructive dynamic of interdisciplinary feminist cultural studies and of course feminist post-structuralism. If the former works towards shoring up a power base for sociology in the academy as well as in politics and culture, the latter works to dissect and analyse the new or emerging practices of power as they come into play in a range of intersecting fields. This new sociology disguises its more combative anti-left and post-feminist agenda through doing what New Labour also does with some adeptness, which is to offer a substitute for feminism to the ranks of ordinary women. To all of those who might anyway have been put off by the radicalism of feminist demands, and now to those younger women sociology students inside the academy, and for those now also in the world of work, for whom a life plan is indeed part and parcel of their more individualised self-identities, we can see how Giddens's sociology and its counter-part in New Labour's policies for women, work together symbiotically, to supplant, eclipse and marginalise the place of strident feminist critique. If this work is then a counter to radical feminist sociology and cultural studies, we might ask, what have the developments been in post-Marxism and in feminist theory which sustain a commitment to equality and gender justice? How can this be drawn on to understand the processes of disarticulation with which I have been concerned in this chapter? Chantal Mouffe and Ernesto Laclau have provided a pathway for re-inventing and developing further left-feminist ideals through their notion of a radical democratic pluralist politics. I want to suggest here that this kind of politics, which draws extensively on Gramsci, and which also shaped a good deal of Stuart Hall's work, proposes a kind of relentless critique of capitalism and of new forms of 'biopolitical' patriarchal power. This new kind of democratic pluralism lies in a strategy of everyday contestation and critique, not as an alternative to old-fashioned revolution, now unviable with the decline of socialism, and not as a kind of theorised version of what used to be referred to as reformism, but instead as a kind of constant mobilisation of the range of radical social movements including feminism where these intersect with each other, learn to take into account the claims being made by each other, and modify their own claims as a result.

Anne-Marie Smith, in her explication of Mouffe and Laclau's writing, argues that radical democratic pluralism incorporates elements of the socialist tradition as well as elements of liberal democracy to forge a post-socialist radicalism (Smith 1998). This entails a battle for meaning, and the need for new radical imaginaries, so that people, for example subordinated groups, can find the means to imagine a way of moving out of privatised or hopelessly individualised subordination, into a social space which allows them to understand their circumstances as a form of oppression which they share in common with others. These imaginaries are a resource, a source of hope, a space that offers vocabularies, concepts, histories, narratives, and experiences which can illuminate the predicament or powerlessness and help to find ways of overcoming such circumstances. Of course the raw materials for the construction of such imaginaries will often exist in cultural forms, in books, films, pieces of music, or in art works. If the memorialised history of past struggles could conceivably play this role (for example the history of the civil rights movement in the 1960s in the US, or the history of the women's movement in the 1970s and 1980s) then the shutting down of such possibilities, is also a kind of aggressive politics of disarticulation. The kinds of mechanisms of disconnect which I have outlined and commented upon in this chapter so far can therefore be seen to correspond with a reversal of the politics of articulation argued for by Stuart Hall. Paul Gilroy, as Anne-Marie Smith reminds us, points to the role played by black music in the passing down, through generations of black people, of the history of slavery and brutal exploitation (Smith 1998). The foreclosing of such practices, the attempt to shut them off, in favour of other more alluring opportunities, is then one of the key means by which radical democratic pluralism is today interrupted, and even pre-emptively dismantled. When important historical moments of liberation become somehow no longer transmissable, or when such moments are caricatured and trivialised, if not forgotten, then there is perhaps a crisis for the possibility of radical democratic politics. If the politics of articulation entails this constant struggle over meaning, then the antagonistic forces which I have been describing have been mobilised to negate or shut down the political imaginary of a radical feminism as a source of political wisdom, which might provide the tools for women to imagine an alternative world to that which is now available to them. My argument so far is that women are currently being disempowered through the very discourses of empowerment they are being offered as substitutes for feminism.

Let me bring this chapter to a conclusion with a more specific instance in regard to what Butler describes as the 'lost horizon of sexual politics' (Butler 2004). This process which Butler refers to takes place within the context of a debate about kinship and the campaigns for gay and lesbian marriage. Butler goes to great lengths to remind her readers that the exclusions and indignities which gay and lesbian people have been subjected to in relation to their non-entitlement of family rights are so substantial as to justify fully the desire for various forms of legal recognition. However one key feature of her argument in the article 'Is Kinship Always Already Heterosexual?' is that this process of sanctification and recognition entails a complex set of new regulatory dynamics being introduced, many of which could be described as boundary-marking. Thus normativity is at work in the granting of marital rights to non-heterosexual people, and this, she argues, has repercussions for not just the involvement of the state within now-recognised gay families, but it also introduces new norms of sexual good health and the dominance of the couple as embodying this within gay culture. Forms of sexual relations which do not subscribe to this model will find themselves more marginalised than before, more undesignated and possibly understood to be more disturbing. But more relevant to the concerns of this chapter is the way in which the move to gay and lesbian marriage has implications for the foreclosing on other radical political imaginaries involving a critique of family norms and the creating of alternatives forms of kinship and community.

Butler's essay in many ways provides the rationale for this entire chapter so far, and the word 'undoing' is one she makes great use of herself. What then is undone in the co-option of gays and lesbians into the world of family, marriage and couples? This is more than simply the extending of rights eventually to an oppressed social group who have for many years mobilised and campaigned for their human rights to be recognised. It is also more than to say that recognition comes with strings attached. It entails the fading away of other arrangements and of the possibility of imagining other forms of kinship and living together and the bringing up of children. Butler rightly points out that a good deal is currently invested in the normalisation of family life on the part of Western societies now concerned about global migration, about the arrival and settlement of diasporic peoples and thus about the future of populations, nation states, and the reproduction of 'culture'. The corralling of gays and lesbians into the happy fold of two-parent households, can be seen as an effort to shore up the nuclear family against whatever perceived threat it now faces. It is for this reason that marriage culture and the various celebrations and rituals which in the past have been unavailable to gays and lesbians now, by and large, attract such widespread publicity and approval, at least in liberal democracies. What Bridget Jones dreams of, in her *thirtysomething* singlehood, that is, a white dress, bridesmaids, confetti and wedding bells pealing out, is exactly what is now also available to all.

The regulation of kinship through the sanctity of family life requires then not just these modes of co-option but the pre-emptive extinguishing of the need for, or relevance of, new feminist, or gay and lesbian alternatives. The very idea of the commune or the alternative family is already nonsensical and absurd. But my point is this, the opting into marriage norms on the part of lesbian couples, also cuts off previous articulations and solidarities across the boundary of gay and straight through the politics of single parenthood. And, it is not coincidental that the most demonised category marking out an alternative to mainstream family life is that of the 'single mother'. In UK political parlance this group of women find themselves most consistently vilified. However it is within what we might call the space of single motherhood that, in the past, it has been possible for women, in a kind of self-determining capacity, to find ways of living and creating communities outside the tight knit norms of the suburban nuclear family. Indeed within feminist political discourse, developing new ways of living outside of patri-archal domination, often entailed such attempts as these. And this in turn linked lesbians, with heterosexual feminists and it also intersected with the non-nuclear inter-generational modes of living which many black women have over the years developed as a survival strategy in the context of poverty and racism. But with kinship arrangements such as these now so disavowed, there is only the couple unit to fall back on, and where this is unviable, or impossible, there is, as Butler suggests, a new index of failure or shame. One would only now try to think of alternatives to normal family life, in desperation, if one failed to find the ideal partner. And for the many young women nowadays who are not having children, or who want to have children, but for whom marriage and the finding of that right person somehow passes them by, and who find themselves unmar-ried, and not living inside these now heavily romanticised nuclear units, there is a shrinking of the range of alternatives, and a fading away of the radical political imagineries associated with previous feminist generations where such things were indeed thinkable. What once might have existed positively as an attempt to re-invent modes of kinship which did not repeat the structures of the hetero-sexual and patriarchal family is now forgotten as something which had any political value, and at present there is it seems little or no writing from within lesbian feminism which continues this kind of debate. This eclipsing of past rad-icalisms in favour of more easily regulated and state supported arrangements for living as part of a sexual minority, corresponds with many of the other similar movements which have been tracked in the course of this chapter.

It should be clear to the reader that the emphasis in this overview of processes of disarticulation is to point to emerging modes of regulation which exist within an overarching framework of capacity, freedom, change and gender equality. I have argued that the disavowing of forms of sexual politics which existed in the fairly recent past, and the replacement of these by re-instated forms of sexual hierarchy, constitutes a distinctive new modality of

gender power. This operates largely through processes of undoing and disarticulation which have the effect of dispersing women across divisions of time and
space, age and class, ethnicity and sexuality so that those who might otherwise
have found some common cause together are increasingly unlikely to do so.

Notes

1 In her journalistic account of the 'new feminism' Natasha Walter describes
the terms used by a group of schoolgirls she interviews about feminism. She
reports them as saying in chorus that a feminist is generally a 'big, fat, hairy,
lesbian' (Walter 1998: 23).

2 BBC Radio 4 *Woman's Hour* 20 March 2007.

3 The *Daily Mail* in the UK runs regular features about young, successful Asian
women who have warmly embraced Western values and have made their way
up the career ladder. The typical story of this sort will describe long years of
conflict and battles with parents, sometimes eventually resolved and other times
resulting in the young woman in question creating a life of her own with an
English, non-Muslim husband. See for example an article titled 'A daughter dis-
owned' by Sofia Hayatt, the *Daily Mail*, 27 May 2004. p. 49.

4 Stacey provides a detailed account of the circulation of the term post-feminism
and the neo-conservative attack on feminism from the early 1970s. She also
refers to the article 'Voices from the Post-Feminist Generation' by Susan Bolotin
in the *New York Times Magazine* 17 October 1982, 28–31. Her own co-authored
article on early anti-feminist backlash is Breives et al. (1978).

5 In feminist cultural studies Elspeth Probyn provided one of the first accounts of
post-feminism as re-traditionalisation in her analysis of *thirtysomething* (Probyn
1988, reprinted 1997).

6 The film has already been subjected to extensive critical analysis by film scholars, for a more recent response see L.R. Williams (2005).

7 For a full synopsis of the film narrative, including this episode where Alex breaks
into the home of Dan and Beth and kills their daughter's pet rabbit and then pro-
ceeds to put it in a pan of boiling water, see en.wikipedia.org/wiki/Fatal_
Attraction (accessed 26 June 2006)

8 In a famous US legal case heard in 1991 Anita Hill accused Justice Clarence Hill
of sexual harassment and testified before the Senate Judiciary Committee
which voted narrowly in favour of Thomas. One of the leading journalists,
David Brock, who later admitted to attempting to smear Hill on behalf of the
neo-conservatives he was working for, wrote at the time that she was 'a little bit
nutty and a little bit slutty', see en.wikipedia.org/wiki/Anita_Hill.

9 For a full synopsis see en.wikipedia.org/wiki/Oleanna_play

10 See the photograph by Annie Liebovitz for *Vanity Fair* (8 December 2006)
which showed actors Scarlett Johansson and Keira Knightley both posed naked
together in the style of the late eighteenth century courtly eroticism. The bodies of the actresses are whitened through a powder puff effect and the picture
suggests a fashion for and also a nostalgia for whiteness. The reader might consider how different the meanings of the picture would be, had the models both
been well-known beautiful black actors.

11 Anthony Giddens and Charles Leadbeater were widely recognised as two thinkers close to the Blair team in its early days, they often took part in panel discussions, conferences and events.

12 There are different nuances in the political thinking, however, of Beck and Giddens, with Beck retaining a liberal democratic commitment to welfare and citizens' income in the light of the unemployment, while Giddens offers a centre-left modernisation position, which provides New Labour with its distinctive post-left programme.

3

TOP GIRLS? YOUNG WOMEN AND THE NEW SEXUAL CONTRACT

Since early decisions on education and employment influence later possibilities, it is only younger women who are able to make many of the major work and life decisions in a context of legally enforceable equal opportunities. Age is thus crucial in new forms of difference and inequalities between women. (Walby 1997: 41)

The education of girls is probably the most important catalyst for changes in society. (Augusto Lopez-Claros Chief Economist at the World Economic Forum quoted in the *Guardian* 18 May 2005: 8)

And now it's quite clear that the danger has changed. (Foucault 1984: 344)

Resurgent patriarchies and gender retrenchment

This chapter presents an analysis of a new sexual contract currently being made available to young women, primarily in the West, to come forward and make good use of the opportunity to work, to gain qualifications, to control fertility and to earn enough money to participate in the consumer culture which in turn will become a defining feature of contemporary modes of feminine citizenship.[1] The analysis interrogates the terms and conditions, the inclusions and exclusions, as well as the social and political consequences of such a contract. A range of technologies are set in motion, so that these invitations to come forward can be issued. Young women are being put under a spotlight so that they become visible in a certain kind of way. The Deleuzian term luminosity is useful here, supplanting Foucault's panopticon as a mode of surveillance (Deleuze 1986). The theatrical effect of this moving spotlight softens, dramatises and disguises the regulative dynamics. I also use the term 'spaces of attention' to examine these luminosities in everyday life.

The chapter takes as a starting point some passing comments by a number of feminist theorists in the last few years. First, as discussed in the previous chapter, there is Butler's mention, in regard to her rich and complex equivocations on gay marriage and her reflections on the politics of kinship, that there has been a decline in radical sexual politics (Butler 2004). Second there is Mohanty's important argument in her article '"Under Western Eyes" Revisited', that the restructuring of flexible global capitalism now relies on the willing labour of girls and women and that this entails both a decisive re-definition of gender relations and also forms of retrenchment on the part of 'patriarchies and hegemonic masculinities' (Mohanty 2002). (Labour and the capacity to work will be key themes throughout this chapter.) Mohanty argues that young women are allocated a pivotal role in the new global labour market, but that this coming forward coincides with the fading away of feminism and the women's movement, such that post-Beijing, the most significant site for pursuing struggles for gender justice has been the anti-globalisation movement.

With feminism giving way to women's rights, and women's rights now largely integrated into the vocabulary of human rights, there is, Mohanty acknowledges, a good deal of scope for feminist scholarship to track, from the perspective of the poorest of women, the chains of expropriation of knowledge and resources on the part of global corporations (e.g. biopiracy) which intensify the disadvantage and dependency of non-First World women. And it is in this kind of scholarship and associated pedagogies that Mohanty sees the possibility again for feminist transnational cross-border solidarity. But when she wrote 'Under Western Eyes' there had been, she recalls, 'a very vibrant, transnational, women's movement, while the site I write from today is very different' (Mohanty 2002: 499). Mohanty suggests that the general shift in global politics towards the right, and the decline of social welfarist models coincides with 'processes that recolonise the culture and identity of people' (ibid: 515). (I will return to the word 'recolonise'.) Both of these observations by Butler and Mohanty chime also with the analysis of gender, media and popular culture presented in Chapter 1. There I argued that emerging from largely First World scenarios, the attribution of apparently post-feminist freedoms to young women most manifest within the cultural realm in the form of new visibilities, becomes, in fact, the occasion for the undoing of feminism. The various political issues associated with feminism are understood to be now widely recognised and responded to (they have become feminist common sense) with the effect that there is no longer any place for feminism in contemporary political culture. But this disavowal permits the subtle renewal of gender injustices, while vengeful patriarchal norms are also re-instated. These are easily overlooked, or else a blind eye is turned to them, by those who are well versed in sexual politics, but who are now weary and perhaps persuaded by the high-visibility tropes of freedom currently attached to the category of young women. On this basis post-feminism can be equated with a 'double movement', gender retrenchment is secured, paradoxically, through the wide dissemination of discourses of female freedom and by what Jean-Luc Nancy has called the 'pretences of equality' (Nancy 2002). Young women are able to come forward on condition that feminism fades away.

Sylvia Walby's rationale for the shift away from earlier and more autonomous forms of feminist practice to the engagement with mainstream politics on a national and global stage stands in sharp contrast to this analysis of the new constraints on female equality (Walby 2002). It is because there have been various feminist successes, Walby argues, that it is now appropriate to re-position feminist politics within the mainstream. Feminism has had a major impact in the field of global human rights and has in effect transformed the human rights agenda. It has also been effective at the level of the nation state so that gender issues are now thoroughly integrated into the wider political field. These changes, along with the participation of women in work, give rise to a new 'gender regime'. Walby's model is therefore accumulative in terms of gains which have been made, and linear, in that feminism moves from localised actions and autonomy onto the world stage and because of this presence and participation, and in the light of possibilities which emerge from globalisation, feminism itself changes to comprise advocacy networks, alliances and coalitions which are capable of being tailored to meet particular or culture-specific requirements. Walby endorses a kind of multi-faceted, gender mainstreaming politics on the basis of institutional recognition. She offers a top down account of the professionalisation and institutionalisation of feminism (her involvement in the UK Women's Budget Group has been important). But this model of gender regime is quite different from what I pose in the pages that follow. This is because Walby implies that institutionalisation and capacity-building and indeed participation as well as the growth of feminist expertise and the presence of women professionals on the world stage, have come about in a progressive way. She does not engage with the wider and punitive conditions upon which female success is predicated. Nor is she alert to the new constraints which emerge as the cost of participation, and, more generally, the re-shaping of gender inequities which are an integral part of resurgent global neo-liberal economic policies. I will return to Walby and the question of gender mainstreaming in the concluding chapter, for now we might also note that Walby acknowledges women's place as workers and producers in the global economy, but overlooks their significance as consumers of global culture, even though it is within the commercial domain that processes of gender change and re-stabilisation are most in evidence.

This chapter asks the question: how do we account for the range of social, cultural and economic transformations which have brought forth a new category of young womanhood? If such changes find themselves consolidated into a discernible trend in the UK (and elsewhere) in the last 10 to 15 years, what are we to make of the decisive re-positioning of young women this appears to entail? Transformations such as those which will be described below, tend to be seen as positive. Across the spectrum from left to right the apparent gains made by young women are taken to be signs of the existence of a democracy in good health, these are palpable reminders that women's lives have improved, living testimony that social reform and legislation has been effective. But the feminist perspective I present here is alert to the dangers which arise when a selection of feminist values and ideals appear to be inscribed within a more profound and determined attempt, undertaken by an array of political and cultural forces, to re-shape notions of woman-hood so that they fit with new or emerging (neo-liberalised) social and economic arrangements. And, within a context where in many parts of Europe and in the US there has been a decisive shift to the right, this might also be seen as a way of re-stabilising gender relations against the disruptive threat posed by feminism. Its not so much turning the clock back, as turning it forward to secure a post-feminist gender settlement, a new sexual contract.[2]

Young womanhood currently exists within the realm of public debate as a topic of fascination, enthusiasm, concern, anxiety and titillation (see Harris 2004). The fact that the volume of attention has reached such an unprecedented level is not entirely attributable to the expansion of both popular and so-called quality media. Nor can it be wholly explained on the basis of there now being a much more substantial female audience, a population of women consumers (mothers and daughters alike) for whom such material is directed. Neither is it only the case that this concern can be understood within the cycles of moral panic, which periodically fix upon and demonise a seemingly dangerous sector of the population, so as to permit an intensification of social control, usually along some new axis of anxiety. The meanings which converge around the figure of the girl or young women, are more weighted towards capacity, success, attainment, enjoyment, entitlement, social mobility and participation. The dynamics of regulation and control are less about what young women ought not to do, and more about what they can do. The production of girlhood now comprises a constant stream of incitements and enticements to engage in a range of specified practices which are understood to be both progressive but also consummately and reassuringly feminine. What seems to underpin these practices is a suggestion that young women have now won the battle for equality, they have gained recognition as subjects worthy of governmental attention and this has replaced any need for the feminist critiques of what Mohanty labels hegemonic masculinities. This abandonment of critique of patriarchy is a requirement of the new sexual contract, the terms of which are established in key institutional sites dedicated to the production of the category of young women.[3] The girl emerges across a range of social and cultural spaces as a subject worthy of investment. Within the language of Britain's New Labour government, the girl who has benefited from the equal opportunities now available to her, can be mobilised as the embodiment of the values of the new meritocracy. This term has become an abbreviation for the more individualistic and competitive values promoted by New Labour, particularly within education. Nowadays the young woman's success seems to promise economic prosperity on the basis of her enthusiasm for work and having a career. Thus a defining feature of contemporary girlhood is the attribution of capacity, summed up, as Anita Harris describes, in the Body Shop phrase the 'can do' girl (Harris 2004). This begs the question, what is at stake in this process of endowing the new female subject with capacity? The attribution of both freedom and success to young women, as a series of interpellative processes, take different forms across the boundaries of class, ethnicity and sexuality, producing a range of entanglements of racialised and classified configurations of youthful femininity. So emphatic and so frequently repeated is this celebratory discourse that it comes to function as a key mechanism of social transformation. From being assumed to be headed towards marriage, motherhood and limited economic participation, the girl is now endowed with economic capacity. Within specified social conditions and political constraints, young, increasingly well-educated women, of different ethnic and social backgrounds, now find themselves charged with the requirement that they perform as economically active female citizens. They are invited to recognise themselves as privileged subjects of social change, perhaps they might even be expected to be grateful for the support they have received. The pleasingly, lively, capable and becoming young woman, black, white or Asian, is now an attractive harbinger of social change.

This is certainly not the first time that such a youthful female figure has been used to signal progress and modernity, the girl was invoked in a similar manner particularly in the 1920s and 1930s. Indeed in a recent study which 're-cast(s) gendered modernity within an international frame' Barlow et al. show, in a way which confounds the more usual equation of the 'modern girl' with Western urban modernity, that 'Everywhere the Modern Girl indexed the racial formation of the nation or colony in which she resided' (Barlow et al., 2008: 247). Later in this chapter the racial inflections of contemporary girlhood will be examined in more depth, but for now it is significant to note that there are novel features in this recent deployment within dominating Western discourse. Seemingly post-feminist vocabularies are drawn upon to establish a kind of gender settlement, a new deal for young women. This is a strategy which forcefully rejects the importance of a renewal of an autonomous sexual politics, with a series of pre-emptive moves. In the pages that follow I examine this new standing of young women by considering four 'luminous' spaces of attention, each of which operates to sustain and re-vitalise what Butler has famously called the heterosexual matrix, while also re-instating and confirming, with subtlety, norms of racial hierarchy as well as re-configured class divisions which now take on a more autonomously gendered dimension. Defining such spaces of attention as luminosities I will propose that these comprise first the fashion-beauty complex (a phrase I borrow from Bartky, 1990) from within which emerges a post-feminist masquerade as a distinctive modality of prescriptive feminine agency. Second there is the luminous space of education and employment, within which is found the figure of the working girl. Third, is the space of sexuality, fertility and reproduction from which emerges the phallic girl. Fourth is the space of globalisation and in particular the production of commercial femininities in the developing world, including impoverished countries, as well as countries like China now undergoing rapid transformation. This luminosity comprises a new deal for the global girl and it is one which seeks to supplant other more social democratic, gender-mainstreaming and human rights based models for gender and social change in the so-called Third World. This is a brash, commercial, updating and translating of a liberal feminist model now being made available as a style of global femininity. The sexual contract on the global stage is most clearly marked out in the world editions of young women's fashion magazines like *Elle, Marie Claire, Grazia* and *Vogue*. The friendly (hence unthreatening), beautiful and somehow pliable, global girl who exudes good will, thus marks out the spaces of undoing of post-colonial critical pedagogy as well as of post-colonial feminist critique. Or at least we might understand this to be the underlying (and re-colonising) aim of the promotion of global girlhood by the global media, the commercial domain (the fashion-beauty complex) and through specifically neo-liberal forms of governmentality.

Shining in the light: the post-feminist masquerade

Young women have been hyper-actively positioned in the context of a wide range of social, political and economic changes of which they themselves appear to be the privileged subjects. We might now imagine the young woman as a highly efficient assemblage for productivity. (This also marks a shift, women now figure in governmental discourse as much for their productive as reproductive capacities.) In the UK the young woman has government ministers encourage her to avoid low paid and traditionally gendered jobs like hairdressing. She is an object of concern when a wide discrepancy is revealed between high levels of academic performance, yet pervasive low self-esteem.[4] She also merits attention of government on the basis of remaining inequalities of pay and reward in the labour market. She is addressed as though she is already gender aware, as a result of equal opportunities policies in the education system. With all of this feminist influence somehow behind her, she is now pushed firmly in the direction of independence and self-reliance (Budgeon 2001, Harris 2004). This entails self-monitoring, the setting up of personal plans and the search for individual solutions. These female individualisation processes require that young women become important to themselves. In times of stress, the young woman is encouraged to seek therapy, counselling or guidance. She is thus an intensively managed subject of post-feminist, gender-aware biopolitical practices of new governmentality. What are we to make of this attention? Does it ultimately seek to re-install re-traditionalised styles of normative femininity to be adhered to, despite these winds of gender change (Probyn 1988/1997, Adkins 2002). This certainly would be one way of understanding the full force of triumphant neo-conservatism in its address to women. But the term re-traditionalisation does not completely capture the incorporation and appropriation of liberal feminist principles which are then taken into account so that they can be acknowledged as no longer relevant. Feminism taken into account is also feminism undone, and this movement permits re-configured and spectacular modes of femininity to come to prominence.

Deleuze, writing about what Foucault meant by visibilities, suggests that they are not 'forms of objects, nor even forms that would show up under light, but rather forms of luminosity, which are created by the light itself and allow a thing or object to exist only as a flash, sparkle or shimmer' (Deleuze 1986: 52). This luminosity captures how young women might be understood as currently becoming visible. The power they seem to be collectively in possession of, is 'created by the light itself'. These luminosities are suggestive of post-feminist equality while also defining and circumscribing the conditions of such a status. They are clouds of light which give young women a shimmering presence, and in so doing they also mark out the terrain of the consummately and re-assuringly feminine. Within this cloud of light, young women are taken to be actively engaged in the production of self. They must become harsh judges of themselves. The visual (and verbal) discourses of public femininity, come to occupy an increasingly spectacular space as sites, events, narratives and occasions within the cultural milieu. The commercial domain provides a proliferation of interpellations directed to young women, with harsher penalties, it seems, for those who refuse or who are unable to receive its various addresses.[5] That is, it becomes increasingly difficult to function as a female subject without subjecting oneself to those technologies of self that are constitutive of the spectacularly feminine. There are new norms of appearance and self-presentation expected not just in leisure and in everyday life but also in the workplace, and government concerns itself with this aspect of self-management through various initiatives.[6]

Drawing on Lacan's concept of the Symbolic as the source of patriarchal authority, the oedipal portal which requires subjection to its presiding order as a condition of acquiring both language and sexual identity, Judith Butler has already conjectured that this patriarchal power (or the Symbolic) has been confronted in recent years by feminism as a political antagonism (Butler 2000a). Butler's analysis can be drawn on here to argue that this feminist confrontation has forced some adjustment on the part of the Symbolic. And this required shift has also coincided with transformations within the economic realm such that countries of the affluent West now find it expedient to employ women, across the boundaries of age, sex, class and ethnicity. Of course women, especially poor women across the world, have always worked, usually for low wages in low status sectors. My point is that work and wage-earning capacity come to dominate rather than be subordinate to women's self-identity, and this inevitably has a ripple effect within the field of power. The Symbolic is faced with the problem of how to retain the dominance of phallocentrism when the logic of global capitalism is to loosen women from their prescribed roles and grant them degrees of economic independence. Of course this raises the question, does access to work and earning a living necessarily permit possibilities of independence? For the global girl working 18 hours a day in a clothing factory in an Export Processing Zone and sending most of her wages home, independence is surely a very different thing?

The Symbolic is thus presented with a triple threat, first from the now-outmoded and hence only spectral women's movement, in the activist sense, second, from the aggressive re-positioning of women through these economic processes of female individualisation, and third, a newer threat which emerges from feminist theory itself, and especially from Butler's work and from its popularity and wider dissemination. This is a threat because what Butler does, after all, is to expose and explain those features of heterosexual power which tend to remain inscrutable and unquestioned on the basis of being so deeply embedded, so resistant to challenge. More broadly we could say this is the danger to the Symbolic posed by queer theory. The Symbolic has had to find a new way of exerting its authority and does so by delegation. Just as power (including sovereign power) in late modernity is increasingly dispersed across many institutions and agencies, and as it, in these dispersed forms, directs itself towards bodies, their well-being, their productive as well as reproductive capacity, then we might surmise that the Symbolic allows itself to be dispersed, or governmentalised. The luminosities of femininity provide the spaces for this authority to be exerted anew. The Symbolic discharges (or maybe franchises) its duties to the commercial domain (beauty, fashion, magazines, body culture, etc.) which becomes the source of authority and judgement for young women. The heightening of significance in regard to the required rituals of femininity as well as an intensification of prescribed heterosexually-directed pleasures and enjoyment are among the key hallmarks of this de-centred Symbolic. In the language of health and well-being, the global fashion-beauty complex charges itself with the business of ensuring that appropriate gender relations are guaranteed. This field of instruction and pleasure oversees the processes of female individualisation which requires the repudiation of feminism which is frequently typecast as embodying bodily failure, hideousness or monstrosity. Repeated incitements to perform a register of restricted acts to confirm the illusion of an appropriately gendered self, have, of course, been understood by Butler, as imperative to the social fiction of sexual difference, even though there is always scope for failure and even though the need for repetition reminds us that femininity is never so easily secured (Butler 1990, 1993). Because the commercial domain is now so dominant, as social institutions are reduced in their sphere of influence, we can detect an intensification in these disciplinary requirements and also we can perceive new dynamics of aggression, violence and self-punishment, as I show in the following chapter.

Confronted with the prospect of women becoming less dependent on men as a result of participation in work and with the possible de-stabilisation of gender hierarchy which might ensue, so it becomes all the more important for the Symbolic to re-secure the terms of heterosexual desire. Great effort is invested in this task of maintaining and consolidating masculine hegemony for the very reason that there are forces that appear to threaten its dominance. Thus the paraphernalia of marriage culture assumes such visibility within popular culture at the very moment that its necessity is being put in question. If for women in the West survival itself, and the well-being of children, no longer rests on the finding of a male partner who will be a breadwinner, then the cultural significance of marriage is much reduced. This is precisely the dilemma which emerges out of social welfare regimes making provision for women and children and so substituting for the male breadwinner so that the role of husband is no longer necessary. As various feminist critics have argued the so-called crisis of welfare especially in the US and the UK can be understood as a fearful response to this scenario (see e.g. Brown 1995, Fraser 1997). For younger women without children this degree of independence introduces a new tension into the field of dominant heterosexuality. This is a case of what is no longer economically central becoming, for this very reason, culturally necessary. Such a scenario also gives rise to a veritable minefield of sexual antagonisms, on the basis that women are no longer intelligible primarily in terms of their exchange in the marriage market. And the social anxieties that arise as a result of this have repercussions right across the cultural field.

Within a framework marked out in various ways, as post-feminist, the commercial domain undertakes to carry out the work of the Symbolic by means of the attention it pays to the female body.[7] The authoritative voice of consumer culture is intimate, cajoling and also encouraging. It produces a specific kind of female subject within the realm of its address. By generating bodily dissatisfaction, the beauty and fashion industries respond directly to the fraught state of non-identity which we all inhabit and which is predicated on unfathomable loss, a loss which is incurred as the cost of acquiring language and sexual identity. The young woman is congratulated, reprimanded and encouraged to embark on a new regime of self-perfectibility (i.e. self-completion) in the hope of making good this loss. And now that she is able to make her own choices, it seems as though the fearful terrain of male approval fades away, and is replaced instead with a new horizon of self-imposed feminine cultural norms. Patriarchal authority is subsumed within a regime of self-policing whose strict criteria form the benchmark against which women must endlessly and repeatedly measure themselves, from the earliest years right through to old age.[8] A key feature of the work of the fashion-beauty complex in this new post-feminist situation is that it wrestles to re-gain control over disrupted temporalities. These have challenged the inevitable cycle of life-events associated with the categories of woman and also girl, through sexual freedom, control of fertility, delay in age of marriage, delay in childbearing, low birth rate, the viability of remaining unmarried, etc. The fashion-beauty complex, standing in for the Symbolic, is charged with the role of imposing new time frames on women's lives. As a result there is a proliferation of activities which impose new temporalities through, for example, beauty products routinely recommended to very young girls as well as so-called age defying treatments for young women who are barely in their twenties. There are also relentless warnings about fertility, and there is also the creation of new age-related categories of feminine pathology (e.g. middle-aged anorexia).[9] The opportunity to work and earn a living is thus offset by the emphasis on lifelong and carefully staged body maintenance as an imperative of feminine identity. Temporality finds itself re-defined according to the rhythms invented largely by the fashion and beauty system to manage and oversee other disruptions brought about by the call of the labour market, which could in turn de-stabilise and put into crisis the heterosexual matrix. There is then a tension in regard to time and this provokes the production of a proscribed new time for young women.

Butler, by means of her concept of lesbian phallus, embarks on a kind of social rendering of Lacan's Symbolic. She does this in her book *Bodies That Matter* (1993) where she subjects to close analytical scrutiny the means by which Lacan posits as universal his concept of Symbolic. There is no space here to discuss how Butler arrives at this more social rendering of the Symbolic, but it is a theme which she also pursues in her later book *Antigone's Claim* (2000a), where there is, she argues, an inevitable entanglement of psychic processes with changes in social and political culture.[10] What I propose here is that a key containment strategy on the part of the Symbolic, faced with possible disruption to the stable binaries of sexual difference, and to the threat posed therein to patriarchal authority, is then to delegate a good deal of its power to the fashion-beauty complex where, as a 'grand luminosity', a post-feminist masquerade emerges as a new cultural dominant. This strategy pre-empts and re-contains the threat posed by Butler's work on gender's fictive status, its artifice and its performative existence in daily life. It permits the possibility of distance from the unbearable proximity of femininity, as described by Doane, through a licensed, ironic, quasi-feminist inhabiting of femininity as excess, which is now openly acknowledged as fictive (Doane 1982). The Symbolic here shows itself to be highly adaptable and capable of operating at high speed, to pull back into the field of constraint, actions which have sought to subvert the subordinate status of femininity. It is as though the post-feminist masquerade is a direct response to the feminist theorising of both Doane and Butler. It openly acknowledges and celebrates the fictive status of femininity while at the same time establishing new ways of enforcing sexual difference. The masquerade, as defined by Riviere in 1929, and engaged with by Doane in her highly influential essay 'Film and the Masquerade: Theorising the Female Spectator' (1982) and then returned to by Butler in 1990/1999, has re-appeared as a highly self-conscious means by which young women are encouraged to collude with the re-stabilisation of gender norms so as to undo the gains of feminism, and dissociate themselves from this now discredited political identity (see Figure 1, advertisement for *Grazia* magazine in the *Guardian* 17 January 2006). As a psychoanalyst, Riviere was interested in how 'women who wish for masculinity may put on a mask of womanliness to avert anxiety and the retribution feared from men' (Riviere 1929/1986: 35, quoted in Butler 1999a, 2nd edn: 65). Riviere understands womanliness and masquerade to be indistinguishable, there is no naturally feminine woman lurking underneath this mask. Butler is interested in the 'homosexuality of the woman in masquerade' and in the question of what exactly the masquerade conceals, if not an authentic femininity. She suggests that Riviere disavows the complexity and ambivalence of desire in the masquerade. Butler claims this to be a site of both 'the refusal of female homosexuality and hyperbolic incorporation of that female other who is refused' (Butler 1999a: 65).

This leads Butler some pages later to develop the idea of heterosexual melancholia. While this is indeed a persuasive engagement with Riviere, I want to introduce the post-feminist masquerade as a new form of gender power which re-orchestrates the heterosexual matrix in order to secure, once again, the existence of patriarchal law and masculine hegemony, but this time by means of a kind of ironic, quasi-feminist staking out of a distance in the act of taking on the garb of femininity.[11] The Symbolic permits the presence of a feminist gesture as it adjusts to ward off the threat of feminism. There is a useful slippage in Riviere's account between the actuality of the masquerade as a recognisable phenomenon which she perceives in her female patients and their encounters, and images of femininity found in the cultural realm. This intersection between the styles of femininity that Riviere observes in everyday life, and those portrayed in feminine popular culture, permits me here to propose the post-feminist masquerade as mode of feminine inscription, across the whole surface of the female body, an

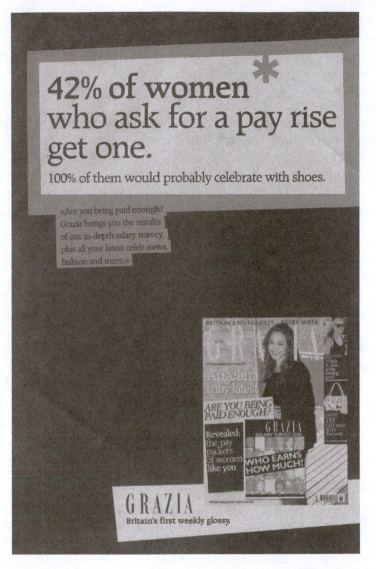

Figure 1   *Grazia* advertisement in the *Guardian* 17 January 2006. Courtesy *Grazia* magazine.

interpellative device, at work and highly visible in the commercial domain as a familiar (even nostalgic or 'retro'), light-hearted (unserious), refrain of femininity. It has been re-instated into the repertoire of femininity ironically (as the wearing of clothes in inverted commas). This signals that the hyper-femininity of the masquerade which would seemingly re-locate women back inside the terms of traditional gender hierarchies, by having them wear spindly stilettos and 'pencil' skirts, for example, does not in fact mean entrapment (as feminists would once have seen it) since it is now a matter of choice rather than obligation. The element of choice becomes synonymous with a kind of feminism. But what the young woman is choosing is more than just participation in consumer culture. No aspect of physical appearance can be left unattended to. The post-feminist masquerade functions with this microscopic attention to detail. As ever more obscure beauty procedures are made available, traditional feminine practices of self-maintenance, like manicures and pedicures, are also re-instated as norms of feminine grooming. Such routine practices as these are required by all women who want to count themselves as such, and these rituals constitute the post-feminist masquerade as a feminine totality.

This new masquerade constantly refers to its own artifice. Its adoption by women is done as a statement, the woman in masquerade is making a point that this is a freely chosen look. The post-feminist masquerade does not fear male retribution. Instead it is the reprimanding structure of the fashion and beauty system which acts as an authoritative regime; hence the seeming disregard for male approval, especially if the outfit and look is widely admired by those within the fashion milieu.[12] The masquerade creates a habitus for women who have now found themselves ensconced within fields of work, employment and public life, all of which hitherto had been marked out as masculine domains. The masquerade disavows the spectral, powerful and castrating figures of the lesbian and the feminist with whom they might conceivably be linked. It rescues women from the threat posed by these figures by triumphantly re-instating the spectacle of excessive femininity (on the basis of the independently earned wage) while also shoring up hegemonic masculinity by endorsing this public femininity which appears to undermine, or at least unsettle the new power accruing to women on the basis of this economic capacity. There are many variants of the post-feminist masquerade (sometimes summed up in the word immaculate) but in essence it comprises a re-ordering of femininity so that old-fashioned styles (rules about hats, bags, shoes, etc.), which signal submission to some invisible authority or to an opaque set of instructions, are re-instated.[13] In practice it can be read as a nervous gesture on the part of young women (think of Bridget Jones's short skirt and flirty presence in the workplace and her 'oh silly me' self-reprimands), who have become aware that their coming forward and competing on the labour market with men as their equals has certain repercussions. They are nervous because they are still unused to power, it ill-befits them, they are inexperienced, they cannot afford for it to be relaxed or casual, they are anxious it will make them unfeminine. It is not so much fear, as recognition that this appropriation of power which they have found themselves assuming, impacts on their negotiation of heterosexuality and potentially detracts from their desirability. The post-feminist (anti-feminist) masquerade comes to the young women's rescue, a throwback from the past, and she adopts this style (assuming for example the air of being 'foolish and bewildered' (Riviere, 1929/1986: 29) to help her navigate the terrain of hegemonic masculinity without jeopardising her sexual identity, which, because she is actually and legitimately inside the institutional world of work, from which she was once barred or had only limited access to, can become a site of vulnerability (she might be made to feel herself too old, past her best, still on the shelf, etc). Or else she fears being considered aggressively unfeminine in her coming forward as a powerful woman, she fears being mistaken for a feminist, and so adopts the air of being girlishly distracted, slightly flustered, weighed down with bags, shoes, bracelets and other decorative candelabra items, all of which need to be constantly attended to. She is also almost inappropriately eager to please. The new masquerade draws attention self-consciously to its own crafting and performance. The post-feminist masquerade (embodied in the figure of the so-called *fashionista*) is then a knowing strategy which emphasises its non-coercive status, it is a highly-styled disguise of womanliness which is now adopted as a matter of personal choice. But the theatricality of the masquerade, the silly hat, the too short skirt, the too high heels, are once again means of emphasising, as they did in classic Hollywood comedies, female vulnerability, fragility, uncertainty and deep anxiety, indeed panic, about the possible forfeiting of male desire through coming forward as a woman.

Both Riviere and Butler refer to the sublimated aggression directed towards masculinity and male dominance in the form of the masquerade. Riviere uses words like triumph, supremacy and hostility to describe the female anger which underpins the façade of excessive feminine adornment, she pinpoints the fury of the professional women who perceives her own subjugation in the behaviour of her male peers. All of this gets transmogrified into the mask of make-up and the crafting of a highly styled look. This strategy re-appears today in very different circumstances. Women now routinely inhabit these masculine spheres, they now find themselves in competition with men on a daily basis. They take their place alongside men thanks to the existence of non-discriminatory policies, and more recently to systems of meritocratic reward as advocated by New Labour. The woman in masquerade wishes to have a position as a 'subject in language' (i.e. to participate in public life) rather than existing merely as 'women as sign' (Butler 1990/1999a). It is precisely because women are now able to function as subjects in language (i.e. they participate in working life) that the new masquerade exists to manage the field of sexual antagonisms and to re-instate women as sign. The successful young woman must now get herself endlessly and repetitively done up, so as to mask her rivalry with men in the world of work (i.e. her wish for masculinity) and to conceal the competition she now poses because only by these tactics of re-assurance can she be sure that she will remain sexually desirable. She fears the loss of her own desirability, so she gets all done up, but where in the past this was a necessity, now it is a personal choice, and male approval is sought only indirectly. And in any case patriarchy and hegemonic masculinities have removed themselves from the scene and are now replaced by the cultural horizon of judgement provided by the fashion and beauty system. This becomes the source of reprimand, this is where punishment is meted out. Women disguise their bid for power by means of masquerade and patriarchal authority absents itself from the scene of judgement and delegates this power to the beauty and fashion system which requires constant self-judgement and self-beratement, against a horizon of rigid cultural norms. This makes it look as though women are 'doing it for themselves'. If patriarchy, at the time when Riviere was writing, objected vigorously to women's bid for power and threatened punishment, the only way in which women could avoid this punishment was by retreating from the bid for power into re-assuring femininity thereby letting men know that they posed no threat. But the need for masquerade in a post-feminist context remains also a source of sublimated anger. This becomes privatised or even illegible for the reason that the critique of masculinity would return complaining women to the camp of the repudiated feminist, thus there is a good deal of searching about for an appropriate cultural space for the venting of this anger. In some ways there is a 'damn you men' gesture in the narcissistic self-absorption of super-fashionable young women today. The controlling and constraining aspects of the post-feminist masquerade, recognises and panders to the sublimated critique of masculinity, and even to heterosexual melancholia as described by Butler. This melancholia lurks beneath the surface, threatening to transmogrify into rage, as will be discussed in the chapter that follows. The heroines of popular fiction (including so-called chick lit) regularly express anger, outrage and frustration in their diaries that they have, once again, to make themselves submissive in order to appeal to men.

Riviere argues that by exaggerating the way in which she inhabits her gender and sexuality so as to draw attention to objects and the accoutrements of her femininity, the woman both masks her bid for masculine power and retreats from it at the same time. She is fearful of seriousness (hence the comedic nature of spectacular femininity) and even when positioned as authoritative she will allude to her inhabiting of femininity so that she remains recognisable within the terms of male desire.[14] Riviere describes how the prominent woman demonstrates her professional skills in a public environment (giving a lecture) but goes on to undermine the effect of proficiency and expertise with an excessive display of 'coquettishness' and feminine gestures. She reassures her male colleagues that she remains nonetheless a real (and thus subjugated) woman. The masquerade functions to re-assure male structures of power by defusing the presence and the aggressive and competitive actions of women as they come to inhabit positions of authority. It re-stabilises gender relations and the heterosexual matrix as defined by Butler by interpellating women repeatedly and ritualistically into the knowing and self-reflexive terms of highly-stylised femininity. The post-feminist masquerade works on behalf of the Symbolic pre-emptively in the light of the possible disruptions posed by the new gender regime. It operates with a double movement, its voluntaristic structure works to conceal that patriarchy is still in place, while the requirements of the fashion and beauty system ensure that women are in fact still fearful subjects, driven by the need for 'complete perfection' (Riviere 1929/1986: 42).

But the next question, which must be asked, concerns the racial underpinning of the post-feminist masquerade.[15] How is whiteness inscribed within this re-ordering of the feminine? How do black and Asian young women find themselves interpellated (or not) by the addresses which seek to encourage the adoption of this bodily norm of 'complete perfection'? The post-feminist masquerade is also a means of re-instating whiteness as a cultural dominant within the field of the fashion-beauty complex. This too is a moment of profound undoing, a mode of re-colonisation through a range of complex strategies which can be identified within the visual discourses of popular culture. What do I mean re-colonisation? What do I mean undoing? In the addresses to young non-white women across the media and culture, there is an insinuation or a suggestion that the fight for racial equality is no longer relevant. Overt anti-racism combined with feminism, is also associated with the past, with the angry period of the 1970s and 1980s which pre-dated the more enlightened time of the New Labour government. As already noted in the previous chapter, this coincides with the shift in governmental thinking away from endorsing multi-culturalism and the policy strategies associated with anti-racism, and instead the encouraging of new styles of integration and assimilation, while also of course celebrating black and Asian success as key features of the new meritocracy. New integrationism has the (post 9/11) ring of the contemporary, and the visibility of black and Asian people including 'modern' young women within the ranks of the talent-led economy would ideally replace the need for arguments about institutionalised racism and the new prevalence and reproduction of racial inequalities. The particular element of undoing relevant to discussions of femininity resides in something as straightforward as the sustained, marked, inattention by predominantly white editors, journalists, and other people occupying important roles in the world of media, culture and inside the social institutions, to what used to be called issues of equal opportunities and to, as discussed in the previous chapter, questions of representation. In the last few years, there is a very noticeable decrease in images of black and Asian women on the pages of the women's and girls' magazines, but equally important, this is no longer a focus for discussion.

Questions about the numerical representation of black and Asian people in the media, takes us right back to the early days of feminist and anti-racist research and scholarship in the humanities and social sciences. It is almost too crude a point to make. My mention here of an observed decline in black models and in coverage of issues relating to non-white women in the field of feminine popular culture bears the hallmark of just that, a kind of instinctive noticing, that even on the pages of the liberal press which now devotes so much space to fashion and beauty and which so forcefully pursues a female readership, most often there are no black or Asian bodies at all to be seen amongst the endless pages of fashion tips, beauty schedules, information about cosmetic surgery and so on. It is as though, in a climate now openly critical of so-called 'political correctness', and thus no longer expected or required to engage with equal opportunities issues, as they might have done in the recent past, editors and journalists, revert to relying on the norms and conventions which governed their practice in the era prior to the rise of feminist and anti-racist politics. Thus there is an undoing of anti-racist feminist cultural politics in the press and across the popular media. Black and Asian girls have a minimal presence as a result in the various styles incorporated within post-feminist masquerade. The luminosities of femininity are unapologetically and invariably white. The clouds of light which fix upon the figures of female success and the top girls can accommodate to black and Asian femininity but only on condition that there is a subsuming of difference (into Western glamour) so that it complies with specific requirements endlessly repeated by the fashion and beauty system. Otherness is also signalled, and there are prescribed pathways for cultural difference to find some negotiated space within the post-feminist masquerade (the occasional black female celebrity featured in the magazines, as a style icon) but overall the post-feminist masquerade implicitly re-instates normative whiteness and it exacts a violent exclusion of diversity and otherness thereby resurrecting and solidifying gendered racial divisions in the cultural realm.

Thus we might say that the post-feminist masquerade re-secures the terms of submission of white femininity to white masculine domination, while simultaneously resurrecting racial divisions by undoing any promise of multi-culturalism through the exclusion of non-white femininities from this rigid repertoire of self-styling. This amounts to a double process of re-subordination, with again, somewhere in the background the hint that of course feminism and anti-racism have been already dealt with, they have been taken into account, young black and Asian women now have the opportunities to succeed alongside their white female counterparts. Of course they are included in the encouragement to achieve 'complete perfection'. This element of confident coming forward, which is so central to the dominant discourses of governmentality, makes it all the more difficult to resurrect a language of discrimination, injustice and exclusion. But the idea of complete perfection embodied within this post-feminist masquerade is elusive, unviable, and beyond reach, it seems, for non-white women, unless they relinquish almost all signifiers of racial difference and subsume ethnicity into the dominant repertoire of normative white femininity.

These current interpellative addresses of the fashion and beauty system to black female subjects has not attracted the attention of feminist scholars in the way such issues did in the 1980s and early 1990s (see Young 2000). The feminine commercial domain operates then with a limited and thus exclusionary address, inviting young (light skinned) black and (respectably demure) Asian women to accept minimal terms of representation within these visual economies. This readership only has the option of adjusting to the norms of dominant white glamorous and high maintenance femininity. There are very few black celebrities whose everyday lives are the subject of paparazzi attention for the gossip magazines. The film version of *Bridget Jones's Diary* evokes a landscape of whiteness with barely a gesture towards London as a multi-cultural city. There was no black girl among the main cast of characters in *Sex and the City*, no black girl in *Friends* (other than the occasional 'date'). There is a successful genre of Asian chick lit, and there are a handful of black models who embody 'complete perfection', but the pool of light which attempts to bring order and stability to the landscape of change for young women by means of a post-feminist masquerade offers young non-white women only the option of mimicry, accommodation, adjustment and modification. This is a kind of racial violence within the celebratory white visual economies of the fashion-beauty complex which goes almost unnoticed. The post-feminist masquerade derives its meaning from the hey-day of (white) Hollywood glamour, and from the conventions of high fashion glossy magazines like *Vogue*. The retro, nostalgia for this kind of whiteness ensures that the new masquerade, if not unavailable to black or Asian women, is then only available at the cost of negating modes of style and beauty associated with blackness, with cultural diversity and ethnic difference (Dyer 1997). The fashion-beauty complex functions on behalf of patriarchal authority so as to ensure the stability of the heterosexual matrix especially when it is threatened by social changes brought about by women coming forward into the world of work and employment. It is also a key mechanism in the active production and reproduction of racialising differences. And likewise the various forms of feminine popular culture whose focus of attention is sexuality, desire, and the conduct of love and intimacy, here too the interpellative address of heterosexuality is simultaneously one which generates and reinforces racial and ethnic difference. These systems of racialised meaning are so deeply inscribed within the dominant language of love, and what young women now need to do to secure a partner or husband (the so-called rules), that the only available logic of difference, within the commercial domain, is the production of an equivalent system of feminine popular culture for black or Asian young women. Hence the proliferation of self-help handbooks for black or Asian women, black fashion magazines, Asian fashion labels, Asian chick lit and so on.

Education and employment as sites of capacity: the visibility of the well-educated working girl

The luminosities of the post-feminist masquerade and the clouds of light bestowed on the figure of the young women by the fashion and beauty system are matched, if not surpassed, by (and frequently intersect with) the visibilities which produce the well-educated young woman and the working girl. Together these comprise two key elements of the new sexual contract. It is the wage earning capacity on the part of young women which is the critical factor that underpins the exuberance of the commercial domain, as commerce embraces the possibilities opened up by the disposable income of young women, who now are expected to not just have an occupation, but to prioritise earning a living as a means of acquiring status, ensuring an independent livelihood, and gaining access to the world of feminine goods and services. And the ability to earn a living is also the single most important feature of the social and cultural changes of which young women find themselves to be the privileged subjects. Governmental activity is put into making young women ready for work, and this requirement takes the form of urging young women towards agency across the whole range of talents and abilities (Rose 1999b, Allen 2008). As I attempt to demonstrate, within the terms of the UK government's modernising project, the prescribed manner of acquiring capacity also ensures the re-stabilisation of gender hierarchies. In this next section I consider some of the ways in which education and employment play this role of re-designating young women as subjects of capacity who will refrain from challenging existing gender hierarchies as they come forward to occupy a position of visibility. Young women are now integral to social change and to processes of social re-structuring with all that entails in relation to social divisions, new polarities between wealth and poverty and the creation of what New Labour labels the new meritocracy.

As well-trained women gain their own more independent middle-class status so also are they encouraged to repudiate their social inferiors and celebrate their own individualistic success. As I show in Chapter 5, the re-appearance of hierarchy, class disdain, indeed hatred, in regard to the habits and appearance of low-income women, gains acceptability in the guise of entertainment, in popular culture and the media, as a mark of women no longer needing the support of each other now that they have access to the means of becoming successful and competitive. Implicit within this discourse of popular culture (BBC TV programmes like *What Not To Wear*) is the idea that women's lives have changed dramatically. Working-class women are urged to abandon fatalistic ideas about the inevitability of ageing, the decline in appearance and the traditional requirement of mothers and wives to be self-sacrificing. This landscape of self-improvement substitutes for the feminist values of solidarity and support and instead embraces and promotes female individualisation and condemnation of those who remain unable or unwilling to help themselves. The new temporalities of women's time mean that they are now called upon to attend to body image and personal skills so that they will remain presentable in the workplace and employable in the longer term. Occupational identity and the acquisition of qualifications mean that young women are no longer classified primarily according to their place within structures of family and kinship. Their highly visible bodies are now marked by the possession of grades, qualifications and occupational identities. As they emerge through the education system, young women, more so than their male peers, come to be associated with the gaining of qualifications. Until the late 1980s, being in proud possession of a clutch of high graded GCSEs and A levels was the privilege of a small number of middle class and largely white young women, so much so that it was not a subject which attracted wide public attention. This has changed dramatically. The impact of class inequalities, racism and the sheer persistence of unsurmountable obstacles for girls growing up in poverty are eclipsed by the emphasis on improvement, success and the significant increase in the numbers of young women going to university.[16] These changes also feature prominently in the process of young women coming forward, and being seen to benefit from the attention of government. The education system now looks favourably towards young women and rewards them for their effort. The result is that the young woman comes to be widely understood as a potential bearer of qualifications, she is an active and aspirational subject of the education system, and she embodies the success of the new meritocratic values which New Labour have sought to implement in schools. This re-positioning is a decisive factor in the new sexual contract. The contractual dimension entails an offer made to young women which cannot be refused, without painful repercussions. But this requires further unpacking and contextualisation. How, for example, have feminist scholars responded to a situation which suggests that young women have now gained equality in the education system and thus might appear no longer to be subjects of injustice or discrimination?

Education has been a site in which years of feminist struggle have indeed reaped some rewards. If second wave feminism paid great attention to the gender inequalities across the school system, with socialist feminists and black feminist scholars also mapping this vector of disadvantage together with those of class and ethnicity, this longstanding commitment to achieving equality in schooling for young women could be understood in Walby's terms as having resulted in the mainstreaming of gender issues as matters for attention within the wider political arena. The increase in educational qualifications referred to above, as well as the growing numbers of girls staying on at school after 16, and going to university, means that it is in effect primarily young women who are providing the New Labour government with reasons to claim that their policies are successful.[17] This could also be seen as an example of women coming forward and feminism fading away on the basis of its work being done, substantial degrees of equality having been won, and enduring inequities are now attended to by mainstream governmental processes. However my emphasis here is rather different. And this is not just a matter of pointing to the unevenness of success, the discrepancy between the rates of achievement and under-achievement on the basis of class, and the continued pernicious impact of racial disadvantage on young black and Asian women across the class divide. The violent impact of racial prejudice on young black and Asian women's educational prospects continues to undermine any straightforward notion of feminist gains in the educational field, particularly as these are described within a vocabulary of gender mainstreaming. We need a much more detailed empirical account of the educational experiences of young black and Asian women in the UK and in Europe which would, we might assume, temper any premature optimism about success and social mobility. What can be argued however is that the coming forward of young women and the attribution of capacity to these now seemingly privileged subjects also plays a role within the modernising agenda of New Labour. Indeed this is a key role, it shows that there remains a solid, social democratic 'heart' to New Labour, and that indeed wise investment in education has proved to reap rewards especially with a social group, i.e. young women who in the past were destined to under-achieve.

There are a range of studies from the US, the UK, Australia and Europe which provide detailed accounts of inequities newly generated by changes to welfare regimes, the decline in state funding of education, and the emergence of meritocratic systems of reward. These show how such policy shifts towards an audit and target-based system, as well as privatisation, impact negatively on the educational achievements of young women from low-income families (Walkerdine et al. 2002). Middle-class girls and those from privileged Asian and black families (who will still of course experience discrimination) will become part of the new competitive elite, while lower middle class girls and many of their working class counterparts will now be expected to gain degree level qualifications and enter the labour market in occupations appropriate to the qualifications gained. As Kim Allen shows, overall in the UK in the early years of the twenty first century there is an exceptionally high level of activity for girls, in schools, in training, in further and higher education and in employment, leaving only 2% of girls who finish school with no qualifications and who are, as a result, now singled out more forcefully as educational failures (Allen 2008). Such a distribution of young women, by means of educational qualifications, looks like a simple reproduction of existing class divisions, with the double proviso, first that women are now gaining their own class identity through work and qualifications, and second that there are specifically feminine pathways of social mobility.[18] The acquisition (or not) of qualifications therefore comes to function as a mark of a new gender divide. Young women are ranked according to their ability to gain qualifications which provide them with an identity as female subjects of capacity. (They can become obsessed with grades.) The principles that underscore the new gender regime require willingness, motivation and aptitude on the part of young women that if instilled within the school system will be sustained and further developed in the workplace. In singling out young women for special attention, New Labour and other governments seem to be fulfilling some of the hopes of earlier generations of feminists, while in fact they are encouraging female activity as a new form of social mobility. Government substitutes for feminism, and instils in place of those now outmoded values, styles of feminine competition which also give rise to new and more opaque entanglements of class, race and gender.[19] Because the language and ideas which circulate across the culture in relation to young women's working lives are so dominated by personal narratives, and by colourful 'self-biographies', and by TV programmes like *Fame Academy* or *The Apprentice*, which emphasise talent, determination and the desire to win, and which feature highly motivated young women, it becomes more and more difficult to discern the real sociological intersections of structural factors of ethnicity, social class and gender, in regard to young women. In the individualising narratives of popular culture, for example in the *Daily Mail*, a good deal of attention is given to the young woman who will step forward as an exemplary black or Asian young woman on the basis of her enthusiasm for learning, her taste for hard work, and her desire to pursue material reward.

High rates of success in gaining qualifications have become the benchmark of equality as achieved. It is assumed that gender inequities have now (more or less) been successfully dealt with, such that young men are now the losers, and they are in effect discriminated against. Thus one form the backlash against feminism takes is to argue that it has gone too far, that it has overstepped its limits and that having succeeded in achieving equality for young women it has indirectly contributed to male under-performance through the feminisation of schooling.[20] And the extent to which this argument is taken up by government, makes it all the more difficult to continue to make a case for young women's inequality despite apparent success in schooling. A range of sociological studies have challenged the sensational headlines in the press about female success and male failure, and have provided important qualifications to such inflated claims, see Arnot et al. (1999), Harris (2004), Driscoll (2002), Safia-Mirza (1997), Bettie (2003),

Budgeon (2001). Arnot et al. writing about UK schooling both contextu-
alise and historicise female success. They point to how feminist practice on
the part of teachers in schooling from the mid-1970s, was gradually supplanted by a more harshly competitive, Thatcherite, target-oriented and
accountability-directed, regime. However, as a result of residual feminist
pedagogic principles still intact, it was possible for the former nonetheless
to be translated so as to accord with the meritocratic logic of the latter, with
young women thus able to reap some benefits from both old feminist and
New Labour policies. Arnot et al. describe the way in which the attack by
the new right on educational practices associated with the left and feminism, forced teachers to abandon the vocabulary that had been in place in
regard to girls and schooling, in favour of one which emphasised results, tar-
gets and external ratings. Feminism was made to fold into the new values of
competition and excellence so that the high-achieving girl came to embody
the improvements and changes in the educational system as a whole.
Notwithstanding the perpetuation within secondary education of glaring
inequities, the authors say 'successive generations of girls have been challenged by economic and social change and by feminism' (Arnot et al. 1999:
150). However this notion of challenge remains rather vague. The new educational vocabulary addressed to young women is actually more aggressive
in its attempts to eradicate the traces of feminism so that feminist pedagogy
is seen to be a thing of the past, frozen in educational history as marking out
a moment of outmoded radicalism. This coincides with recent parallel
efforts to associate anti-racist educational practices with similar meanings,
in the move, in the aftermath of the events of 9/11 to find ways of re-instating
vocabularies of assimilation and integration rather than those of cultural difference and muticulturalism. For black and Asian girls there is the impact of
a double process of discrediting the radical values which had been established in the school system from the mid-1970s to the mid-1990s and
which had also shaped at least parts of the curriculum.

The account I have presented so far of educational changes is certainly
schematic, and aims more at drawing attention to the shift away from
debates which historically focused on questions of girls and schooling, to
those which now assume that young women are being relatively well-catered
to by education and consequently understood as subjects of capacity, subjects
who are in a position to do well. The actuality of the schooling process for
young women and the re-drafting of inequalities clearly require a good deal
more analysis. But in regard to the process of young women as subjects of
capacity we might also point to the convergence in values between the UK
endorsing of competitive female individualisation and the comments made
by Gayatri Spivak about the forms of pedagogy advocated within Western
aid programmes ostensibly to the benefit of the new global girl. Spivak (in
contrast with Nussbaum) urges caution in endorsing the seeming support for

girls' education on the part of governments in impoverished Third World as well as wealthy countries of the West (Nussbaum 2003b, Spivak 2002b). The investing in girls as subjects of educational capacity as a sign of progress, she argues (contra Walby), must be countered with recognition that they will now most likely be educated according to pedagogic principles which are completely compliant with the values of neo-liberalised global capitalism. Spivak questions the role of such forms of knowledge and the paternalism which underpins the categorising of the girl as worthy of investment. Of course she is not saying that young women should reject the possibilities for becoming educated, rather that the terms and conditions within which this provision is made be subject to critical scrutiny. The attention of Western government to the category of girl shows the extent to which the global girl is now a figure who promises a great deal within the new international division of labour. Where once she was simply known for her nimble fingers, the global girl now emerges as a subject of micro-credit worthiness, gender training, enterprise culture as well as an active practitioner of birth control (Spivak 1999, 2002a, 2002b, Mohanty 2002).

If education remains the privileged space within the countries of the affluent West for promulgating female participation, the recent attempts on the part of government to create more direct links between education and employment by emphasising work experience, internships, employability, and enterprise culture, have particular resonance for young women. Right across a range of recent studies of young women's self-identity it is apparent that occupational status has become an overriding factor in the presentation of self. Interviewees, across the boundaries of class and ethnicity, are motivated and ambitious, they have clear plans about what direction they might hope to follow from a young age and they frequently refer to the support they receive from their parents, especially from their mothers (Budgeon 2001, Harris 2004). Having a well-planned life emerges as a social norm of contemporary femininity. And conversely the absence of such styles of self-organisation becomes an indicator of pathology, a signal of failure or a symptom of some other personal difficulties. As Harris and others have pointed out this governmental vocabulary of self-responsibility also personalises disadvantage and marks out poverty and economic hardship as issues connected with family and dysfunctionality rather than as socially generated phenomena. For those young women who appear to be in possession of the social skills of confident self-presentation and ambition, the question that arises is how these are transposed into the workplace? For those without such advantages, the transition to work will surely entail being pushed towards low pay, low skill work but with the proviso that for those who wish to improve their chances in the labour market there are indeed pathways to further education, day release schemes and training. The result is that those young women under-achievers, and those who do not have the requisite degrees of motivation and ambition to improve themselves, become all the more emphatically condemned for their lack of status and for other failings, than would have been the case in the past.

At the opposite end of the scale, we might ask how the middle class and lower middle class young women, who have, as Arnot et al. argue, benefited both from the feminism of the earlier period, and then have been designated as subjects of immense capacity through the ethos of meritocracy and competition by the New Labour government, find themselves positioned within the field of work and employment? If this section of the female population are the winners, can they also be losers? Are their grounds for claiming that here too gender retrenchment takes place, despite a façade of opportunity and capacity and despite the various attentions which produce specific visibilities around the figure of the working girl or the young career woman? Certainly it is the hard working and aspirational young woman who in popular culture transmogrifies into the luminosity which surrounds the figure of the 'working girl'. She has benefited from feminism, and can now afford to wave goodbye to its values, in favour of pursuing her own personal desires. She again is invariably white and finds herself the subject of countless narratives in film, TV drama as well as within the repertoire of features in girls and women's magazines. Charlotte Brunsdon writing in the 1990s on films like *Working Girl* (directed by Mike Nichols in 1989), shows exactly how postfeminist meanings emerge in popular cinema directed at a female audience through narratives which acknowledge, or make some gestures to the impact of the women's movement, on ordinary women's lives and their current investment in work and careers. Brunsdon reflects on the disavowal of feminism in a number of 1980s and early 1990s Hollywood women's genre films, and in many ways my argument in this book takes Brundson's notion of disavowal further by looking at how feminism is actively taken into account, in order that it is also undone, and so that it might never happen again (Brunsdon 1991, 1997). The prevalence of powerful and attractive working girls across the landscape of media and culture and the incorporation of working identity as integral to the post-feminist masquerade comes to provide a benchmark against which young women are invited to measure their own capacity in the world of work.

The film *Working Girl* provides a narrative account of young women's movement, or coming forward, to occupy these spaces of luminosity. Indeed this film enacts a passage from masquerade to post-feminist masquerade by means of two competing female figures. The middle class, feminist-influenced executive figure, Katherine, played by Sigourney Weaver is eventually eclipsed by her rival and social inferior in the typing pool (played by Melanie Griffith) who studies her closely, and learns how to dress so that she too embodies 'complete perfection', but who remains endearingly feminine and succeeds in work and in love by these means. In the film Melanie Griffith plays Tess McGill, an office girl with poor taste in dress. An opportunity arises (her boss has a skiing accident) which allows Tess not just to emulate the immaculate style of her boss Katherine, but also to seduce her boyfriend and turn herself into an equally high-powered executive by means of a combination of old-fashioned feminine conniving and instinctive intelligence. Tess's post-feminist masquerade entails learning and applying all the fashion rules, but she remains nervous, unsure of herself, and eager to please, and playing these qualities up, she attracts the attention of the handsome executive and Katherine's long-term boyfriend played by Harrison Ford. This is only one of many working girl narratives, but, as is often the case with mainstream Hollywood films, it anticipates with perspicuity many of the key thematics of gender and social as well as cultural change of the last 20 years. These include post-feminist competition and unbridled rivalry among women, female social mobility, working-class ambition, and the post-feminist masquerade as feminine performance which succeeds for Tess for the reason that she works out why Katherine, despite her expensive wardrobe, will fail when it comes to men and sexuality. Katherine is too near to being a feminist. In her style as well as her manner, she presents herself as equal to men, and she is beaten in love by her less well-educated rival who is better able to adjust to the requirements of masculine domination.[21]

The post-feminist masquerade exacts then on the part of the working girl a kind of compromise, she takes up her place in the labour market and she enjoys her status as a working girl without going too far. She must retain a visible fragility and the displaying of a kind of conventional feminine vulnerability will ensure she remains desirable to men. This compromise enacted in the cultural field also finds expression, as social compromise, in the field of work and employment. I borrow this term from Rosemary Crompton to account for the way in which the new sexual contract operates in the workplace, setting limits on patterns of participation and gender equality (Crompton 2002). Rosemary Crompton focuses on women who are also mothers and their re-positioning in the labour market on return to work after the birth of children. The relevance of this work to the discussion here lies in the implicit abandonment of critique of masculine hegemony in favour of compromise. Young working mothers, it appears, draw back from entertaining any idea of debate on inequality in the household in favour of finding ways, with help from government, to manage their dual responsibility. This links with the previous discussion of the post-feminist masquerade as a strategy of undoing, a re-configuring of normative femininity, this time incorporating motherhood so as to accommodate with masculine domination. In the social compromise there is then, once again, a process of gender re-stabilisation. Rosemary Crompton points to the significant rates of retention in employment or return to work shortly after having children by UK women. This corresponds with government's focus on women's employability and the transition to lifelong work for women as an alternative to traditional economic dependence on a male breadwinner. The compromise requires that woman play a dual role, active in the workplace and primarily responsible for children and domestic life (Crompton 2002). Instead of challenging the traditional expectation that women take primary responsibility in the home, there is a shift towards abandoning the critique of patriarchy and instead heroically attempting to 'do it all' while also looking to government for support in this Herculean endeavour. The transition to this feminine mode of activity comes into existence by means of a series of luminosities (the glamorous working mother, the so-called yummy mummy, the city high-flyer who is also a mother, and so on) images and texts which are accompanied also by popular genres of fiction including best selling novels such as *I Don't Know How She Does It* (Pearson 2003).

The UK government substitutes for the feminist, displaces her vocabulary and intervenes to assist working mothers who are coming forward, and to avert the possibility of critique by women of their double responsibilities and thus of possible crisis within the heterosexual matrix.[22] Government thus acts to protect masculinity hegemony by supporting women in their double role, while the media and popular culture endeavour to re-glamorise working wives and mothers through post-feminist styles of self-improvement, hyper-sexuality and capacity. This feature of the new sexual contract requires compromise in work as well as within the home. Despite the rhetoric of heroism in the combining of primary responsibility for children with maintaining a career, in practice the emphasis by various agencies whose subject of attention is the young working women, entails the scaling down of ambition in favour of a discourse of managing following the onset of motherhood. In the light of these new responsibilities the young woman is counselled to request flexibility of her employer. Government is certainly not encouraging women back into the home after having children. The new sexual contract instead offers support and guidance so that the return to employment (often part-time) is facilitated in the form of a work-life balance. There is an implicit trade off, what the working mother wants or needs from her employer is recognition of her dual role, and some degree of accommodation in this respect. The work-life balance is now underpinned in the form of better safeguards in law for part-time workers and also pension rights for women.

Government also makes strenuous efforts to encourage men to become better fathers and to make family life important. Important as these initiatives are, this looking to government for support for working mothers brings a new dimension to feminist public policy debate about the state replacing the husband i.e., 'the man in the state'. But in this scenario the state intervenes not to replace the husband (by supporting single motherhood) but rather to allow the husband the chance to pursue his working life without female complaint, without the requirement that he curbs his working hours so that he can play an equal role in the household. A kind of post-feminist realism, or governmental pragmatism prevails. Ideally men will devote more time to the family, but that must be a personal choice. Thus we might argue that in this case women come forward as willing subjects of economic capacity, while also undertaking to retain their traditionally marked out roles in the household, rather than radically challenge the division of labour within the home, as feminists did with noticeable effect from the mid-1970s onwards. How successful the individual heterosexual woman might be in achieving equality in relation to domestic labour and childcare then becomes a private affair, or rather evidence that she has chosen well or fortuitously from the range of possible partners. Her life-plan in this regard has worked to her advantage.

The social compromise defined by Crompton is then a key element of the new sexual contract, which is premised on the management of gender and sexuality by a wide range of biopolitical strategies which pre-empt the possibilities of renewed feminist challenges to patriarchal authority. Of course this settlement could also be understood as part of the process of gender mainstreaming, New Labour have now fully incorporated women's needs into their wider political programme of modernisation, and feminist issues of the past have been taken up and are now being seriously addressed at the level of national government. However true this may be, it is also the case that what is quite absent from these discussions are any elements drawn from the old feminist 'demand', that men be prepared to relinquish some of their privileges and advantages in work and in the home, in order to achieve equality in the domestic sphere. A decade ago Nancy Fraser argued that men must again become more accountable to gender inequities in the household, while what I have attempted to demonstrate here are the forces which prevail against this kind of expectation re-emerging as a possibility (Fraser 1997). Fraser also argued that the Universal Breadwinner Model increasingly takes precedence over the Caregiver Model which was associated with the older welfare regime which took into account womens's role as care-givers and the limits that role put on possibilities for economic activity (Fraser 1997). This care role was central to feminist debate from the mid-1970s onwards and still figures in feminist discussion today (Lister 2002, Williams 2002). At the heart of these debates was the tendency towards maternalist essentialism on the part of those who defended the Caregiver Model. But what the social compromise now suggests is that the Universal Breadwinner Model requires of women a joint responsibility which also, more or less, guarantees subordinate status in terms of wage earning capacity in the realm of work and employment over a lifetime. At the same time the coming forward of women into work offers government the best opportunity of cutting the long-term costs of welfare.

If we extend this model of assumed activity into the field of the new flexible economy the question arises as to how women fare under these new more competitive often casualised and precarious conditions? Armed with good qualifications and having been encouraged to display enthusiasm and willingness to pursue careers as a mark of new and independent sexual identities, this female participation becomes an important feature of the success of the new economy. Labour market participation over a lifetime reduces the cost of welfare to women as traditionally low paid earners, and it will ideally bring down the high rate of female poverty in old age. And in addition this immersion in work also creates a thriving and re-energised consumer culture directed towards women. It is for these reasons that we can make a claim that young women are privileged subjects of economic capacity and it is on this basis that we can also expect degrees of social mobility to be more marked among women without children.

We have already discussed how gender re-stabilisation is achieved through the social compromise on the part of working mothers, but do young women without children also find themselves subjected to a new work regime where their presence and their coming forward is also however the occasion for their re-subordination? The most obvious indicator of enduring inequality in employment is of course the pay gap, the substantial discrepancy between male and female wages, a feature of the labour market which has indeed given rise to close governmental attention in recent years. But the decline of bureaucracy, public services and trade unionism in the light of privatisation and de-regulation, the growth of enterprise culture and the so-called cutting of red tape all contribute to the diminishing role and significance of sex discrimination policies in the workplace. As already discussed in Chapter 2, Scott Lash remarks that women are 'reflexivity losers' in the context of the information society (Lash in Beck et al. 1994). And Lisa Adkins has explored in more detail they way in which re-traditionalised gender relations re-emerge in the de-regulated workplace and with the return to small-scale family-run enterprises which are integral to the production processes which underlie global consumer culture (Adkins 2002). There are also various exclusions generated by the informal networking practices which come to dominate the freelance precarious economies in the cultural and creative sector. Wittel's analysis of 'network sociality' overlooks the way in which these reproduce social elites and create material barriers to those who lack the social and cultural capital to participate (Wittel 2001, McRobbie 2002). Project work, informal recruitment procedures, the opacity of structures and pathways into new media and cultural work, as well as the long hours culture based on competition and aggression (see for example Nixon's recent account of grossly unequal gender relations and the unashamedly resurgent hegemonic masculine cultures inside the UK advertising world) are all features which become more widespread in an era of de-regulation and privatisation (Nixon 2003). Thus there is a paradoxical situation that the young women who are so visibly coming forward, and flowing into the labour market, are doing so just at the point in which the social democratic conditions which were recently propitious to their arrival are being dismantled. The new sexual contract to women requires that they compromise career aspirations to fulfil domestic obligations which in effect means complying with existing gender hierarchies. They must also acquire the individualised capacities to fulfil the demands of the new flexible economy by emulating the pathways to achievement associated with the competitive values of corporate culture rather than by attempting to retrieve or uphold the more anonymous cultures of the workplace and the less individualistic values of the public sector and bureaucracy.

Phallic girls: recreational sex, reproductive sex

The post-feminist masquerade, and also the figure of the working girl, are two of the means by which the new sexual contract, as an urging to agency, makes itself available to young women. Here I introduce a further figure, the phallic girl,[23] and then in the final section, the global girl. Butler envisages the 'phallic lesbian' as a political figure who wrestles some power from the almighty Symbolic. In an interview Butler is asked if heterosexual women might also be able to pick up the phallus in this way and she responds that this might be an important thing to do (Butler 1994). But now, more recently, and within the terrain of Western post-feminist culture, the Symbolic reacts swiftly to the antagonism which not just feminism has presented, but also which Butler's lesbian phallus and queer theory per se present by pre-emptively endowing young women with the capacity to become phallus-bearers as a kind of licensed mimicry of their male counterparts. This also precludes any radical re-arrangement of gender hierarchies despite, indeed because of this 'pretence' of equality, that permits spectacles of aggression and unfeminine behaviour on the part of young women, seemingly without punishment. The phallic girl gives the impression of having won equality with men by becoming like her male counterparts. But in this adoption of the phallus, there is no critique of masculine hegemony. I have already rehearsed some aspects of this scenario, which, within the landscape of UK popular culture, culminates in the figure of the so-called 'ladette' (McRobbie 2005). This is a young woman for whom the freedoms associated with masculine sexual pleasures are not just made available but encouraged and also celebrated. She is being asked to concur with a definition of sex as light-hearted pleasure, recreational activity, hedonism, sport, reward and status. Luminosity falls upon the girl who adopts the habits of masculinity including heavy drinking, swearing, smoking, getting into fights, having casual sex, flashing her breasts in public, getting arrested by the police, consumption of pornography, enjoyment of lap-dancing clubs and so on, but without relinquishing her own desirability to men, indeed for whom such seeming masculinity enhances her desirability since she shows herself to

83

have a similar sexual appetite to her male counterparts. But this is a thin tightrope to walk, it asks of girls that they perform masculinity, without relinquishing the femininity which makes them so desirable to men. If the post-feminist masquerade undercuts the power of young women coming forward into the world of work and employment through the encouragement to once again adopt the mask of submission and servitude and to invest time and effort in the crafting of a self which ensures desirability, youthful female phallicism (and it cannot be old) is a more assertive alternative to masquerade. It can also be understood as a kind of strategic endowment to young women, a means of attributing to them degrees of capacity but with strict conditions which ultimately ensure gender re-stabilisation. The taboo-breaking phallic girl also emerges as something of a challenge, not only to the repudiated feminist, but also to what Butler again calls the spectre of the 'phallicised dyke' (Butler 1990). By being able to take up some of the accoutrements of masculinity, the drunken, swearing and leering young woman who is not averse to having sex with other girls, demonstrates that within the presiding realm of Symbolic authority, many things are possible. A version of lesbian desire can be accommodated within this space of female phallicism, as long as it remains visually coded to conform to the requirements of the fashion and beauty system which, as has already been demonstrated, sits in judgement, substitutes for hegemonic masculinity and presides over the management of the capacity, in this case sexual capacity, with which young women are endowed. (In the novel *Brass* by Helen Walsh the main character Millie adopts a 'licensed' lesbian phallicism which entails consuming large quantities of drugs, alcohol and picking up prostitutes, Walsh 2004.)

This licensed transgression is also facilitated not just by the fashion and beauty system but by the wider leisure industries which have responded vigorously to the possibilities opened up by women's disposable income, daring indeed, to define themselves as champions of women's rights. Consumer culture, the tabloid press, the girl's and women's magazine sector, the lads' magazines and also downmarket, trashy television all encourage young women, as though in the name of sexual equality, to overturn the old double standard and emulate the assertive and hedonistic styles of sexuality associated with young men, particularly in holiday locations, or in the context of the UK city centre leisure culture which has developed around late night drinking and the relaxation of the laws in regard to the consumption of alcohol. This assumption of phallicism also provides new dimensions of moral panic, titillation, and voyeuristic excitement as news spectacle and entertainment. The phallic girl is epitomised in the so-called glamour model, who earns most of her money posing naked for the soft-porn pages of the press and magazines and who, if successful, will also launch herself as a brand, lending her name and image to various products, usually ranges of underwear, make up, perfume or other fashion items. But for her ordinary counterpart, the girl on the street, assuming phallicism more often simply means drinking to excess, getting into fights, throwing up in public places, swearing and being abusive, wearing very short skirts, high heels, and skimpy tops, having casual sex, often passing out on the street and having to be taken home by friends or by the police. Under this pretence of equality which is promoted by consumer culture, such female phallicism is in fact a provocation to feminism, a triumphant gesture on the part of resurgent patriarchy. There is also hostility to women underpinning this particular form of freedom. In coming forward and showing herself to be, in common parlance, 'up for it', the phallic girl also allows herself to be the target of old-fashioned sexist insults and hostility from the men she seeks both to please and to emulate. The Symbolic uses the field of popular culture and entertainment to accommodate some prior feminist demands in relation to the right or entitlement to sexual pleasure, for example challenging the old sexual double standard, so that women are no longer punished in quite the same way for pursuing sexual desires, but this 'right' is then totally disconnected from any notion of a renewed feminism, quite the opposite. The champions of this new freedom, the phallic girls like TV presenter Denise Van Outen, glamour model Jodie Marsh and even Spice Girl Geri Halliwell are all vociferously disparaging of feminism.[24]

So as long as she does not procreate while enjoying casual and recreational sex, the young woman is entitled to pursue sexual desire seemingly without punishment. Indeed the appropriate uses of sexual pleasure are prescribed within the many manuals and forms of instruction which constitute the terms and conditions of this new sexual contract. Delay in age of marriage and also delay in the birth of a first child on the part of young Western women, are directly connected with their being able to come forward into the labour market. It is this movement on the part of women, which has accelerated in recent years, that gives rise to the focus on reproductive capacity. Young motherhood, across the divisions of class and ethnicity now carries a whole range of vilified meanings associated with failed femininity and with disregard for the well-being of the child. Poor white and black young women alike are targeted by government because the high rate of teenage pregnancy (set against the falling birth rate among older and better educated young women) is almost exclusively concentrated within this group. Middle-class status requires the refusal of teenage motherhood and much effort is invested in ensuring that this norm is adhered to. If the young woman is now envisaged as an assemblage of productivity, then she is also now more harshly judged for inappropriate reproductive activity. The concept of planned parenthood emerges in Western liberal democracies as an address to young women so that they may postpone early maternity to accrue the economic advantages of employment and occupational identity and thus contribute to the solving of the crisis of welfare. Single mothers are seen as feckless or else are charged with depriving a child of his or her 'human right' to a father. As Harris and others have described, the subsidised availability of IVF treatment and the investment in reproductive technologies implicitly address this postponement of childbirth into the 30s and the encouragement of this as a mark of respectability, social responsibility and citizenship (Harris 2004).

Despite, or rather because of the proliferations of different modes of kinship in increasingly multi-cultural and sexually diverse cultures, the marital couple re-emerges as the favoured form for family life. Here too there is a case to be made for the re-stabilisation of gender norms against a perceived threat of disruption from non-Western forms of kinship, from feminism and from the gay and lesbian movement. Interventions to ensure that help is given to those who abide by the rules of responsible parenthood, means that those young career women in the UK who have followed the advice of New Labour, and have postponed childbirth until they have secured wage earning capacity, become deserving subjects of investment in scientific research.[25] More so than in the past the reproductive years are intensely monitored by government, from the debate about 12 year old girls being given the pill, to lesbian couples hoping for genetic parenthood, to older women in their 50s also having access to IVF treatment. And it is on condition that she does not reproduce outside marriage or civil partnership, or become the single mother of several children, that the young woman is now granted a prominence as a pleasure-seeking subject in possession of a healthy sexual appetite and identity. In the UK such is the importance to government of discouraging teenage motherhood, that contraceptive and morning after facilities are easily available to most teenage girls. The enjoyment of sexual pleasures on the basis of practising effective birth control as well as safe sex, is one of the most visible features of so-called female freedom today. However this activity, when set within a wider social environment where de-regulated dominant (consumer) culture intersects sharply with already-existing patterns of class and racial inequalities, gives rise to unanticipated consequences such as rising rates of sexually transmitted diseases, alcohol abuse, as well as conflicts and anxiety on the part of young women in regard to what they might now expect of sex and intimacy within the heterosexual matrix. The seeming freedom of the phallic girl, her openness to sexual adventure, is also, in fact, a means of re-constituting and shoring up divisions between heterosexual and lesbian young women, in the light of the perceived threat that such boundaries might also come tumbling down. The 'real lesbian' is reviled in much the same way as the repudiated feminist. The rigorous requirements of the commercial domain addressed to young women are radically uninhabitable by young lesbian women, and so the phallic girl like her counterpart who inhabits the post-feminist masquerade, functions on the part of dominant culture to re-instate boundaries, with the effect that life outside the heterosexual matrix requires the production of distinctly other queer spaces and temporalities, despite the illusion promoted within the commercial domain that gay and lesbian identities are now also mainstreamed (Halberstam 2005).

The global girl

The account so far of recreational sex as practised by phallic girls, and then of reproductive sex now the subject of even more intense government attention than in the past, offers further illustration of how the terms and conditions by which young women come forward, take the form of invitations to specified modes of self-actualisation. Female phallicism is as restrictive as the post-feminist masquerade in that its endorsing of licentiousness and bad behaviour also ensures this plays out in a field of leisure activity which assumes a white female subject. These figurings of young womanhood are also boundary-marking practices within popular culture. It is one thing for young white women to playfully disrupt the divisions which underpinned the old double standard between the good girl and the whore, but adopting the appearance and the street-style of whore, brings starkly into visibility, the divisions which exist between white privileged femininity and its black and still disadvantaged counterpart. For Afro-Caribbean young women, whose sexuality is always regarded as suspect by the state, being drunk and disorderly while also dressed like a prostitute is not a risk worth taking. As various black feminists have argued, within a context dominated by the prevalence of the racist imagination, notions of respectability and constraint in the field of desire have been embedded within black women's sexual identities, a response to the virulent racism which assumes sexual availability, appetite or else which assumes that poverty makes prostitution or addiction a likelihood (Noble 2000). It is not surprising then that expressions of sexual autonomy and enjoyment on the part of young black women tend to be channelled towards black music subcultures such as hip hop, or else are located more specifically within leisure forms associated with the black community (e.g. Jamaican dance-hall culture).[26] For young Asian women we could surmise that white female phallicism functions as a provocation to the assumed norms of submissiveness to patriarchal and religious authority, typically attributed again within the racist imagination, to those Asian girls who do not embrace Western styles of fashion and sexual display. The phallic girl is a summation of the sexual freedoms which have been granted to young Western women. Her activities appear to transgress all the boundaries of feminine docility, even though as I have argued above, her active pursuit of sexual pleasure, remains not just thoroughly subjected to patriarchal authority and judgement, but is also completely compatible with the requirements of a re-adjusted and seemingly liberalised heterosexual matrix. There are good reasons then why the spectacle of skimpily dressed, drunken, shouting, black or Asian girls, baring their breasts on the street at closing time in city centres to groups of passing boys, black and white, and eventually getting picked up by the police and bundled off to the police station to dry out, is an unlikely scenario.

These considerations suggest that both the figurations of the post-feminist masquerade and the phallic girl mark out by subtle means processes of exclusion and re-colonisation. There are patterns of racialised retrenchment embedded within these re-configured spaces of femininity. The post-feminist masquerade fulfils this notion of re-stabilisation by extolling the virtues of dissembled feminine weakness, and fragility. But playing at tradition in this way, adopting a style of femininity which invites once again a display of masculine chivalry, gallantry, power and control, resurrects norms of white heterosexuality from which black women and men have historically been violently excluded. Since the first post-war waves of migration, black women in the UK have always worked and earned a living, usually in menial jobs. Black feminist history has over the years demonstrated that in the context of labour exploitation of black women, from slavery to the modern international division of labour, the feigning of feminine fragility has been a mark of racial privilege. The post-feminist masquerade as a cultural strategy for re-stabilising gender relations within the heterosexual matrix produces a new interface between working life and sexuality which is implicitly white and which assumes kinship norms associated with the Western nuclear family. In line with the new ethos of assimilation and integration rather than the now failed multi-culturalism of the 1980s and 1990s, aspirant young black women are invited, as readers of magazines like *Grazia* or viewers of television programmes like *Friends*, or films like *Bridget Jones's Diary*, to emulate this model.

The global girl comes forward, primarily in the advertising images from fashion companies like Benetton, and also through the different editions of global fashion magazines like *Elle*, *Marie Claire*, *Vogue* and *Grazia*, which are customised from one country to the next, as emblematic of the power and success of corporate multi-culturalism. This envisages young women, especially those from Third World countries, as enthusiastic about membership of and belonging to, a kind of global femininity. There is both difference and homogeneity in this fashion and beauty system in a way which is very similar to that analysed by Barlow et al. in the course of their study of the Modern Girl of the 1920s and 1930s (Barlow et al. 2005). The modernity of the global girl today is expressed in her new found freedoms, her wage earning capacity, her enjoyment of and immersion in beauty culture and in popular culture, and in her pleasing and becoming demeanour which lacks the ironic inhabiting of femininity of her post-feminist masquerading counterparts, and the aggression and sexual bravado of the phallic girls. Indeed global girls are defined in terms of an intersection of qualities which combine the natural and authentic, with a properly feminine love of self-adornment, and the playfully seductive with the innocent, so as to suggest a sexuality which is youthful, latent and waiting to be unleashed. This marks out a subtle positioning, a re-colonisation and re-making of racial hierarchy within the field of normative femininity. But there is also a different spatial and temporal momentum invoked in the mobilisation of the global girl. Unlike her American or British counterpart there is less underpinning of this figuring of femininity by the full range of governmental discourses, precisely because this young women is increasingly mobile herself and thus often inhabiting a kind of transnational status. The idea of a sexual contract as a convergence of attentions, spanning a range of bodily activities, and permitting modes of coming forward on condition that any residue of sexual politics fades away, is a Western formulation addressed to those who are assumed to have full citizenship and the right to remain in the country of abode. In this contract economic activity is foregrounded and politics reduced to the margins of significance in favour of the seeming attractions of consumer citizenship. However we might surmise that for those who are excluded from this privileged model of freedom based on the state provision of education, followed by participation in training and in the labour market, there are other spaces of attention, and also undesignated spaces and liminal zones marked out by brutalities, cruelties and hardship. We might point here to the global flows of young women, who, as they somehow find the means of moving from the country to the city, or from the east to the West or from south to north, as they also find themselves in various border zones, are the subjects of a globalised political economy which orders and re-orders these other femininities according to fears and anxieties about 'immigrant' fertility. In such a context the consumer-led discourse of the global girl functions as an ideal, these are girls who do not threaten the West with migration and uncontrolled fertility, instead they stay put and yearn for the fashion and beauty products associated with Western femininity and sexuality (Hoefinger 2005).

In conclusion, this chapter has provided an account of the means by which young women in contemporary sociality, in a post-feminist gesture which implies that feminism has been taken into account, and that equality is in the process of being achieved, are called upon by a range of commercial and governmental forms of attention, to come forward as subjects of agency and capacity on the basis that there is also a relinquishing of political identities accruing from perceived inequities of gender or sexuality associated with those styles of feminism which have, as well as being taken into account, also been repudiated and vilified. The chapter charts the process of feminism being undone through high levels of intervention and attention being directed towards the young woman, whose significance in terms of wage earning capacity is now substantial. There is a new sexual contract issued to young women which encourages activity concentrated in education and employment so as to ensure participation in the production of successful femininity, sexuality and eventually maternity. The commercial domain requires that young women prioritise consumption for the sake of sexual intelligibility and in the name of heterosexual desire, and this in turn intersects with and confirms the neo-liberal turn by contemporary government (especially in the UK) with its emphasis, as we shall see in the chapter that follows, on consumer-citizenship. The spaces of attention and the luminosities I have described, supplant and substitute for the various forms of political mobilisation which were associated with feminism as a social movement, they also relegate politics to the margins of women's lives, and political culture comes to be dominated by a technocratic style of 'corporate managerialism'. As Chantal Mouffe has argued this marginalisation of the sphere of formal politics puts the 'civic bond in jeopardy' (Mouffe 2000).

By focusing on the links between governmental and commercial discourses it has been my aim to demonstrate in this chapter how sexual politics is presented as irrelevant. This chapter also reflects on the young women who as global girls are the subjects of different forms of attention but whose wage-earning capacity within the international division of labour marks them out as emergent and becoming. I have argued that these 'movements of young women' or 'coming-forwards', in the various figurations I have described, which are also created through specific 'spaces of attention', function as a kind of shadow feminism, a substitute and palliative for the otherwise forced abandonment of a new feminist political imaginary.

Notes

1   I use the phrase sexual contract in the manner which Stuart Hall might use it, i.e. to refer to a form of power which entails negotiation at the social and cultural level with the objective of a settlement within the field of sexuality. In this current context the term permits an analysis of a combination and intersection of forces constitutive of an address to young women, a 'space of attention', the regulative dynamics of which are subsumed within a language which implies this attention as the outcome of a progressive concern for sexual equality.

2   The term is associated with Pateman's important book *The Sexual Contract* (1988). However I use the phrase in a quite different sense.

3   I use the term patriarchy with some hesitation. It has been used within feminism as a universalising and homogenising strategy, a means of proposing that women across the world share the same forms of subjugation. This has been subjected to extensive critique and bearing this in mind it I propose it can be

re-employed particularistically by drawing on Mohanty's terminology and her use of the word patriarchies.

4   The Rt. Hon. Tessa Jowell (Minister of Culture from 2000–2007) made comments to this effect in the context of the Body Image Summit 21 June 2000, see www.sizenet.com

5   For how the contemporary fashion-beauty complex intersects with lesbian sexuality, see Lewis (1997).

6   The UK New Labour government adopted a model for assisting unemployed single mothers into the workplace similar to the US Dress for Success initiative which encouraged well-paid working women to donate cast-offs suitable for office wear. The UK version comprises second-hand clothes shops and outlets such as the Camden Job Train shop in London NW5.

7   See also *The Beauty Myth* by Naomi Wolf (1991).

8   Butler makes the point in *Gender Trouble* (1990) that the Symbolic merges with, to become indistinguishable from, dominant culture.

9   Recent reports in the press indicate anorexia extending beyond teens and twenties into middle age, not unconnected, we might surmise, with the above discussions and with the prevalence of advertisements like those discussed by Ros Gill (in conference June 2006) showing an older woman in a bikini shot from behind with the caption, as though spoken by her daughter looking on at this unsightly body, that although she loved her mother she didn't like her cellulite (See Gill 2006).

10   See McRobbie 2003.

11   Mary Ann Doane's essay shapes my own thinking here. Drawing on feminist psychoanalytic writing which problematises femininity as 'claustrophobic closeness', as 'presence to itself', as 'spatial proximity', as a place of either masochistic or narcissistic over-identification, then, argues Doane, that dangerous closeness which locks women into this rigid position, can somehow be opened up and loosened through distance-producing strategies, such as the masquerade. 'The masquerade, in flaunting femininity, holds it at a distance' (Doane 1982: 135). Doane argues that the masquerade in effect skewers or re-aligns femininity so that a gap or a distance is produced, this in turn re-positions the woman away from simply occupying that subordinated, powerless, space of male desire within dominant heterosexuality. This is achieved through the 'hyperbolisation of the accoutrements of femininity', (ibid: 139) which throw the male gaze off course, which make it strange and unfamiliar, perhaps unseemly. In short the masquerade is a distance-producing strategy, and my claim here is that this subversive possibility has now been incorporated, indeed promoted by consumer culture, as a sign of female independence and empowerment.

12   This is a regular theme in *Sex and the City*, Carrie's date may not care for her silly hat which she knows only fashion experts would appreciate. Thus the wearing or not of the hat provokes much self-reflexivity. Should she or shouldn't she? Carrie tends to cling onto these seemingly ridiculous items, as a mark of her own independent identity. But we (the audience) know that in the end these items work to the advantage of her femininity. They actually make her more endearing to men. Their excessive quality shows her vulnerability, and her child-like enjoyment of dressing up. If she gets it wrong and she looks a little foolish, it is because she is still a girl, unsure of herself as she takes on the mantle of womanliness. Indeed getting it wrong is a mark of her girlishness, and this failing makes her all the more desirable to men.

13   Fashion journalists in the serious press, especially in The *Independent* and The *Guardian* frequently adopt a self-mocking tone when they are making recommendations about what to wear and how to look. They imply that, along with their readership drawn from the liberal to left middle classes, they share some ironic distance from the more didactic, authoritative and judgemental language of fashion writing. But this use of irony also has the effect of safeguarding such journalists from critique.

14   Cherie Booth QC, the wife of former Prime Minister, Tony Blair, exemplified this inhabiting of the post-feminist masquerade. At every available opportunity she drew attention to her investment in the paraphernalia of femininity, as though to deflect attention from her status and power as a barrister. In July 2003 she allowed a *Marie Claire* journalist into her bedroom, and even let her have a quick look inside her chest of drawers, which was predictably full of frilly feminine lingerie.

15   Riviere in her masquerade work uncritically draws on the racist stereotype of white women's fears (and fantasies) of being attacked by a 'negro'.

16   For detailed accounts of changes in educational qualifications see Arnot et al. 1999 and Allen 2008.

17   See Kim Allens's PhD Thesis, Goldsmiths College 2008, also thanks to Kim Allen for pointing me in the direction of www.dfes. gov.uk/regateway/DB/SFR/s000708/SFR04 for information on activity rates of young school leavers.

18   This is a certainly a topic on which there are different views. While most sociologists dispute the reality of social mobility in the UK during the New Labour years, i.e. from 1997 onwards, the activity rates of young women in the labour market and the staying on rates in further and higher education, taken alongside the cultural emphasis on doing well and on becoming aspirational subjects suggests that, what I here refer to as the new sexual contract, comprises an encouragement to young women to themselves become socially mobile, or to aim for some degree of upward mobility. This may take years to become visible statistically, but if so many young women are now gaining university degrees, then the argument that there is no social mobility seems questionable (Devine et al. 2004, Walkerdine 2004 and Skeggs 2005).

19   Arnot et al. 1999 refer to a study which showed the Asian young women interviewed to be aiming for upward social mobility into professional occupations.

20   Making it also more difficult to insist that it remains important and relevant to engage with the new as well as the old inequalities facing young women today, for example significant under-achievement in science subjects, across all member states of the European Community, see www.europa.eu/reseach/science-society/women/wir/pdf

21   Several essays by Charlotte Brunsdon (1997, 2005) analyse, with prescience, the emergence, in film and television of a post-feminist sensibility .

22   See the work undertaken by the Women and Work Commission 2006 (www.womenandequalityunit.gov.uk/women_work_commission) which implicitly blames women themselves for making the wrong choices of career which in turn locks them into the low pay sector.

23   See Bennett and Woollacott (1987) for an analysis of the phallicism of the Bond Girls in the fiction and films based around Fleming's James Bond 007 character.

24   In a recent interview with the glamour model Jodie Marsh in the *Guardian* following her humiliating experiences on *Big Brother*, where her 'tarty' appearance and her reputation as a 'slapper' made her the butt of a series of hostile

and misogynist comments, she nevertheless directed her own anger against 'those feminist bitch women'.

25　The London *Evening Standard* ran a headline in May 2006 'Fertility Test For Career Women' as though to imply that these women were the only deserving subjects of this new test.

26　The exuberant sexuality of Kelis in the video for her single 'Milkshake', as well as the more explicitly soft-porn videos for a range of hip hop acts, requires more extensive sociological and cultural analysis than is available to date (see Rose 1994, Noble 2000).

4

ILLEGIBLE RAGE: POST-FEMINIST DISORDERS

The state cultivates melancholia among its citizenry precisely as a way of dissimulating and displacing its own authority. (Butler 1997a: 191)

Introduction: normative discontent

In this chapter I return to feminist psychoanalytical writing from the 1980s and early 1990s and I bring this together with Judith Butler's notion of gender melancholia, in order to address the contemporary field of 'female complaint'. My aim here is to initiate a new debate about current female malaise, but not in a conventional sociological way. I will not be giving an analysis of moral panics, nor will I focus on media coverage of binge drinking among teenage girls, or on other apparently deviant or self-harming behaviours. My focus of attention is indeed on this realm of female disorders, from the mildest to the most severe, but not with a specifically empirical eye. Instead I offer a cultural reading in the form of a series of reflections, where, among other things, I propose that feminism has become, for young women, in rather indiscernible ways, an object of loss and melancholia. In fact in each of the chapters so far in this book I have touched on feminism as loss. The question then must be, what exactly is lost? What is this thing 'feminism' that has been lost? Certainly it has not been my intention to suggest some kind of nostalgia for a sanctified past, and for a golden age of second wave feminism. There is a version of feminism in the public imagination which is created by the right, and by the media as well as by the New Labour government, as a hideous thing, which can then be easily vilified. But this feminism-that-never-was, is also of course different from the feminism-as-object-of-desire which I will be referring to here, as something that is lost and becomes melancholically preserved. This takes us near to the terrain of left melancholia as discussed by Wendy Brown (2000). But there is a different inflection in what follows in this chapter, since I am also arguing that young women in the social world, are forced to give this up, in order to count as real young women. Feminism, with its critique of masculine domination, is given up, and then preserved unconsciously, it is privatised, internalised, with only a few occasions (inside the feminist academy) to be opened up and re-considered. This takes us into the realm of feminist psychoanalysis and I want to draw attention to the importance of Butler's re-working of psychoanalysis as a necessary tool for understanding the illegible rage of young women, and for helping us to think about how this rage can be acted on politically.

I wish to foreground, once again, 1980s and early 1990s feminist psychoanalytical theory to examine the relation between fashion images, their fascination for female viewers, and the self-harming practices of young women. This means moving away from the common sense and pragmatic cause and effect debates which endlessly 'blame the media' for these disorders. Moralistic and empiricist perspectives induce repetition, circularity and double standards. No matter how many debates there are about the harms caused by the fashion industry, and despite all the pressure put by governments and regulatory bodies on the magazines to only show images of healthy female bodies, the same images of virtually emaciated girls, whose arms and legs show clear signs of anorexia continue to appear on the pages of not just *Vogue* magazine, but also the newspaper fashion pages and supplements. It is not my intention here to engage in depth with the topic of anorexia, although of course it has long been a matter of interest for various feminist scholars (Probyn 2000), but I do want to interrogate through a reading of Butler's work, how we might think afresh about self-harm and femininity in the context of heterosexual melancholia and the loss of feminism. It is as though most commentators on the subject of young women's self-harming practices somehow know these to be about gender per se and even about what used to be called women's oppression, now recast as her subordination to the power of the image, and yet such knowledge simply becomes a weary cliché, interrupted only by the sense that young women's situation, in recent years, has surely improved? It cannot quite then be the fault of society, it must be somehow their own doing. Actually I want to argue the opposite. The more change there is to the gender regime, let us say the need on the part of capitalism for young women's labour power, the deeper is the anxiety on the part of the less visible 'patriarchies'. Thus these disorders are more social than ever. Indeed if it is the case that the anorexic girl is frequently embroiled in her own family dynamics, and is also tending to be a girl who is seeking approval, in terms of school work and other activities, then we might propose that, at the very least, her disorder is still at least a mark of her femininity and her rightful place within properly oedipalised families, which in turn leads me to suggest that these disorders come to be a way of freshly demarcating the boundaries of sexual difference. These girls may be unwell, they may sometimes try to end their own lives, but at least they are surely normal girls in this respect? Cutting themselves, endlessly on diets, fearful of their weight, prone to low self-esteem, frequently anorexic? These are all now healthy signs of unhealthy femininity, normalised in the Foucault sense, but also dynamic features of the heterosexual matrix in the Butler sense. Better to be an ill girl than a girl who gets up out of her sickbed and challenges the power of the heterosexual matrix. Pathology as normality is preferable to a new form of women's movement. In this chapter I ask a number of questions. Can we talk about 'post-feminist disorders'? Is Butler's notion of heterosexual melancholia useful in this regard? Indeed can some of the ideas in Butler's *The Psychic Life of Power* (1997a) provide insight into female self-beratement, low self-esteem and post-feminist discontent?

The spiralling of feminine discontents and disorders in relation to body image has reached new heights in the last decade, and the routine accusations that the media, in particular magazines, play a key role in the 'cultural production of female psychopathology' have achieved the status of sociological banalities (Blackman 2004). What we might call the popular feminine public domain comprises of these phenomena and creates a kind of tolerance to them, as though to say this is what we now must expect of young women today, from reporting on the pro-anorexia websites, to magazines like *Grazia*, which, in a slightly more reflective mode than the downmarket celebrity magazines, looks for ways, each week to subject the female body to new forms of assessment and harsh judgement. There are also the Sunday supplements like *Observer Woman* (informed by feminism) as well as the wider press eagerly seeking out new angles in the coverage of routine events like the new season's fashion collections. We could call all of this the 'making-up' of young womanhood in such a way as to institutionalise pathology (Hacking 2006). There is an increase in the range of demarcated pathologies associated almost exclusively with young women, and in the numbers of those who suffer from a spectrum of conditions seemingly connected to body image and low self-esteem, i.e. self-starvation, bulimia, self-harming including cutting, binge drinking resulting in hospitalisation, drug abuse, suicidal behaviour, aggression, depression and feelings of worthlessness.[1] We need not look far to be confronted with reports, images, testimonies, narratives, fiction and non-fictional accounts of 'female complaints'. From short-lived stories in the press (for example, two overweight working class girls meet through the internet, seem to get involved in a relationship with each other, but isolated and experiencing bullying at school plan a suicide pact, one girl dies and the other survives),[2] to graphic factual TV like Channel 4's *Brat Camp for Girls* showing extreme degrees of mental distress on the part of teenage girls whose excessive drinking, drug taking and violent behaviour in the home, prompts fear, anger and despondency on the part of their mothers as well as themselves. Alongside this there are of course the celebrity stories which, because of the entertainment value produce new dimensions to old double standards. For example, in the same week in December 2006 that Amy Winehouse topped the charts with a song where she described, with 'ladette-style' bravado, not wanting to go into rehab despite the advice of her record company, there were press reports on the five young women sex workers murdered in Ipswich describing their addiction to heroin and crack cocaine and the lack of rehab provision for ordinary girls like these.

There is of course enormous variation in these illnesses, from the middle class girl or woman (e.g. 'self-confessed' 34 year old journalist Polly Vernon in the *Observer*, 14 January 2007) who is mildly anorexic, to the girl who has a full-blown drug habit and is also vulnerable in other ways including being poor. But for the sake of this discussion, I want to draw this spectrum together and consider them under the heading of illegible rage. The most common non-medical responses to these various forms of distress by medical practitioners and various other experts often involve making reference to cultural norms of female perfectibility promoted and endorsed in girls' and women's magazines and by consumer culture. As the British Medical Association put it, 'today's young woman is expected to strive for perfection in all spheres' but, the report continues, 'achieving and maintaining a feminine identity doubly compromises the mental health of females' (BMA 2000). Thus it is acknowledged that seeking to achieve a feminine identity makes women and girls ill. Being, as Butler would have it, 'culturally intelligible' as a girl makes one ill. But by today's standards, that is almost acceptable. The forces of social regulation operate in this context to normalise this post-feminist scenario, so as to avert the possibility of questions being asked of the sort associated with second wave feminism and certainly questions like those asked by Butler. There is pre-emptive mobilisation which again takes feminism into account by borrowing from some of its best-known figures (usually Susie Orbach). There is no shortage of advice and support, and there is a vast proliferation of expertise in this field of female pathology. The magazines are asked to self-regulate, in regard to the use of extremely thin models, and every so often, usually in response to a widely publicised death, government gestures in the direction of support or resources. A tragic event gives rise to any number of follow up stories, for example in *Grazia* a cousin of the Brazilian model Ana Carolina Reston who died in November 2006 of anorexia, got the opportunity to provide her insight into the case, and then her mother was also interviewed in the *Observer*. In her study of young women Budgeon shows how women now find solidarity among themselves, that these complaints are normal, part and parcel of being a woman (Budgeon 2003). They become the ways in which 'we' understand ourselves as women, hence also a way of excluding those women who dis-identify with these normalising strategies. This is mirrored in the world of magazines which foreclose on any socio-political critique in favour of endless genres, which because of the repetition, because of the cycle of disorders which are reported, because of the very obviousness of the contradiction, with super-slim models on one page, and good advice about overcoming low-self esteem on the other, confirm a notion of female confinement or entrapment. She who suffers (along with her fellow-sufferers) is no longer passive, indeed she is expected to be highly active in her struggle to overcome her afflictions. But these patholo-gies remain part of her make-up, her personal reminders about what it is to be a woman. The production of the category of girl along these lines and by means of these new norms of classification which include her ambition, her desire to achieve, her willingness to try hard etc., is presented not as the 'violence of reg-ulatory norms' as Butler might put it, but as enabling, and this is reinforced through an accompanying discourse which suggests that girls have never had it so good, and that after all their male counterparts are also now experiencing new dynamics of hardship. The common sense running through this kind of language also serves to undercut the need for any new feminist initiative since in many regards women are after all doing better than some of their male peers. This also deflects attention away from any idea of a patriarchal authority, or from any socio-political rationale which is responsible for feminist disorder, in favour of pragmatic consternation or concern that achievement and freedom seems to have produced, by some mysterious process, such high levels of dis-tress. The attributing of normative discontent to young women has become a key mechanism for the production of sexual difference, it provides a vocabu-lary for understanding the female bodily-ego as prone to anxiety, as lacking in certain respects, as insufficient in regard to self-esteem. But feminism has had some existence, especially in large social institutions, it is something that young women are likely to have literally bumped into, particularly in education. They become gender aware, at some level they perhaps even know that these pathologies are actually connected to the kind of society we live in, and the expectations of heterosexuality and consumer culture. So even when it is reviled or ignored, feminism has some kind of shadow presence. It must be actively abandoned or relinquished for a certain quality of life to proceed, the cost of which is self-violence, which, Butler argues, is 'a refracted indictment of social forces'.

Fascinated looking and desiring

'A little bit anorexia, a little bit of bulimia. I'm not totally OK now but I don't think any woman is'. (Amy Winehouse interviewed in the *Daily Mirror*, October 2006).[3]

The fashion image is constantly blamed for encouraging eating disorders among young women. And yet neither inside the academy, nor in the world of public debate and policy, has there been a sustained discussion about the cultural significance of these images in the lives of young women. The degree of complexity in the act of consuming these images is constantly overlooked in favour of surveys often commissioned by interested organisations or companies and usually undertaken more for their headline potential than for serious purposes. Or else there are studies which are wholly empirical drawing on simplistic cause and effect models. In the following pages, my intention is to return to an earlier moment in feminist scholarship and to retrieve and update some of that material. Throughout the 1980s, and into the early 1990s, there was a series of animated debates about the social relations set in place through the consumption, on the part of the woman (or young woman), of the high fashion image, the fashion spread or indeed the glossy magazine genre as a whole. This work was mostly drawing on feminist psychoanalytical work in film studies, with its emphasis on desire, looking and fantasy, and applied this to the photographic image and then to the women's magazine. These essays are located within a field of feminist scholarship that is far removed from debates about the causes of eating disorders among young women. They provide an analysis of what is entailed in the processes of looking at and consuming these cultural forms. In contemporary feminist theory and in media and cultural studies, this scholarship appears to have been forgotten. Thus my aim here is to recover this work, since it helps us understand the interface between pleasure and pain, which this process of fascinated-looking, as well as the fantasy of identification with and in these scenarios, permits.

This world of fashionable images changes relatively little over the decades. As a genre of popular images, the fashion photograph remains remarkably static. They increase in volume as women's consumption habits expand, they have certainly spread rapidly in post-communist countries for example, in Russia and in East Europe and also now in China, and they cross-fertilise into other media forms, including advertising, film, video and television genres. The settings, the fantasy scenarios, the narrative sketches, the idealised female shape and body images remain remarkably constant. And within this narrow repertoire, contemporary, or up-and-coming fashion photographers regularly raid the archives, and put back into circulation, albeit with some new twist, the kinds of styles associated with key archetypal or iconic moments in the history of this cultural form (the most frequently recycled being the work of Helmut Newton and Guy Bourdin). Feminist psychoanalysis helps us to understand the grip this genre has over generations of young women, and it also helps us to locate the threshold of pain, self-punishment and loss which these images appear to be connected with. Whether it is images of models striding down the catwalk, or shots which conform with one of the many narrative styles which are so familiar they hardly warrant a second look, the features which are most marked are, extreme thinness, stick-thin legs and arms, almost completely flat chests, with barely a hint of breasts, narrow boyish hips, flat tummy, sculptured facial features, large eyes and chiselled cheek bones. There is also a limited range of expressions, from apparent boredom, through sullenness, to narcissistic self-absorption, to aggression and disdainfulness towards the assumed viewer, and most often an air of indifference and melancholia.

In a seminal article Diana Fuss (1994) argues that the institutionalised invoking of female homosexuality in this genre is a necessary strategy on the part of heterosexual patriarchy (or the Symbolic) to ensure its proper repudiation, in favour of the achievement of a normative sexual identity on the part of young women. This process is far too important to be left to chance, the successful fixing of the heterosexual desire must be overseen, presumably at that point in the teenage girl's life where questions about sexuality and identity become so significant. I would want to extend Fuss's account to propose that this strategy she describes also keeps failing, prompting renewed attempts to manage this cultural moment marked by distance from heterosexuality. As a result the genre is one of endless disturbance, a field of tension and anxiety locking the viewer into looking, and keeping her just there, over the years, and well beyond anything marked out as a teenage phase. This ghostly invoking of non-normative sexual desire has a productivity that takes the form of a loss. The fashion photograph gives dramatic form to feminine melancholia. Butler follows up her account of heterosexual melancholia in *Gender Trouble* with a claim in *The Psychic Life of Power* that gender per se is melancholic. The fashion photograph is exemplary in this respect, and as a result it is a troubling genre (Butler 1990/1999a, 1997a). There is always, as Rabine (1994) points out, in her analysis of fashion images, an oscillation between possibilities of freedom from the constraints of gender subordination, and the re-establishment of order and control. Kaja Silverman also hints at this tension when she writes that it 'requires the male subject to see himself (and thus be seen) as 'the one who looks at women' (Silverman, 1994: 187). But the narrative presence of the male subject, even in the background, is these days largely removed. Nor is his indisputable place as *auteur* photographer so revered, he no longer has such God-like status in a context where women appear to have won the right to become active themselves. (The bullying, triumphant macho of the fashion photographer in the iconic 1960s Antonioni film *BlowUp* seems today inflated and comic.)

It would be unfair to judge Rabine's article as simply pre-Butler in the assumptions it makes about femininity as, socially constructed but nevertheless belonging to women, and masculinity likewise belonging to men, and while it is true that she does adhere to binaries within a social and psychic constructivist framework, she also presciently touches on many of the themes raised here. She recognises the way in which by the late 1980s ideas about feminism and women's empowerment have been adopted and integrated, to an extent, within fashion magazine editorials. She comments on how this also impacts on a style of freedom visible in the fashion shots themselves. She uses both psychoanalysis and elements of Derridean deconstruction to investigate how fantasy operates in this genre. She explains how in this field of femininity, the absent signifier of phallocentric power, finds substitution in fetishistic fashion items and objects, thus ensuring that in this women-only sphere, things do not get out of control, since the fetish is the reassuring reminder of that phallic power. According to Rabine this terrain is also nowadays characterised by knowingness or reflexivity that power relations are at stake in the sexuality of the fashion image. The genre enacts sexual difference anew, but always, inevitably, and ultimately, in favour of existing gender hierarchies. We could say then that this women's genre mounts a valiant struggle, it is imbued with the desire for freedom, and this is partly what makes it pleasurable for consumers, but awareness of the external omnipresence of constraint, and of something which must be relinquished, gives rise to exhaustion and loss which can then be read across the bodies of the models.

Rabine uses words like semi-hallucinatory to refer to the atmosphere evoked by this genre of photographs. She argues that there is a particular proximity between the fantasy scenarios of the fashion image and the 'pleasure of re-creating the body and the pleasure of masquerade' (Rabine 1994: 63). This pleasure she traces to the different meanings invoked in the move from being naked ('unmastered biology') to that of being dressed (the fiction of a 'self-produced coherent subject') but, Rabine continues, this 'dream of producing a self as a whole' is invariably frustrated, the body image which is produced is not a coherent self, but a body which still signifies lack (ibid: 64). Rabine, in an argument close to my own here, argues that what marks the present moment of women's fantasy and dressing (for her the 1980s) as different from earlier periods, is that, with the advent of feminism women find themselves addressed by the popular media in terms which indicate their entitlement to forms of subjectivity which previously were only available to men. They are addressed as if they are equals to men, while in reality there is no radical adjustment to the gender hierarchy. The dilemma or frustration is that women still do not have the means to challenge the Symbolic order. Writing again in a pre-Butler strain, she sees this as producing a kind of bisexuality, the woman can have the subjectivity of a man, and even act in ways which have in the past been his privilege, but she still remains locked within the constraints of subordinated femininity. 'She has ended up reproducing a self as alienated …a self conscious Oedipal subject founded on lack' (ibid: 64). She is increasingly portrayed as independent, and attention is drawn to the idea of her being aware that she is the object of the male gaze in the photographic image, but this endless self-reflexivity remains locked within the terms posed by the Symbolic, so that she can only reflect on herself as object. This, argues Rabine, is a kind of fictitious invitation to empowerment as she is encouraged to 'assume custodianship' of her look and to manage the power which nevertheless 'reduces her to the second sex'. The photograph seduces the woman, to ensure that she remains the seductress of the male look. The additional level of fantasy, argues Rabine, is that the woman dressing herself to enact the fantasy of wholeness or coherence, also now imagines the gaze of the male as less controlling, as indeed non-dominating. She is thus an emboldened subject and he almost disappears from the scene. There are rarely male figures to be seen in the fashion image. This then corresponds to a fantasy of social change and transformation, she feels herself to be no longer subordinate to men, where in reality according to Rabine what the fantasy produces is a women with two bodies, one which can become seemingly 'confident, free' the other which is still totally entrapped within all the external social and economic relations which require that she remain subjected to patriarchal power. The effect of the dramatic and visually powerful fashion photograph is to provide women with a 'sense of invulnerability and exuberant female sexual power that they can dramatize through their bodies'(ibid: 65).

Later in the same article Rabine examines a glamorous Paris *Vogue* shot of a woman in an archetypal little black dress (see Figure 2). The head is cropped out of the photograph so that all that can be seen is her slim body and long legs, and she is bending to adjust the sling-back of her stiletto. The visual emphasis is on her legs and in particular her feet and Rabine suggests that this foot fetish in fact stands in for the woman as fetish. Despite the seeming carefree appearance of this woman, as well as her confidence, the photograph, like the culture as a whole, resolves the threat posed by women being without the phallus and her seeming 'indifference to this lack' by 'making the woman into the phallus, i.e. men give themselves the "illusion of possessing the phallus" by the illusion that they possess women'. This, she claims, through a deft reading of the image, is construed through the abundance of jokes in the image about the threat to phallic power posed by the desirable woman who is nevertheless contained by the light-hearted re-invoking of phallic power through the excessive signifiers of this power which literally frame the image. But the key phrase here is 'indifference to this lack' because this implies that in the fantasy women have somehow lost their sense of inferiority, their deference to patriarchal authority. The fashion photograph provides a momentary sense to women that they can escape the requirement to be subordinate and that they can be self-sufficient. (This also accounts for the non-conformity of the fashion shot with the conventional terms of male desire, there is an absence of the signifiers associated with what men are known to like.) This in turn is suggestive of a kind of alternative sexual economy, which overturns the obligation to assuage male anxieties about the phallus by betraying

Figure 2   Photo from Paris *Vogue* (November 1989). © F. Scianna/Magnum Photos.

an obvious sense of inferiority and lack. This is the fantasy, but as Rabine argues, the image also enacts a double bind, the woman can enjoy this fantasy, and can also through certain forms of labour on the self, act the fantasy out, while the empowerment which underpins the fantasy and the acting out is nevertheless regulated by the wider patriarchal relations which are as resistant to change as ever, even though the relations permitted within the economy of the image suggest otherwise, even though in this new landscape of desire and feminine empowerment, masculinity is less dominating. This framing is dramatically apparent in the image Rabine chooses for analysis where the cropped figure of the young woman is set in a palazzo-style courtyard surrounded by ancient walls upon which is mounted a 'Church Father' carved from stone.

The seductive power of the fashion photograph is based on the affirmation it appears to offer to its female consumers, that they are subjects of change, and are, within these repertoires, emboldened, unthwarted and endowed with capacity.[4] There is a play for power then within these images, a dangerous oscillation and a tension. To pull women into the web of glamorous consumption, her desire for freedom must be engaged, and this is done by having her enact in fantasy, an indifference to her lack, but this license is inevitably threatening and can only be tolerated within certain limits. Hence the sense of tension, excitement and anxiety in this genre. There is a feminist desire invoked as she is encouraged to take up some freedoms in these images, to be in the city, to be alone, to be self-contained, to be in some emancipated scenario, and this connects with possibilities for gender equality, which are now referred to and engaged with, as Rabine points out, in the popular media. There is also a way in which this desire for feminism is hinted at in her indifference to lack, her turning away from the need for male approval, and instead her location, seemingly self-sufficient, within a women's world, dominated by a particular fashion and body aesthetic. The self-contained world of the fashion magazine and its images permit this indifference to, or turning away, even if just temporally, from the incessant demands of male desire. The question then is what fills the spaces made available when male desire is removed from the scene? The many genres of fashion photography which direct themselves to mechanisms for invoking fantasy and pleasure, correspond to this hermetically-sealed feminine sphere, where desire is constantly generated. But, seemingly, indeed necessarily, without an object, desire in the fashion image becomes both hallucinatory, for the reason that there can be no resolution to this desire, and it becomes melancholic where, under the regulative norms of the heterosexual matrix, the lost object of same sex desire, is incorporated onto the discrete bodies of the models who are in effect consumed by this prohibition. The fashion image enacts a particular rendering of the complex entanglements of freedom and prohibition which have emerged in response to the threatening presence of young women, their coming forward into public worlds as economic actors in their own rights, and their embodiment as beneficiaries of feminist entitlement.

The way in which feminist theorists in the 1980s, and early 1990s, examined the interplay of psychic forces mobilised in this genre is helpful to contemporary attempts to understand tensions, anxieties and manifestations of pain on the part of young women. Rabine's analysis provides a useful way of exploring this realm of pathology, anger and illegible rage. Illegible because almost all images produced now for this market assume and also celebrate equality and empowerment. And these circulations of meanings also take place in an environment marked by the absence of patriarchal signifiers, there is a sense of feminine self-sufficiency, and within certain familiar conventions, a turning away from heterosexuality. Understanding the psychic underpinnings of this genre of visual images enables us to engage with why the source of pain remains so nebulous and opaque. There is endless displacement in relation to precisely where subordination and subservience 'kick in'. What does it mean for young women to live out a situation which tells them they are now equal, and that for sure there is no longer any need for sexual politics, and yet which also suggests that this equality has been mysteriously arrived at, without requiring adjustment or dramatic change on the part of patriarchal authority. Far from patriarchy divesting itself of power, in a re-distributive and democratising move, so as to permit equality, in many instances it seems to be shoring itself up once again, in the aftermath of feminist politics. Hence the opacity about the source and meaning of pain. Hence the extent to which young women are perhaps driven mad by the situation within which they now find themselves.

This 'madness' is mirrored in the delirious genre of fashion photography, where styles of psychic disturbance are endlessly circulated. There is also a contradictory undermining of gender norms at the core of this visual regime whose ostensible objective is, as Fuss has pointed out, to direct women towards the required goal of successful heterosexuality. But if, as Butler has regularly reminded us, the achieving of femininity invariably fails in some respects, then we could say it also fails within the deployment of these particular technologies of gender, where unlike commercial Hollywood cinema, the male gaze does not have a presiding presence. The fashion photographs, tucked into the centrefolds of the many forms of magazines from the glossies for women, to the Sunday newspaper supplements, betray many evident signs of this instability. Evans and Thornton (1989) describe fashion as a 'hysterical discourse', whose fantasy structures permit the portrayal of endless scenarios of 'desire, depression, ecstasy'. The conventions of the fashion photograph describe not just states of sexual ecstasy, but also of psychic disturbance; it is a slightly deranged world. Models are pre-occupied, neurotic, they walk away from the camera, they appear to be despondent, or alienated, or detached as though in a drug-induced reverie. The images create an atmosphere of desire through the very opacity of the needs of the women portrayed. There is no apparent object that will satisfy this need. They are mysteriously insatiable. The object is not simply to arouse male sexuality, quite the reverse, since those well-known cues are totally absent. The logic of the fashion image is that it speaks primarily to women viewers, it is thus mediated through the codes of femininity and it must address the nebulous or illegible desires of women which are not specifically, in this genre at least, focused on masculine approval.

Diana Fuss tackles most directly the mobilisation of a lesbian gaze within this cultural field which 'provides a socially sanctioned structure in which women are encouraged to consume, in voyeuristic if not vampiristic fashion, the images of other women' (Fuss, 1994: 211). For Fuss this process by which women come to look as though they were lesbians entails, as she puts it, 'consuming' images of women whose poses range from the coy to the aggressive. And this spectatorial position is triggered by the distinctive codings which are specific to fashion photography many of which rely on, as Rabine points out, the fragment of the body, showing body parts in pieces, cropping the body to show either torso, or legs or in the case of the images Fuss looks at, seemingly disembodied faces 'detached from any visible body'. These images of body parts return the viewer to a pre-mirror phase and this goes some way in accounting for our obsession with them, they 'reenact, obsessively, the moment of the of the female subject's earliest self-awareness' (Fuss 1994: 214). They recall moments when we all asked, is this a me? Do I actually exist? These are questions which remain with us as recurrent reminders of our fragmented selves. But this showing of parts also corresponds with women's lack and the anxious compensation for this fearful lack on the part of dominant masculinity through the substitute of the fetish. But since the fashion photograph itself has a fetishistic quality all of these features come to be concentrated into this genre so that it is literally overloaded with sexual anxiety in regard to the production of sexual difference, the threat posed by women and the need for that threat to be managed and contained. Fuss develops her argument about the non-heteronormativity of the fashion image by connecting the pre-mirror phase and the earliest moments of self-awareness, with Kristeva's notion of the 'homosexual-maternal facet'. This suggests a homosexual attachment to the mother on the part of the pre-oedipal daughter which is extinguished as a requirement for the acquisition of language and identity, but never so thoroughly since her oedipalisation is inevitably imperfectly realised, as we recall from Freud. This primary homosexuality is constitutive of female subjectivity in that she, the daughter, identifies in a primary way within a 'same sex continuum'. But being reminded of this pre-oedipal moment is also a source of panic and anxiety, because she is reminded of being utterly powerless, terrified and dependent. The memory provoked by the images is intense but also inspires abject terror of 'not being'. The various codes which comprise the conventions of fashion photography play out, over and over again, these feminine anxieties. Fuss describes in detail how the image of the beautiful (dewy?) woman's face, shot to emphasise 'soft focus radiance' functions psychically as the restoration of the lost object of desire, and to the extent that it promises satisfaction, it also threatens dissolution of the boundaries of the self. This beauty shot is taken as though the spectator is looking towards the face of a beautiful, adoring mother. 'Often …we see the face from the distance and perspective that an infant might see it'(Fuss1994: 218). These faces of angelic mothers are made up and shot as if to convey something excessive, an overabundance of jouissance which also provokes this memory ('pre-oedipal nostalgia') of being totally overwhelmed, in a state of pre-identity' (see Figure 3). Hence the panic and anxiety.

Fuss demonstrates how fashion photographs have to be able to generate homosexual desire so that it can be properly eliminated, but in so doing there is also a production of 'lesbian desire within the identificatory move itself'. However, as she goes on to say, this lesbian eroticism is so apparent, so visible for all to see, that this obviousness actually also immediately negates the 'homoerotic structure of the look'. The illicit desire is 'harnessed' in the very process of being invoked as something that exists and that has to be contained and controlled. Thus there is a mobilisation of homosexual desire within an overarching visual economy which at the same time forbids it, producing it in order to say no. Or as if to say 'better get it over and done with here and by these means'. These photographs therefore flirt with the viewer in a game which both allows the desire expression, and then reminds the viewer of the high cost attached to abandoning herself to such desires. Fuss describes this as the 'strategic deployment of a homo-spectatorial look' (ibid: 227). So precarious is the passage for the woman or girl into required heterosexuality, that, especially in a commercial field given over to expanding the pleasures of feminine consumption, it takes immense efforts to bring this unruly terrain to order, and in a marvellous passage Fuss explains that the work of the fashion image is to provoke this desire so that it can be 'channeled (or *Chanel*led)' (ibid: 227). And unlike the viewing position supposed by the medium of film, the position 'mapped by contemporary commercial fashion photography can be read...as feminine, homosexual, and pre-oedipal' (ibid: 228).

All the writers discussed so far (and others besides) have referred extensively to repeated themes in the fashion photograph involving processes of turning away from the camera, as though in search of some other source of recognition, or else they describe states of dejection, boredom, moodiness, fatigue, self-absorption. It seems the genre enacts a kind of hysteric, grand feminine repudiation of dominant sexual norms, 'a refusal to be the object of another's desire'. Griggers carries this in a different direction from the other authors mentioned so far, when she reminds us of Irigaray's notion of mimesis which contains within it, the possibility of 'joyful reappropriation' of the differences buried within the attributes of femininity itself, and with which the feminine subject might reinvent her selves' (Griggers 1990: 82). This suggests that there is a distancing from the everyday life of heterosexual culture, indeed a dissatisfaction with this motivates not so much a narcissistic turning in upon the self but rather an embracing of the possibilities that 'Woman's essential difference can be and must be reinvented' (ibid: 82). This possibility becomes the source of alternative pleasure and fascination. What is played out in the images is 'the cultural construction of feminine subjectivity, and its splittings, which the fashion discourse articulates' (ibid: 87). Such a perspective suggests an investment in the kind of femininity which Kristeva would equate with pre-oedipal dissolution of self, a kind of feminine psychosis, but which Irigaray turns around to become a site of joyful appropriation. If it is the case that the fashion photograph is a cultural form which is capable of generating this range of tensions and anxieties, and if it has the power to create fantasy worlds for female viewers, then we should not be surprised that being charged with this function, the genre is also a site of struggle, the illusion of feminine autonomy is the means by which the underlying power of patriarchy disguises its presence.

Fashion photography is culturally asymmetrical, there is no equivalent form of institutionalised looking within the field of masculinity. Men do not look at each other in this fascinated, prolonged and uninterrupted way. For this reason it has something very compelling to tell us about the formation of feminine subjectivity. My concern here has been to reflect on the place of this genre set within a socio-economic context, where there appears to have been a shift in the balance of power between men and women, where women have gained some degree of economic power and independence, and where there is legislation in place to protect them from discrimination, violence and harassment. The feminist theorists above have each pointed to the presence, or the invoking in the world of fashion photographs, of a homosexual fantasy scenario, often so obvious that this can be very easily discounted, is meant to be discounted. Fuss argues that these images are in effect safety valves, they mark out the official site within which female homosexuality can be portrayed, only so that it can be swiftly dealt with and satisfactorily disavowed. But what is at stake in this disavowal? And if it is invoked only so that it can be all the better contained, what are the consequences of the inevitable failure of this containment? Even if, set against the substantial power of patriarchal society, this is only a slim margin of failure, it is nevertheless that slim margin which counts, at least for the purposes of this discussion. The tension in these images surely emerges through the dilemma which commercial culture is confronted with in its desire to sell vast mountains of commodities in the form of fashion and beauty items, to young women, but to do this effectively it finds itself having to acknowledge the embedded desire for distance from heterosexuality which fuels this desire for looking.

The pictures then inevitably, and especially in the light of the emboldened stance of young women in recent years, display an abundance of tensions which cannot be reconciled. My argument is that they speak a kind of normative pathology on the basis of the impossibility of femininity in its struggle for autonomy. There is a sense of psychic turbulence across the world of fashion photography, as these images re-enact repetitively and obsessively both pre-mirror and post-mirror phases in the lives of girls and young women. The madness of fashion photography resides also in the effect of containment or confinement. Within its frames femininity is made to become too much, yet endlessly desirable. There is nostalgia for girlhood (especially apparent in *Prada* fashion photographs), before that point in which the demands of heterosexuality become so palpable, when the female body is still pre-pubertal. Distance from heterosexuality is then magically resolved through yearning for a time before its effects were so tangible and unavoidable. As Griggers also points out this genre has particular attraction for middle class or aspirant middle class viewers, for whom some degree of freedom or economic independence has been encouraged through the impact and efforts of feminism, education and consumer culture. To sell clothes, cosmetics and the magazines themselves, these images must engage with and tap into feminine desire, indeed they must positively produce feminine desire while also contain it, so that it does not threaten the basis of masculine hegemony. This act of containment operates within the frame of the image, within the genre itself, within the world of the fashion image. The effect of the fashion photograph is that it is always threatening to spill out of its frame, but it never quite does, instead it is always brimming, always immanent.[5] The genre is somehow pregnant with undirected and impossible desire, which, exhausted, turns inwards, or against itself, in some kind of illegible rage, or in a kind of drug-induced ennui (Kate Moss), a disdainful aloofness, a specific melancholia, a nostalgia for something that is lost, and that is associated with time immemorial. The archetypal fashion photograph conveys a certain coldness, *froideur*, disappointment, a profound reluctance to embrace domesticity, and a preference for some undisclosed state of otherness. Of course there are also differences between the feminist theorists referred to here. Irigarayian approaches, for example, focus on femininity as a site which in its subordination can nevertheless be mobilised as a quasi-autonomous force, can emerge or become, as a fragmented subject who is 'not one, but many, and not all' (Griggers 1990: 100). Griggers argues that the power of these images correspond with 'the reader's perpetual confrontation with her own retreating and regrouping desire, with her own splittings as a subject. ... for the female reader the experience ... is the experience of ambivalence ... towards power, towards motherhood, towards marriage, towards a homoeroticism dressed in leather and pearls, toward fashion, toward social investment, towards representation itself' (ibid: 101).

A more transparent reading of the fashion photograph, especially the kind of images found in the glossy pages of magazines like *Vogue*, would suggest the disdainful turning away from the everyday, as a profoundly narcissistic gesture, indicating not just a preference for the self, but an inflated sense of the self, as a more beautiful and hence more socially valuable subject, than any other. The model looks down with contempt on those who do not and

can never aim to achieve her exceptional beauty. And such a style comple-
ments the value system of magazines like *Vogue* which elevates the world of
luxury consumption and the social capital accruing from great wealth, talent and physical beauty. This would be to understand the fashion photograph as producing and sustaining a social and symbolic hierarchy based on
norms of feminine beauty which are to be traded as an asset on the elite
market. But this is an insufficient account in that it does not provide an
analysis of the narrative settings, the style of photography, nor the kinds of
changes in the genre which have made it something more than just a reflection of the values of what is referred to as high society. Rabine shows how
this previous elite function of fashion photography was replaced by styles
which seemed to articulate with dynamics of social transformation, including those changes associated with sexual politics. And on the basis of the
centrality and omnipresence of this cultural form, and its pervasive styles
which extend far beyond *Vogue* into the more popular and distinctly non-
elite pages of the fashion weeklies like *Grazia*, I have here provided an
account of what seems to be at stake in managing and regulating the flows
of desire which are unleashed by the images and the practices of looking. I
have suggested that the fashion photograph marks a site of normalised pathology, a kind of institutionalised madness which accrues from the impossibility
of femininity. Young women find themselves positioned in a post-feminist
frame where notions of equality are routinely invoked, while, at the same time,
new terms and conditions are being set. This is a socially induced imbalance
accruing from the female subject having become 'gender aware' as a result of
previous feminist activity and struggles associated with sexual politics, while
also now being expected to disregard this awareness.

The young woman has been a beneficiary of these struggles, she is now
routinely interpellated (as I have argued in the previous chapters) as a subject of capacity, the commercial media and consumer culture champion
her as a subject of popular feminism. But insofar as such knowledge or
awareness also meets its limit when confronted with only minimal adjust-
ments to the bid for gender quality on behalf of dominant patriarchy, the
injury can only be compounded. Post-feminist disorders are thus the site
for new and even more subtle modes of regulation. The defining and diag-
nosing are, *pace* Foucault, regulative practices. It becomes normal to be
injured in new kinds of ways, and there are various techniques and treatments now made available for these post-feminist pathologies. The world
of fashion photography visualises this turmoil and disturbance. Its women
(Kate Moss, Naomi Campbell) are inevitably harmed, suffering, deviant,
injured in some way. But what I have been arguing is that this kind of
pathology is normalised and even glamourised, its symptoms and styles
are readily available, and with them there also comes into play, any number of feminist-influenced psychotherapies, as well as techniques drawn

from cognitive and behavioural sciences. In some respects these operate as a self-perpetuating regime, which refutes and disavows the asking of questions which pertain to the critique of masculinity, patriarchy, and the enforcement of norms emanating form the heterosexual matrix. They keep young women locked into a hermetic world of feminine ambivalence and distress.

In the concluding sections of this chapter I will draw on Butler's account of heterosexual melancholia, and I will designate these pathologies as illegible rage, as female complaint, where the values of feminist sociality are disavowed and replaced by a bolstered post-feminist self which is unviable, this unviability ensuring its status as subject for attention and treatment in accordance with the values and norms set by various experts, self-help gurus and professionals. The fashion photograph, let us say the brimming maternal jouissance of Kate Moss's face, shot from just below, or the pre-occupied disdain and angry sexual unavailability of Naomi Campbell (beauty with a sneer), or again the self-absorption of Kate Moss posing naked as though for the sole gratification of her self, and her teen girl fans),[6] these endless stagings of femininity conjure psychic landscapes and scenarios of loss, melancholia and illegible rage. In the following section I will examine the definition of and the limits of selfhood, that is routinely made available to young women, as a technology of contemporary individualisation. These interventions offer support in times of stress, and they overwhelm the subject with choices, possibilities and advice in pursuit of control, self-esteem, and success. They regularly draw on elements from well-known feminist discourses in terms of independence and the desire for agency, but subject these qualities to further transformation so that they more fully conform with the dictates of a post-feminist sexual contract which seeks resolution to sexual inequality without challenge to or contestation of masculine hegemony and the heterosexual matrix. If pre-feminist female selfhood was previously understood in terms of absence of autonomy and dependence on male approval, its post-feminist counterpart requests of the female subject that she, with the support available to her, finds the resources within herself to regain the self-esteem which is always and inevitably lost. As I will show in the sections that follow it is precisely this mobilisation of a self with esteem that is part of the problem.

From masquerade to melancholia

The tension I have referred to which pervades the field of fashion photography, which is also contained by this same field, which entails a turning away from male desire, but in no perceivable direction, indeed in a directionless way, not in preference for a same sex choice of sexual object, and not either in favour of narcissism,[7] can be perhaps best understood as heterosexual melancholia. In *Gender Trouble* and also in *The Psychic Life of Power* Butler examines this terrain of melancholia and illegible rage. Butler gets to these ideas through a persistent engagement with notions of masquerade. As we have already seen in Chapter 2, the masquerade has been a source of fasci-nation for various feminist and psychoanalytic theorists. Butler is less con-cerned with the injuries sustained by those women who are inside masquerading femininity, than with the wounds which accrue to those women who find themselves unable to take up such positions. For Butler a key axis is between those who appear to be able to take up these positions without trauma, and those for whom this expectation is itself traumatic. In demarcating my own field of inquiry at this moment as inside this field of normative femininity, I am making the point that there are also traumatic injuries pertaining to the seeming inhabiting of this position. Concessions are made on the part of patriarchal authority in the direction of responding to desire for autonomy, or desire for distance from heterosexuality, but all the more so that unruly or disorderly desires can be safely contained, even if this requires the endorsement of normative pathologisation, such that symptoms of gen-der distress (self-harming, drug addiction, eating disorders) come to be estab-lished as predictable, treatable, things to be managed medically rather than subjected to sustained social scrutiny. They are in effect incorporated into the current definitions of what it is to be a normal female, and in this sense they are everyday attributes, part and parcel of femininity. Fashion images occupy a special place in this process of normalisation of feminine melancholia, they are a cultural sign of its institutionalisation. The fashion image shows over and over again, the incorporation of the same-sex object which was once loved, but which must be abandoned, and is then incorporated as loss into a space which, as Butler puts it, is, if not in the body, then possibly on the body. This process is also a way of maintaining the loss as unspeakable, and that unspeakability comes to be codified and presented back to female viewers, in the 'turning-away-from' gesture and in the profusion of clothes and items whose function it is to be 'on the body'.

How does feminine melancholia comes to feature as a condition of young womanhood today? What does it mean to be constrained, or stuck, or immobilised by a loss that must remain unspeakable? Butler provides us with a vocabulary for understanding how cultural values, new forms of regulation and constraint, predicated as they are on various incitements to become active, serve to position young women so that they accommodate to pathology, so that they become used to the idea that self-harming, or being depressed or grieving that they have 'left it too late' to have children, that these are all part and parcel of women's lives, and that there is no other solution beyond those on offer, no radical alternatives. It is in this context that the fashion photograph, with all of these conflicting sexual desires, threatening to spill over and out of the frame, but nevertheless remaining somehow locked just inside those frames, registering, in this instance, other emotive bonds that could have been pursued, but which under the circumstances are instead preserved as a source of melancholic longing, comes to serve as a metaphor for the various post-feminist disorders which are now so familiar that even we feminists become used to them and maybe even immune to their significance, so that we too turn away from them.

Butler is it seems thrown by, mystified by, perhaps also fascinated by the masquerade. This seems to provide the key to understanding gender's failure and melancholia. She takes the lead from Lacan who is likewise derailed somewhat by the masquerade. And, since this idea of masquerade, if it is to take meaningful social form, must surely point us in the direction of fashion, make up, beauty and the body, then inevitably we might be expected to look at the fashion image to understand something of its operations. Lacan says that the masquerade is the 'effect of a melancholy feminine position' (quoted in Butler, 1990/1999, 2nd edn: 59) If he appears to remain perplexed and unsettled nonetheless by this formulation, if he vacillates in his account of this position as a substitute for not having the phallus, a 'reassuring strategy', protecting the male from his own lack or his fear of castration, if it is an enactment of the position that femininity must occupy as 'being an appearance' i.e., an object which promises fulfilment to a masculinity which is also wanting, since it too is defined in lack, then Riviere was surely right to equate the masquerade with womanliness itself (Riviere 1929/1986). Butler asks so many questions of the feminine masquerade (more than ten) over the space of a few pages in *Gender Trouble* that the reader might reasonably conclude she sees it as critical to the understanding of female sexuality, yet at the same time endlessly, infuriatingly recalcitrant and elusive. As we have already seen, it is a theme in the writing of Riviere, then Lacan, and then again in Irigaray and in Doane, and Butler recognises that it both seems to answer various questions which have proved obstinate, and it also presents new difficulties. She wonders (and here I summarise only a few of her questions), is the masquerade in effect 'dressed up' female desire which, because women must personify lack, is otherwise disguised and negated? Does this take shape in the form of a magnificent wardrobe? Or is it the product of the denial of lack, a presence which comforts men as an 'appearance' of the Phallus? Is the mask a kind of flawlessness that does the work of being the Phallus with perfect efficiency? Does it offer a full confirmation of the femininity which is forced to be the binary opposite of its masculine counterpart, so as to refuse any 'bisexual possibilities which would interrupt the seamless construction of heterosexual femininity' (ibid: 61)? Butler recalls that Riviere sees it as a production of femininity which transforms anger into seduction and flirtation, but there is also the possibility that this dramatic style of self-presentation conceals or glosses over those other possibilities of more autonomous female desire, which, were they to surface, would reveal masculine failure. Does the masquerade provide a template for the position which must be occupied by femininity, or does it cover up the masculinity which women might also possess (a phallicism) but which they must renounce, for fear of punishment, which in turn might account for some elements of the anger of the masquerade? ('I must get done up like this in order to be recognised as a women and to function in the world but in being forced to do so I am also renouncing some masculine possibilities which might otherwise be rightly mine, why not?'). And fear of masculinity is also fear of being one who refuses men, which carries reprisals.

Butler comes back time and time again to Lacan's claim that in the feminine masquerade there is an identification in which refusals of love are resolved. Lacan connects this with female homosexuality and sees the refusal of love as one in which it is the male who is being refused and who is disappointed in this asexual femininity which turns away from him. He is disappointed about what she doesn't or will not give him, i.e. a pleasing appearance and availability. This refusal on her part is thus a preservation of another love, and a seeming preference for it. The melancholic state that ensues takes over feminine identity, dominates it and also resolves the loss forced upon it, by preserving it, incorporating it as an ego-ideal which berates and scolds the ego for failing to live up to the requirements of this lost love. Feminine melancholia is thus a state also of endless self-beratement since the love that is lost, or that must be abandoned is also a source of anger and ambivalence. The woman inevitably castigates herself both for having renounced this love and also for failing it, and for failing to measure up to its high expectations. But in donning the masquerade she refuses a female homosexuality while at the same time she hyperbolically incorporates the 'female other who is refused'. Following the drift of Riviere's argument Butler suggests that she in effect 'becomes the object she forbids herself to love'. This analysis of heterosexual melancholia emerges then from Butler's close critical reading of Freud as well as Levi-Strauss. They lead her to argue that a prohibition against homosexuality precedes the incest taboo, and it is this prohibition which then institutes the very necessity of the opposition between masculine and feminine positions as dispositions, indeed even more radically she suggests that masculinity and femininity are processes of becoming the lost same sex object through incorporation, and with this a construction of an ego ideal which is in effect the voice of that preserved but renounced love. What seem to be primary drives are produced effects 'of a law imposed by culture and by complicitous acts of an ego ideal'. This means that the perfect femininity upon which the fashion magazines stakes its own existence tells a story about disavowed love and gender identity as a 'melancholic structure'. At this point it is perhaps useful to recall that in Chapter 2 I argued that the post-feminist masquerade, in the figure of the working girl who wears her ultra-feminine wardrobe both ironically, and also to re-inscribe herself within a field of the reassuringly feminine, emerges as a new mode of regulative gender power, one which is alert to and quick to respond to the dangers posed by feminist theorising like Butler's as it filters through various social channels and institutional sites.

Illegible rage

The step I wish to make now, is to use some of Butler's thinking on these matters, translating it into a more explicit social currency, and to propose that what is at stake in young women's contemporary melancholia, is a double loss, first the loss of the same sex object of love which is, as Butler argues, a pre-requisite for acquiring a gendered position, which then is directed through the Oedipal process, the outcome of which (always imperfect for the girl), is subjectivity and language. But the second loss is, I would suggest, the loss of the feminist ideal of liberty and equality into which was always incorporated the possibility of love between women. My argument is that the landscape of popular culture, including the world of the fashion image, facilitates each of these losses, providing instead and pre-emptively a kind of compensatory containment for gender melancholia within this now-more-familiar even predictable field of psychic pain and distress. Popular culture is asking young women to get used to gender melancholia, and to recognise themselves and each other within its terms. Indeed popular culture and the world of magazines establishes a kind of surrogate feminism predicated on normalising melancholia, but, as I show below, the consequences of this can be fatal. I will take the reader through Butler's chapter titled 'Psychic Inceptions: Melancholy, Ambivalence, Rage' in the *Psychic Life of Power*, bearing in mind that while she does not herself point us in this direction, that is to the terrain of contemporary girlhood, nevertheless it seems to me she provides us with this opportunity (Butler 1997a). It seems to leap out of her pages. She finds a persuasive way of connecting the social with the psychic so as to permit an analysis of gender melancholia, as the outcome of social processes which work to institutionalise and consolidate this state for young women, so that seemingly inexplicable anxiety, pain, rage, and self-harming behaviour, become accepted ways of being. The media and popular culture find reason to be both titillated and entertained by self-destructive young women, who speak out their pain loudly, and yet whose rage appears to be illegible. And since, just as Butler points out, the melancholic person will publicly self-berate, since she will be someone prone to shameless self-exposure, it becomes all the more difficult, especially in the time of blogs and websites like *MySpace* and *YouTube* (and pro-anorexia websites) to differentiate between what appears to be female agency in the many opportunities for self-advertisement of pain, anxiety and self-loathing, and those mechanisms which are pre-emptively deployed across the commercial media which produce the framing for the institutionalisation of melancholia. (For example on her website Amy Winehouse says to her young teenage girl fans 'I am an ugly drunk dickhead, I really am' and, commenting on her tattoos, 'I like pin up girls, I'm more of a boy than a girl. ... I'm not a lesbian tho' ... not before a Sambuca anyway')[8].

Butler proposes that the enforced abandonment of same sex love becomes an unavowable loss, the effect of which is melancholia which is characterised by ambivalence and anger and the production of an ego which substitutes for the lost object by incorporating it. Following Freud she reminds us that what is lost can also be 'country or liberty', i.e. an ideal, which in the context of this debate I draw on to propose that feminism might count as such a lost object. Melancholia marks a withdrawal from the social world, and a seeming retreat into the landscape of the psyche where the process of incorporating and preserving in an opaque way the lost object produces a kind of spatialisation of the psyche and a division between the ego and the ego ideal. This latter takes up the role of berating 'critical agency' which is forever castigating the ego for failing to live up to some unattainable standard. It is also the means by which, as Freud famously put it, 'by taking flight into the ego, love escapes extinction'. It is, according to Butler, this very process, instigated by a regime of social prohibition, which actually produces psychic life (as we don't know it) and its capacity to report back, as it were, from this location. The inner life of melancholia then takes the form of a series of non-communications in the form of self-reproaches, at the same time there is loud denial about any such loss, as Butler puts it, it is as though the melancholic subject is saying 'I have lost nothing'. However, although these angry outbursts remain opaque (the sullen models turning away from the male gaze, the drunken aggression of young women like Amy Winehouse) Butler then suggests that, despite this opacity, such activities are also 'nascent political texts'. She explains, 'the violence of social regulation is not to be found in its unilateral action, but in the circuitous route by which the psyche accuses itself of its own worthlessness' (1997a: 184). These assaults on self-esteem takes the melancholic subject to the brink of survival, she is virtually suicidal, she experiences worthlessness, and yet, there is also in her despair something of a 'crushed rebellion' (Butler 1997a quoting Bhabha). Even if the state has already interjected to 'pre-empt an insurrectionary rage', if in my terms it has orchestrated the terms of gender melancholia such that in a post-feminist context, young women have made some advances, they seem perhaps not to have much to complain of, some might even see them as 'having it all', there is still, amidst this illegibility of their 'plaint', some trace or residue of that lost feminist rebellion. It is this which provides a small window of escape, like a long forgotten and only momentarily accessible memory which nevertheless offers an understanding of the tormented landscape of contemporary femininity. Young women's melancholia, with its ambivalence and indifference, its undirected anger, or its anger directed against the self, these are in Butler's terms 'faded social text(s)', where the 'violence of the loss is redoubled in the violence of the psychic agency' in the harm the young woman is now capable of inflicting on herself (ibid: 196). There are rarely, these days (where there might have been in the past) questions raised about the social aetiology of such phenomena, they remain dealt with as though illegible, something to do with being a girl. This is an index of the extent to which this state of being stuck, and alone in a terror of anxiety, is an instituted and normalised alienation.

Butler sees that melancholia can drive its subject to a point where she no longer wishes to live, and yet, even in this state there remain some signs of attachment to and dependence on others. The loneliness of the anorexic girl, the isolation of the young woman who cuts herself, the cut-off-ness of the alcohol or drug-dependent girl, can possibly, in the nick of time, be overcome. But she must lose her attachment to the preserved object and re-enter the world not as an ego bolstered with self-esteem but as one who understands her dependency on others, this is the social tie, still there even in the loneliest of moments, it is there in the wish to convey, in the suicide note, a remaining attachment to the world of social relations. To live she must 'claim life back, not by an act of will but by submission to a sociality' (ibid: 197). I referred earlier to one such suicide letter, left to a mother, written by a girl who was overweight, bullied, who had desires outside the frame of heterosexuality. Her letter is extraordinarily painful to read. It entered the public domain through the decision by her parents to allow it to be published, this letter is a social indictment of the cruelty of her male peers at school and their aggressive judgemental masculinity, it is also a critique of prevailing cultural norms which make those women with bigger bodies experience themselves as worthless and repugnant. Exactly what happens on the basis of that letter, if for example it is taken up by gay and lesbian groups, by a new wave of young feminist activists, or by parents of teenagers who commit suicide, all of this is uncertain, but the point is that the letter was written and it was recognised as a social statement, a 'nascent political text' by the grieving parents. The same point could be made in relation to the suicide letter addressed to her mother, by the model Ana Carolina Reston, but this time with more explicit feminist and psychoanalytic overtones which correspond to many of the themes I have explored so far. It read ' If I could I'd like to go back to being four, clinging onto you as if I were still in your womb, so that nobody could harm me' (quoted in Philips, *The Observer Supplement* 'Skin and Bones', 14 January 2006).

Raging to 'avoid death'

I have claimed that there is an awareness among young women that female bodily anxieties are intricately tied up with the need for social approval and more generally with the high value which society places on spectacularly coded styles of feminine beauty and sexuality, at the expense of other capacities. There is also recognition that same sex love carries the full weight of social disapproval, even when officially there are rights and entitlements for gay and lesbian people. If feminism disputed the overwhelming emphasis placed on this narrow range of feminine attributes, then knowledge of that critique is what must also be stifled and lost. In abandoning or repudiating (as is required by the State and by consumer culture) these feminist ideals which would seek to challenge this narrow grid of intelligibility, something is lost and what exactly it is that is lost becomes opaque, and the 'violence of regulatory norms' gives rise to a melancholia. This female melancholia and its attendant patterns of self-beratement can be understood as responses to such a loss. The self-violence which follows and the outpourings of anger against the self are a 'refracted indictment of social forces'. Of course Butler is not talking explicitly about young women, nor about feminism. Her focus of attention is on how we are made into subjects, how subjectification works upon the psyche, with how 'the fiction of identity is constituted through an originary violence that turns the will against itself in a mode of subjection' (Colebrook 2002a: 88). Butler attempts to knit together an analysis of social structure with that of psychic structure, how does the power of social norms impact on the psyche? How are practices of subjectification actualised? How does critical agency turn the ego against itself, 'animating its emergence in the form of a power over the self'? And this turning in against the self, she argues, can be understood as a 'recasting of social plaint as psychic self judgement'. For Bhabha this state of violence against the self or self-loathing is a kind of anti-colonialist rebellion put down, and the greater the power of the state or its agents to cultivate this melancholic self-loathing, the more 'shameless is the self-exposure' of those who wish to proclaim their self-worthlessness. At the same time the nature of this loss must remain elusive and 'nameless', opaque and silenced. The ideal, whether it is for liberty, freedom from oppression, freedom from racial hatred or freedom from sexual injustice, must remain 'unavowed'. In this chapter I have made a case for feminism to have been such an ideal, one which challenged as a political antagonism the normative narrow ideal of femininity that now finds itself so triumphantly re-instated. Repudiated and vilified in dominant political culture, despite having gained degrees of effectivity (in legislation and as gender awareness) its only existence for a younger generation of women today is as unavowable loss. The State, media and popular culture converge in the production of female melancholia and illegible rage to pre-empt the re-invention of feminist politics through a wide range of individualising strategies and technologies of the self, many of which draw on and even cite with a degree of approval early feminist books and interventions. These include the endorsement of a narrow range of appropriately feminine attributes (achieving a perfect body shape), expectations of individual excellence and competition (achievement), within an environment where support guidance and help are available.

Butler's analysis of gender as melancholia also helps us understand how this desire for images of perfect femininity coexists with expressions of animosity, antagonism and loathing to unfeminine, masculine women, feminists and lesbians together. The enforced loss of homosexual desire as a requirement of the heterosexual matrix contributes to melancholia and the namelessness or unspeakability of such a loss. The fact that it is a lesbian feminist theorist like Butler herself who disentangles this state of confusion, ambivalence, anxiety and self-hatred accounts also for the ambivalence directed in a post-feminist context to similar feminist figures, since they appear to hold some of the keys to explaining the sources of such anger. The 'unthought known' of gender awareness resists such accounts not just because the melancholic does not want to be robbed of the loss which now has a place in her psyche which she is so attached to, but also for fear of punishment and the threat of abjection. Therefore the young woman prefers to keep her feminism a private matter, something personal, something internalised. Feminism is a private concern, a kind of secret life, a devouring of classic feminist novels, for example, a love for Jane Austen, a passion for Emma Bovary. If the 'violence of social regulation' gives rise to impossible demands while also foreclosing on a form of power which might challenge these punitive norms of social approval, the young woman's illegible rage expresses the powerlessness in the forced abandonment of this public feminist ideal. Such forms of self-rebuke span a wide spectrum from normative discontent to suicidal behaviour. But where survivability itself comes into question, where the young anorexic woman is at the brink of self-annihilation, Butler sees anger as not being entirely without ambivalence. The angry defiant girl, now also the subject of competitive individualised aloneness rages also to 'avoid death', the girl cutting herself, or starving herself almost to death, or drinking and taking drugs so as to create an inner world of self-gratification, has not completely severed her attachments to the 'allocutory bond', to the social world and thus to life itself.

'Survival does not take place because an autonomous ego exercises autonomy in the face of a countervailing world (i.e. autonomy is not the solution),
on the contrary no ego can emerge except through animating reference to
such a world' (Butler, 1997a: 195). The social terms which make survival
possible suggest neither coherence or mastery 'indeed by forfeiting the
notion of autonomy survival becomes possible' (ibid: 196). However con-
science negates this social horizon 'as though to infer that survival depends
on an act of will' (ibid: 197). Quite the opposite argues Butler 'to claim life
in such circumstances is to contest the righteous psyche by submission to a
sociality that exceeds the bounds of the ego and its autonomy' (ibid: 197).
The insistent bolstering of the female ego, the requirement of feminine coherence and mastery, are as Butler says forms of violent constraint and female
confinement. It is by these dictates that forms of gender re-stabilisation are
secured at a cost. Young women now find themselves, if no longer trapped
within the home, then confined to the topographies of an unsustainable
self-hood, deprived of the possibilities of feminist sociality, and deeply
invested in achieving an illusory identity defined according to a rigidly
enforced scale of feminine attributes. The question then is what social and
(sub) cultural resources are available to young women which are capable of
challenging or contesting the violence of prevailing social norms?

Let me conclude this chapter with some speculative comments. Butler's
account of the anguish of a locked-in self, for whom readily available and normative notions of the self are part of the problem, might lead us to imagine
some other more socialised youth cultural spaces where there is the possibility of a dissolution of this self, or a suspension of self in favour of ritualised
communality. Such a re-reading of 'subcultural style' is actually already
rehearsed by Butler in her response to Stuart Hall's engagement with youth
culture in the mid-1970s (Hall et al. 1976, Butler 2000b). In her article Butler
suggests that for stigmatised sexual minorities, subcultural lifestyle can be a
matter of survival itself. She asks 'what sort of styles signal the crisis of survival'? I would like to transpose this reading of subculture, as a way of illuminating what are often seen as themselves dangerous spaces for young people
on the basis of a cocktail of drugs, alcohol, dancing, music, and casual sexual
encounters. But if these are all conducted within a space of intense sociality
which is outside of the nuclear family, and hence away from tight oedipalised
relationships then already we can see that maybe subcultures have the capacity to display and even celebrate our radical dependency on others. While at
a simple level this could be reduced to ideas like 'peer group bonding', actually the intensity of gang culture, the giving over of the self to the hip-hop
family, or to the 'House' (in the film *Paris Is Burning*), is something much
more than that, a kind of desire for sociality, for dependency on others which
is acknowledged, which is reciprocated.[9] Returning to the questions I have
been posing about 'illegible rage' we could say that subcultures permit that

rage to become legible through intense sociality, and through the collective production of cultural forms such as music (being in a band) fashion (creating styles) films (making DIY movies) as well as novels , blogs, art, photography, fanzines and other accoutrements. We could add to this by saying that for lonely melancholia to be overcome, the lost objects of both same sex love and the feminist ideal need to be killed off, for the sake of re-attaching to social life and creating a new kind of feminism. If survival also requires detachment from the self-berating ego, then perhaps for young people, in this case girls, subcultures have also historically provided this possibility. We might read activities like *riotgrrrl* and *the f word*, also *Ladyfest* and the queer subcultures which Halberstam documents, in exactly these terms. But let us not get carried away too quickly in this respect. No market is more precious to contemporary capitalism and its consumer culture than that of young women, and increasingly subcultural spaces find it hard, if not impossible to evade the surveillance of a seemingly friendly-capitalism which will employ similarly-minded young women to work on behalf of the big brands which are so eager to plug into what in the past might have been an underground of hidden-away sociality and creativity. In a sense subcultures, with the promise for young people, of escape and possibilities of dissolving a self in favour of collectivity and communality, have also become things of the past, given the high value they now have as a source of innovation and creativity. They are almost instantly tracked, charted, documented and publicised through these practices of corporate theft. This, alongside the incessant discourses of female individualisation transform the landscape of what once would have been subculture, into a different kind of space altogether, where young women's rage becomes once again illegible.[10]

Perhaps the best example of many of the themes examined in this chapter, is the work of the artist Tracey Emin. Working class and half-Turkish, Emin's work is haunted by a history of feminist art that came before her, and which she was presumably taught while at art school, but which she must seemingly disavow. Indeed she mimics this work while also railing against it. Her regular denunciations of feminism, made in the right-wing tabloid press, bear the mark of a knowing betrayal, while her work itself, reflects both ambivalence and rage about that which cannot be named. It cannot be named but Emin's concerns are absolutely the same as those which have been at the heart of early second wave feminist art, for example, autobiography, testimony, narrative of the self, the woman's body, sexual abuse, rape, menstruation, mental illness, suicide attempts, the sexual double standard, abortion, pleasure, danger and desire. However, in her art work there is displacement, and a logic of substitution, which says 'this is about me, rather than this is because I am a woman'. Emin's 'shameless self exposure' in place of social critique, which is frustratingly absent, a kind of deliberate, obstinate and disavowed absence, locks her into reliance on her own self-biography, which both reflects and refutes many of the concerns of feminist (sub)cultural studies, in the 1970s, as well as the issues which dominated feminist art history. Emin's art fulfils many of the features which I have in this book so far attributed to a post-feminist disposition. Emin's anger only goes so far, for example, she attempts to get vengeance on the local men who abused her and exploited her sexual vulnerability when she was a young teenager in Margate. She does this in the form of a short film where she ritualistically names those men, who named her as a slut, whore, or slapper, back when she was too young to understand what was going on (Emin, Why I Never Became a Dancer, 1995). While the viewer will see this as an indictment of the sexual double standard and against male violence, this is never the vocabulary which gets to be attributed to her work as a whole. She is in effect more acceptable as a top artist when she expresses anger against herself, than in those moments when her anger is about sexual injustice and violence.

Let me conclude this chapter then with the figure of Emin, since she embodies the new feminine subject who is endowed with capacity, a working-class girl who through her own determination got into Maidstone College of Art and then won a post-graduate place at the Royal College of Art. She exemplifies and outstrips those other young women who have won a string of entitlements, but who will also display a series of ailments and anxieties, if not full-blown pathologies. The loss of feminism, the loss of a political love for 'womanhood' which feminism advocated and encouraged, which also allowed a certain suspension of the self in favour of 'the collective' or 'the communal', creates new forms of female confinement. The young woman in contemporary political and popular culture is asked to reconcile autonomy and the possibility of achievement with compliancy with a patriarchal order which is dissolved, de-centralised, and nowhere to be seen. What I have sought to do in this chapter is to examine modes of regulation within the popular domain which make impossible or at least unlikely the critique of the heterosexual matrix and masculine domination and which normalise illegible pathologies as culturally intelligible, if not always survivable.

Notes

1 See also the Depression Report 2006.

2 A report in the *Guardian* (23 September 2004: 12) by Sam Jones titled 'Suicide Pact Teenager's Parents Release Letter Telling of Bullying', described the aggression and violence which resulted in two girls running away together and taking an overdose leading to the death of one of the girls, Laura Rhodes and the hospitalisation of her friend. Laura's suicide letter told of how boys would trip her up in the school corridor daily, heckling her that she was fat and a dyke. She described herself as 'this fat lump which is myself' and she wrote 'while I got fatter and fatter and sadder and sadder, everyone got meaner and meaner'.

3 Accessed at www.wikipedia/Amy Winehouse 1 January 2007.

4 For example the energetic and exuberant images of 1960s 'Swinging London' girls in mini-skirts.

5 This immanence is seen in the work of Cindy Sherman in her most famous film stills which also evoke the world of fashion photography (see Williamson 1986).

6 On what grounds can this claim be made? The images are without the fetish signs (items, fish nets, heels, etc.) which typically accompany the pin-up directed to the male gaze, these pictures instead belong to the internalised world of the girl's bedroom, which in the last few years has found a mass public forum with MySpace and Facebook. See also Kate Moss teen girl fan sites.

7 We might ask the question, what is the relationship between narcissism and gender melancholia? I have ignored the place of narcissism in this reading of the fashion photograph because I am concerned with an implied but lost relation with an other, in these images. This makes them social forms, addressing a relation with another which nevertheless must be disavowed.

8 www/amywinehouse.com

9 Gilroy writes about the survivalist aesthetics of black music, Hebdige talks of subcultural rage, with style as refusal, and as 'noise' (Gilroy 1987, 1993; Hebdige 1979).

10 See for example *Thirteen* (dir. C. Hardwicke 2003) and *Morvern Callar* (dir. L. Ramsay 2002).

5

'WHAT NOT TO WEAR' AND POST-FEMINIST SYMBOLIC VIOLENCE

A gardener is thought to have made legal history after being convicted of racially aggravated harassment for using the word 'pikey'…. The Crown Prosecution Sevice said it was unaware of any previous convictions for using the word 'pikey' in a racial context. In September Marco Pierre-White was rapped for using the expression 'pikey's picnic' on ITV reality show *Hell's Kitchen*. It sparked a row with ex-Blue star Lee Ryan who walked out of the show. (A. Radnedge, *Metro*, 14 December 2007: 16)

Introduction

In this chapter I examine a 'movement of women' which is a requirement of the contemporary socio-economic system, and I propose that one site for the overseeing and orchestrating of this movement is the terrain of popular culture, in particular the genre of 'make-over' television programmes. This is a key function of the make-over format of programme, to move women from one state, now deemed unacceptable, to another, which is a greatly improved state of good looks and well-being.[1] The 'movement of women' refers to the need for women, particularly those who are under the age of 50, and thus still of potential value to the labour market, to come, or move forward, as active participants in these labour markets, and also in consumer culture, since the disposable income permits new realms of buying and shopping. Both of these activities, working and spending, become defining features of new modes of female citizenship.

The television programmes do not just open up the field of consumer culture to women, in particular working-class or lower middle-class women, they actively direct such women so that they learn to make the right choices. The transformative effect results in healthier subjectivities, cheerfulness, better 'self-esteem' and an improved quality of sexual relationships. National television has been put to work on the self-images of women who, in the past, would have been easily overlooked and made invisible as they moved through the lifecycle of marriage, having children and growing older. But now it has become a feature of women's lives, indeed almost an entitlement, to move from out of the shadows, into a spotlight of visibility, into a luminosity which has the effect of a dramatisation of the individual, a kind of spectacularisation of feminine subjectivity, which becomes the norm. This make-over format is a new 'space of attention', a form of gender power which has the effect of offering to women a specific form of freedom and a particular idea of independence. Luminosities of momentary visibility or short-lived celebrity are forces of change, forms of power which re-define the landscape of class and gender. Working-class women and lower middle-class women, who once tried to achieve simply 'respectability', as Skeggs (1997) argued, as a class-appropriate habitus of femininity, a solution to the tyranny of imposed yet unachievable norms of femininity, which eluded them and made them feel ashamed, are now urged, or so I claim in this chapter, to aspire to 'glamorous individuality'. They are encouraged to feel special and to pamper themselves. This is what I mean by a 'movement of women' from being hidden and unimportant to becoming visible, and with a new sense of self-importance. A movement of women is also suggestive of a form of social mobility that entails some re-designation in terms of class and status. And the intersections of class with gender and ethnicity are central to how changing places or changing locations for women are organised. If the socio-economic system requires this mobility it is inevitable that there is a new landscape of class for women. This does not mean that class inequalities lessen or that class no longer matters. The urgent issue for the social order is that women must, when confronted with this opportunity for change, know how to deal with it, know how to accept their new station in life. And as women come forward as more active agents in the socio-economic system, they are charged with carrying out different, more aggressive, roles especially in the context in the UK where there is a shift towards a more competitive neo-liberal order. As subjects of the new meritocracy a question arises, how are women supposed to compete with each other? By what means will women conduct new class antagonisms? How will middle-class women retain their advantages and ensure that their social inferiors do not encroach upon their patch of class privilege? What weapons are at their disposal? How do lower middle-class women and working-class women navigate this terrain of managed gender movement? How do white, black and Asian femininities operate in this 'space of attention'? We can begin to reflect on these questions by looking more closely at women's genres of television. A case study of Oprah Winfrey would provide a golden opportunity to study the 'movement of black women' in the context of American society. In the UK, the media, and especially television, have become instrumental in overseeing these processes, they are charged with this responsibility. They act, within a field, not of coercion or compulsion, but of consent, participation and enjoyment, that is, in leisure, in popular culture and in entertainment.

These complex social processes require close examination, and the writing of Pierre Bourdieu is particularly relevant since it encompasses the world of consumer culture and the function it plays in managing and reproducing class hierarchies. Bourdieu is also a social theorist who engages with the relations between the state and the large social institutions of modernity. His work has been a renewed focal point for discussion in media and cultural studies, as well as sociology, in relation to the increasing dominance of the institutions of the mass media by television, and also more broadly on the question of 'media power' (Couldry 2003). Bourdieu's field theory has also been used to develop a fuller understanding of the interrelations between media and other social institutions, notably the state. My own concern in the pages that follow is with the relationship between television and feminine consumer culture, and with corporate organisations, such as the world of fashion, beauty and lifestyle products. Bourdieu turned his attention, in a more polemical mode than was his usual style, to the field of journalism, and to the way in which television not only was taking precedence over print journalism, but was also, itself, increasingly subjected to the battle for ratings (Bourdieu 1998). He was concerned with what was entailed in chasing audiences, and with the abandonment of seriousness in favour of the cult of personalities. This, he argued, had a significant effect on styles of journalism. Traditional professionalism and the status of news reporting was giving way to informal styles of freelance lifestyle journalism, and the huge increase in the numbers of journalists being trained meant that wages were being undercut by new entrants willing to work for very little. In relation to the issues I have been raising so far, it would be important to use Bourdieu in the context of a specifically feminist inquiry. It is surprising that this kind of work has not been already done, for the reason that many of the areas of concern which provided a specific subject matter for analysis in Bourdieu's work, e.g. *Distinction* (1984), as well as the more recent writing on journalism and on television, are actually now female-dominated spheres, or rather spheres of recent feminisation.

The chapters on lifestyle in *Distinction* are concerned with the kind of questions of taste and fashion, and with trends in home decoration and interior design, which were always women's concerns, but which in the light of the vast expansion of consumer culture in the last 20 years have more fully drawn in women, including young women, as producers as well as consumers. Bourdieu was well aware of this, even then, and he presciently understood the impact of both the increasing presence of middle-class young women in higher education, as well as the feminisation of certain, particularly cultural, labour markets. In addition his empirical and theoretical

126

work in *Distinction* pinpointed just how important the massive growth of lifestyle and consumer culture was for the post-Fordist capitalist economy. In his own lifetime however he did not bring together the study of television with that of consumer culture and women's particular role in consolidating this convergence. Nor did he foresee the way in which the staple formulaic contents of women's magazines would take flight and find a new home within broadcasting, first as daytime television and then as prime time, such that this whole feminine terrain has in the last two decades been transplanted into television, providing new genres of domestic and lifestyle programmes, taking the form of 'zones' addressed at a primarily female audience. And Bourdieu was not himself so concerned with the intersections and entanglements of gender with class and with race and ethnicity, entanglements we now assume to be both integral to our understanding of gender, per se, and also inseparable, i.e. they cannot be conceptualised in isolation from each other. Charlotte Brunsdon has documented this sphere of domestic television culture, including American as well as UK programmes, as have various other feminist writers.[2] I hope here to supplement Brunsdon's work by raising a series of additional issues which stem directly from Bourdieu, for example his account of the symbolic violence accompanying the creation of new hierarchies of taste and style, and the embeddedness of class conflict at the heart of the absorption by television of consumer culture and lifestyle, but this time focused at the point where women appear as class agents, as well as gendered subjects, in their own right, that is, independently of their status as wives, mothers or daughters. I am concerned with the way in which the production and reproduction of social divisions are increasingly feminised and with how the social categories of class are now materialised through reference to the female body.

In the pages that follow these processes will be charted in more detail, but I also want to provide as a response to Couldry's notion of 'media metacapital', some reflections on the relations of power which underpin the class-inflected forms of instruction provided by the new 'cultural intermediaries' (again a Bourdieu category), both male and female, whose audience is, however, predominantly female (Couldry 2003). In fact the full array of Bourdieu's conceptual schema is of assistance in aiding the understanding of the genre of 'make-over' television, in particular, field, habitus, cultural capital and symbolic violence. These prove useful in understanding the forms of intra-female aggression in these programmes and what they tell us about the current post-feminist climate where solidaristic bonds between women on the basis of perceived interests and shared oppression are noisily disavowed in favour of what seems like a more 'modern' set of behaviours including competitiveness, bitchiness and verbal violence. The programmes also demonstrate many of the points Couldry makes about meta-capital and media power, insofar as this genre of television not only acts as a shop window and thus promotional device for the vast world of fashion and beauty procedures including cosmetic surgery, but is also instrumental in creating new forms of social policy and consequently enters into a new kind of relationship with the state (Couldry 2003).

Class, aspiration and glamour

My main focus of attention here is on the forms of female symbolic violence found in the mid-evening television programmes that are given over to the so-called 'make-over', i.e. the transformation of self with the help of experts, in the hope, or expectation of improvement of status and life chances through the acquisition of forms of cultural and social capital. The public denigration by women (and a handful of men) of recognised taste (the experts and pre-senters) of women of little or no taste, brings a new (and seemingly humor-ous) dimension to this kind of primetime television. The reprimands by the presenters span the spectrum from the schoolmarmish ticking off for poor grooming, bad posture and unattractive mannerisms, to the outright sneer, or classroom snigger (bullying) directed towards the unkempt young, single mother wearing stained trousers as she drops off her child at school. Over the last few years this genre of popular television has achieved huge ratings and has attracted a great deal of publicity on the basis of a format which brings experts in taste and lifestyle together with willing victim in need of improve-ment. My interest here is primarily in two BBC TV programmes *What Not To Wear* and *Would Like To Meet*, both of which have had series running from 2002–2004,[3] but I will also consider the more recent programme broadcast by Channel Four titled *Ten Years Younger*.[4] The format in *What Not To Wear* comprises a victim/participant who wishes to be made-over by the two presenters, Trinny Woodall and Susannah Constantine, whose spin-off book based on the series reached the number one slot for Christmas book sales in the UK December 2002 (see Constantine and Woodall 2002). The experts take a very close look at the victim, they ask her to show them her wardrobe, and she allows herself to be paraded for scrutiny, usually in her underwear in front of a full-length mirror (so that 'the girls' can get an idea of shape and proportions) and then she is taught how to shop, what to look for, what colours would suit, how to buy a better fitting bra ('no more saggy boobs'), and so on. Then she is left on her own, with a budget, to buy new outfits. Under the watchful eye (hidden video camera) of the girls, she goes shop-ping, and every time she tries to buy the bad old look, the girls laugh and then pounce and stop her, guiding her towards more flattering purchases. The two presenters are extremely tactile with the victim, they breach the usual boundaries of inter-personal interaction by touching body parts including 'boobs', as they are called, and bottoms also. In one programme they pulled at the unflattering underwear of a victim, encouraging her to throw away unsightly knickers, and in another where the woman in question had very prominent breasts they made a great fuss over her cleavage.[5] By the end of the programme the woman has been given a full make-over which is then shown off to her friends and family who are invariably both supportive and delighted by the new look.

Would Like To Meet comprises three experts, two female, one male, whose job it is to dissect the problems of a victim who is failing to find a partner, get dates or enjoy a lively social life. Here too the victim is scrutinised for body failings, and also for unappealing characteristics including voice, manners, facial expression, etc. The experts train the victim into new habits of self-presentation, arrange a dummy date and then on the next occasion expect the now confident victim to pluck up courage and ask someone out of her own accord. Throughout the proceedings the experts spy on the victim from a van equipped with a hidden video camera. The woman (or man) in need of improvement is usually overwhelmed by the changes in her life and outlook. Even if the date does not lead to a full-blown relationship, what is important is the new appearance, the sense of personal style and new found confidence. *Ten Years Younger* produced by the independent TV company, Maverick, is more sensational by virtue of the recommended use of cosmetic surgery. The woman who is the victim, typically, has a very unkempt and prematurely aged appearance, including lines and wrinkles, sun-damaged skin, poor body shape including being overweight, badly cared for hair and lack of style in fashion and make-up. Every item about the woman's appearance is judged wanting, and this is confirmed by passers-by on the street who usually judge her to be about 20 years older than her actual age. Being presented with this evidence about how she is seen (and almost always bursting into tears) is swiftly followed by the intervention of the team of experts including a cosmetic surgeon, a cosmetic dentist, and a top hairdresser all orchestrated by the presenter and stylist. The outcome of this work is that the woman is transformed and unrecognisable, and is finally judged by people on the street to be ten years younger than her real age.

The programmes I am concerned with draw attention to and legitimate forms of class antagonism, in the forms of aggressive words and disparaging gestures and expressions between women, and by impeccably middle-class women, who serve as models, against poor and unattractive working-class women, in a way which would have been socially unacceptable until recently. The programmes actively produce newly defined social hierarchies on the basis of gender attributes and femininity. In the past the rules of television, and especially public service broadcasting, were such that public humiliation of people for their failure to adhere to appropriate respectable and middle-class standards in speech or appearance would have been considered offensive, discriminatory or prejudicial. (Likewise it would have been considered unacceptable for television presenters to swear at people using four letter words, in the way that is now common especially by macho TV cooks such as Jamie Oliver and Gordon Ramsay). This new style of denigration is done with a degree of self-conscious irony, both the presenters and the audiences are assumed to know that no harm is intended, and that, in post 'politically-correct' times, this is just good fun. It is now possible, thank goodness, to laugh at less fortunate people once again. And the message is that the poor woman would do well to emulate her social superiors. These programmes mark out the contours of a new de-regulated era of television, where public service broadcasting is forced to become more competitive and to increase their market share through introducing more popular formats. In the case of these and other similar genres, many of the rules of public service broadcasting are broken, in favour of a populist or tabloid-inspired television vernacular. The programmes I am concerned with deliver shock value. What makes them new and apparently exciting is this level of insult and humiliation directed against bodily failings. While men are involved, as both experts and victims, this is largely a female genre of TV and the overall address is to women (see Brunsdon et al. 2001). Indeed the presence of men for such make-overs is normally so that they become more pleasing or palatable to women. This primarily female address corresponds to the changing identity of women in contemporary Britain. No longer defined in terms of husbands, fathers or boyfriends, women and in particular younger women are urged to compete with each other, sometimes mercilessly.

The question is, in a post-feminist context (and bearing in mind that I define post-feminism as a kind of anti-feminism, which is reliant, paradoxically, on an assumption that feminism has been taken into account), how do women actually compete with each other? What forms does this take in the new meritocracy? The answer provided by these programmes relies on a return to old-fashioned 'school-girl' styles of feminine bitchiness, rivalry and bullying which are updated to comply with the postmodern ironic styles of contemporary popular entertainment. But what this means is that public enactments of hatred and animosity are refracted at a bodily or corporeal level against weaker and much less powerful people, with impunity, on the grounds that the insult is made in a playful spirit and that it is not really meant. The way in which class relations are conducted within make-over programmes is exactly compatible with and contributes to the meritocratic model of social mobility and consumerism so strongly promoted by the Blair government during its time in office. A word that was frequently used during the Blair years was 'aspirational'. These programmes dramatise and feminise this political ideal. People are increasingly individualised, they are required to invent themselves, they are repeatedly called upon to shape themselves so as to be flexible, and to fit with the new circumstances. In terms of the workplace this means keeping oneself employable, and being willing to adapt to the requirements of the rapidly changing labour market. Appearance and self-expression take on new importance when so many jobs are located in the service sector, at the interface with clients and customers, and where customer service and sales require all sorts of enhanced techniques including the self-presentation skills of staff. Thus, class makes a decisive re-appearance in and through the vectors of transformed gendered individualisation, with the result that class relations are themselves changed by the performative force of femininty.

Walby has suggested that with full participation in the workforce, differences between women are actually becoming more marked. 'There are new divides opening up, between younger and older women ... older women ... face an older life in poverty' (Walby 1999: 3) so that 'age inequalities can compound those of class' (ibid: 6). There is an enormous disparity of income between younger and older women (with the latter much worse off). Walby's point is that women are increasingly divided by class and by age, and her point of reference is the labour market and pay levels. But race and ethnicity must also be understood as critical factors effecting women's access to jobs and economic opportunities. Older black women remain in work in a more sustained way than their white counterparts across their lifetimes, but at low pay levels and low skill levels. Young black and Asian women do not get jobs and opportunities commensurate with their qualifications and ambitions. Their importance as potential consumers is therefore less than that of their white counterparts. In the UK there is still no substantial black middle class, and it is only recently that Asian communities in the UK have been able to see their children benefit from higher education. Asian and black women are also marginalised by the large corporations and advertisers that constitute the fashion-and-beauty complex. Those sectors of women who are deemed capable of benefiting from a make-over, and who will become the ideal consumers of products and whose presence on the make-over shows, will not just attract large audiences but will also create the right format to attract television advertising (for the commercial channels), will be lower middle-class women and upper working-class or aspirational and predominantly white working-class women. As I will show later in this chapter, the way in which the presence of black or Asian women is managed in the make-over format is shaped by their race and ethnicity, especially since the forms of insult and aggressive strategies might easily be construed as racist.[6] Older women have also been excluded from the world of make-overs, although very recently, in search of a new idea, the Trinny and Susannah team, having moved away from the BBC to ITV, came up with a series which would improve the look and appearance of the nation's 'grannies'.[7] But bearing in mind this map of more widely dispersed class divisions, the programmes do not seek to unite women under traditional class identities, or through images of sameness and conformity, but instead create new gendered meanings about class and status more generally. If glamour is celebrated as a mark of aspiration and sexual identity, then this becomes a gendered marker of class and an attribute which properly middle-class women must eschew, since they will in contrast be in possession of 'effortless elegance' or 'simple chic' which, in Bourdieu terms, shows the 'glamour of aspiration' to be the result of having to try hard, in contrast to the style which comes so easily and naturally to middle-class women, young and old alike. Glamour carries all the marks of hard work, it is what the victims are congratulated upon, where elegance, or chic, or fashion sense or instinct, remain beyond their reach. This then shows the subtle degrees of class differentiation which come to be played out around the bodies of the female victims in these programmes.

And as I argue throughout this book, racial antagonisms and inequalities are intensified in a new context where anti-racist politics are silenced and sidelined in favour of assimilation and integration. One result of this is the lack of political attention paid to the existence of both old and new gendered forms of racism, and the way in which the new competition between women legitimates discrimination. There is nothing approaching gender equality for non-white women. However, this does not mean they are not urged to achieve, nor does it not mean that they are featured in the press and on television in terms which celebrate success and achievement. Black and Asian women co-inhabit the 'spaces of attention' with their white counterparts, but it is always understood that they are exceptional and thus might act as role models for their less successful black or Asian peers. This is conveyed through the scripted interactions and the bodily gestures of both presenters and participants. Those who come forward as victims for a make-over are treated with less overt contempt and ridicule than white women but the result is that the format of the programmes are slightly modified so as to account for difference, a point I return to later. Overall this scenario would suggest gender transformation, in particular a movement of women towards securing new lower middle-class positions which are now signalled not through respectability, but through more individualised styles of glamour, requiring conspicuous consumption on the self, e.g. manicures, fashion, pampering and so on. Change and movement are thus a feature of women's experience in recent years. But how are these changes refracted within the format of the programmes themselves? Of course, as Bourdieu and many others have shown, women have by no means been immune to the articulation of sharp and often cruel class distinctions (Bourdieu 1984). There is nothing new about harsh and wounding words being directed at poor or working-class girls or women by their social superiors. Working-class women have been very aware of the denigratory judgements made against them by their middle-class counterparts particularly in regard to their appearance and non-respectability (Skeggs 1997). Middle-class women have played a key role in the reproduction of class society not just through their exemplary role as wives and mothers, but also as standard bearers for middle-class family values, for certain norms of citizenship and also for safe-guarding the valuable cultural capital accruing to them and their families through access to education, refinement and other privileges. The questions are, when women become more detached from traditional family roles as a result of movement into the labour market over a lifetime, how does this effect class society? What are the cultural forms and the wider repertoire of mean-ings which seek to give shape to and retain control over new gendered hierar-chies? Is it the case that through the prism of individualisation class differences are re-invented, largely within the cultural and media field, so as to produce and re-produce social divisions now more autonomously feminised? Are women being more intensely re-classified on the basis that they now occupy positions of key importance in the wider political economy? Does the move into the workplace displace the masculine inflection of class values, with a wide range of more feminised meanings? Perhaps it was an easy mistake for femi-nists to make, to assume that the gains of feminist success in terms of the win-ning of certain freedoms (to earn your own living, to be entitled to equal pay, etc.) would bring with it for women, an interest in and commitment to extend-ing the possibilities for socialist-feminist values. Female individualisation in contrast is a process bringing into being new social divisions through the den-igration of poor and disadvantaged women by means of symbolic violence. What emerges is a new regime of more sharply polarised working-class and lower middle-class positions, epitomised through shabby failure or glamorous success. The pre-welfare rough and respectable divide is re-invented for the twenty-first century.

Let me consider briefly two illuminating journalistic moments, each of which is indicative of a social dynamic which re-iterates these specifically feminine modalities of symbolic violence, as processes of class differentiation now thoroughly projected onto and inseparable from the female body. From now on the young, single mother will be understood to be an abject person with a 'mismanaged life'. She is a social category, a certain type of girl whose bodily features and disposition betray her lowly status. This marks a reversal of the language of welfare liberal values for whom the teenage mother was someone to be provided with support. A new virulent form of class antago-nism finds expression through the public denigration of the bodily failings of the girl who at a too young age embraces motherhood. Thus Christina Odone (at the time Deputy Editor of the *New Statesman*) provides a more serious-minded (if inevitably laced with some irony) version of this recent form of boundary marking practice by writing that 'top range women ... prefer to leave reproduction to the second eleven ... a bump risks becoming as clear proof of a working-class background as the fag hanging from someone's lips'. She goes on to say that a teenage mother produces a 'socially autistic child with little expectation and even less talent' (Odone 2000). In the same vein, but this time emerging from within the heartland of tabloid pop culture, one of the girl singers from the pop band *Atomic Kitten* (Kerry Katona), finds herself widely referred to on the *Popbitch* website as 'pramface' (which in turn circulates across the wider pop media). That is, she is deemed to look like the kind of poor, low-class girl with a baby in pushchair. Other derogatory forms of female social classification include 'minger' or 'pig' as *The Sun* newspaper labelled runner up for the *Big Brother* 2002 TV contest, Jade Goody. What does pramface mean? A kind of girl. What kind of girl? Not dressed for work, therefore not earning an honest living. But not a student. With a baby, but looks single, that is, not sufficiently attractive and presentable to attract a long-term partner. She must be unmarried and dependent on benefits. As a seemingly recognisable social type it is assumed there must be many like her. The insult is thus indicative of a renewed and injurious practice of social re-ordering. The bodies of young women are now to be understood according to a scale running from welfare-dependent, single, with maternity marking failure, to glamour marking success. The pramface girl who is pinched, and poor-looking, common and cheaply dressed, and with a child in a buggy, is in sharp contrast to the 'A1' girls who can spend a disposable income on themselves and aspire to full participation in consumer culture, and through this differentiation class distinctions are now more autonomously (i.e. these are all single girls) generated, within what Bourdieu might call the media or journalistic field and refracted through the youthful female body. This is a relatively recent phenomenon. Denigratory speech unashamedly, and spitefully directed towards girls by other girls is associated with pre-feminist old-fashioned 'bitchiness'. In the past hurtful comments about body image, shape, style or poor taste would be considered as belonging to the school playground, and vociferously condemned by liberal-minded adults, parents and teachers as a form of bullying. Likewise sniggers about living in a council estate or having a mother who does not look well off, might be met with a sharp reprimand. The prevalence, once again, of this kind of language is a mark of the cultural undoing of the anti-discriminatory and anti-racist policies which had an institutional life in the UK from the late 1960s until the mid-1990s.

Butler and Bourdieu

I have drawn on Bourdieu for his understanding of how class differences are reproduced in the arena of taste. But it is the television programmes themselves which call out for a Bourdieu analysis, even though there are also problems in his sociology of class stratification which Judith Butler reminds us of (Butler 1999b). The question that the dialogue between Butler and Bourdieu raises, is whether programmes like those discussed are effective in managing change and the movement of women according to the requirements of the dominant social regime and its values, or whether there are points of tension, moments of possible disruption, and of 're-signification' or 're-territorialisation' on the part of the socially dominated women who take part in them. I argue that the programmes offer few possibilities for re-signification of the denigratory comments. This might be a defining feature of television's media power! Instead they repetitively show the working-class women to be deferential and grateful to their social superiors for guiding them in the direction of self-improvement. Nevertheless Butler's critique of Bourdieu alerts us to the limitations of his model of power and domination (Butler 1999b). Butler may be less persuasive in relation to possibilities for social critique emerging from within the space of the television programmes themselves, but her Foucauldian model of power permits greater understanding about how wounding words and hate speech gain currency and legitimation, and then circulate more widely in different social spaces (e.g. playgrounds, classrooms and shopping malls) far beyond the carefully edited and highly scripted space of television. I would suggest that these programmes constitute a new and expansive form of gender power which oversees and takes charge of an economically necessary movement of women, by utilising a *faux*-feminist language of 'empowerment of women' so as to defuse, refute and disavow the likelihood of a new solidaristic vocabulary being invented which would challenge these emerging forms of gendered, racialised and class inequalities. Butler's response to Bourdieu allows us to clarify the power relations of both gender and class that are at stake in this television format.

Butler reminds us that Bourdieu is concerned primarily with social class, influenced but not fully shaped by a Marxism, which he amends and expands by foregrounding the market (for example consumer culture) and by introducing a spatialising concept of field theory. However it is the concept of habitus and the way in which this permits an analysis of the body within what is at the same time a macro-sociological framing, which is most interesting to Butler and which here provides the key insight on the way in which women bring their bodies into the television spotlight for improvement. Butler comments that the habitus is a space of 'embodied rituals of everydayness', such rituals also being the way in which a culture 'produces belief in its own obviousness'. The body for Bourdieu is marked by its own habitus, it bears the marks of its own 'incorporated history', it is then always a social body, inclined to act in certain ways as a result of the force of this impregnated history. Thus we could say that the woman victim brings to the genre of the programme her own bodily hexis already marked as inferior or flawed. Although there are very occasionally middle-class women who allow themselves to be the subject of a make-over, this is unusual, when they do come forward they present themselves apologetically, as out of kilter with the norms of their own habitus, for example as eccentric, or else as having 'let themselves go' following a divorce, or family crisis. The victims tend to be working class (ranging from poor and in unskilled jobs, to white collar clerical or administrative work), or else they are from lower middle-class backgrounds. What they share in common is the fact that the habitus they present, with its rituals and regularised actions, such as styles of speech, styles of deportment, styles of dress and appearance, is now publicly deemed to be 'in poor taste' and in need of change or adjustment. This has become a matter of national interest, insofar as domestic television creates a form of 'imagined community'. If, in the past, this gendered habitus of the working-class woman was a familiar and recognisable feature of social difference, reproduced over time so as to confirm the existing social hierarchies, the question is why at this point in time, do these inadequacies come to be a matter of public debate? Why now? These bad habits, have in the past, been carried out in an un-thought way. That is, part of the function of the habitus, is to inculcate in a mechanical way, dispositions and ritualistic forms of social practice which fulfil what is required of these types of social subjects within a given field, while also permitting some realm of autonomous action which when repeated over time, describe and give identity to a culturally distinct social formation. The body of the working-class woman has known its place in the world, and it is, and has been visible on the basis of this limited capacity, it has known how to abide by what Bourdieu would say are the rules of the (class) game. It knows what to expect and how far it can go, mostly it is a deferential body. This class habitus does not exist in isolation from the wider social field that informs and limits the practices that the habitus is able to generate. If the habitus creates or gives rise to the kinds of actions and expressions which ultimately encourage the subject to conform, then this subject is also conforming to the demands set by the field. The habitus becomes recognisable and visible by virtue of the woman having, over the years, learnt how to play this game of acting, hence, as Butler suggests it more or less presupposes the field, or takes it into account, such that over time the habitus reproduces those rules and norms, it does the work of the field for it. The field then is what establishes the terms and conditions for what is possible and what is impossible for the habitus, even though there is a 'mutually formative' relation between them. Indeed the habitus is understood by Butler in terms of its adaptive capacities, it will re-direct itself, even though it is capable of autonomous improvisation and invention, to become congruent with what the field requires of it, it will bow to necessity and abandon possibilities which are always out of reach. But this means, according to Butler, that since the field does not 'alter by virtue of the habitus', the field (in this case the social world) becomes an 'unalterable positivity'. This tendency to faithfully reproduce the rules established by the field persuades Butler that the status of Bourdieu's habitus is questionable, the idea of it encountering the field which is what Bourdieu proposes (while avoiding an obvious dualism of 'subjective' habitus encountering the 'objective' field) is conceptually difficult to accept since it is only by accepting the rules of the field, already set in stone, that the habitus is able to operate with some autonomy ('the habitus presupposes the field from the start'). The richness of Bourdieu's attempt to flesh out what is the socialised space of the subject, called into being, and which is otherwise, at least in Althusser's work, a kind of empty space, is for Butler, in the end incompatible with a theory of power which is broadly discursive.

Butler argues for an interpellative account which refuses the distinctions which Bourdieu creates both between habitus and field and between the domain of social reality with its 'institutional conditions', and the realm of linguistics with its performative words and rituals. The effectivity of injurious words relies for Bourdieu on the official weight of the institutional conditions behind these words, and with who has the authority to speak them. This is usually a matter of class privilege and social authority, which for Bourdieu carries a kind of absolute weight. This would suggest that the experts in the programmes are given, through the rules of television and its institutional structures, the authority to reprimand and scold the victims in a cruel and insulting way, often by using wounding words, or by using what elsewhere would be considered 'hate speech'. This licensed authority also complies with the rules of popular entertainment which are scrutinised by the appropriate authorities (e.g. The Broadcasting Standards Commission). Butler operates with a much less centralised, and more diffuse understanding of power, which for her is a micrological process operating in ways which are not tied to the rigidities of fields of authorisation, but instead move widely through and across a multiplicity of sites and social spaces. Power works around the body for example, but also on the street, in unauthorised locations, in the school playground, in the supermarket, in the normative practices of everyday life. This would lead Butler to argue, perhaps, that the effectivity of 'harmless' programmes like these is to give legitimation to the uttering of injurious words and 'hate speech' well beyond the confines of ritualised television genres. What Trinny and Susannah can say to the poor-looking unkempt single mother in the spirit of self-improvement, becomes a new social norm. It becomes an acceptable way of identifying and labelling poor or disadvantaged people. A more general endorsement of prejudice and discrimination and a recognition of class inequalities as unchanging facts of life, re-enter the public domain, against the grain of social democratic and leftist values, with the novelty of such traits being that they are now thoroughly feminised.

Butler inquires into the wider interpellative processes that authorise subjects to speak. She queries the more rigid sociological idea of 'social position in the field' and the objective determinations which permit some to speak and others not, 'for the question of how social positions are produced and reproduced will raise the question of the "temporality" of positions themselves (Butler 1999b: 124). For Butler the social position of field is too monolithic, power in Bourdieu's model is over-directive, moving it seems rather mechanically between habitus and field, where Butler instead draws attention to the multiple and dispersed socio-linguistic and discursive processes which bring subjects, who are authorised to speak in wounding ways, into being. (What is it, for example, which permits the white teenager with his friends on the street, to shout racial abuse at the veiled Muslim woman and to get away with it?)[8] This is of course a more Foucauldian model, which understands power to be decentred and fluid and traversing the whole world of social relations including those that swirl around gender and the body. Butler disputes Bourdieu's model of habitus and field, arguing nevertheless to retain a re-defined idea of habitus as a space of bodily hexis that carries specific histories within its corporeality. This habitus of the body is also a social rather than a personal space and it can become the site for contesting the injuries which are sustained. If the 'racial or gendered slur lives on' this provides the possibility for re-working the slur itself, and turning it into a political instrument. The reality of 'having been called a name' comes to be, as she puts it, impregnated in the 'flesh of the addressee', this is one of the ways in which 'subjects are called into being'. I take her here to be saying that years of denigration and verbal abuse cast a kind of physical shadow over the body of the poor black woman, it is etched in her features, and shapes the way she walks, and how she makes her way through a white-dominated city. Verbal violence is then, a key feature of contemporary power, not just in the process of 'subject formation' but also as a site for 'political contestation and reformulation of the subject as well'. Butler, unlike Bourdieu, sees some possibilities for challenge and opposition within what might seem like micro-social processes, or in seemingly small things like the repetitive speaking of wounding words. The body of a man or woman who has been 'called a name' seems to carry that insult incorporated as a history, but at the same time this wound can become a site for the production of an oppositional politics, as the wounded body finds ways of turning around those words which have wounded it, using these to challenge the power responsible for its injury.[9] Butler also sees the habitus as being a generative space for the production of change, it is where subjects are made, but also re-made. This provides us with two points of re-entry into the world of the make-over television programme. The bringing about of social change within this specific format, and the degree to which these social performatives, these verbal slurs, these forms of symbolic violence are also refuted or contested, while also being absorbed and embodied by those who are being addressed, can be applied directly to these programmes. Indeed they are key to the political power and influence of the programmes, and what is at stake in their production values. We could say that what the programmes dare to allow to be said, legitimates in the wider culture, the saying of similar offensive things, with the proviso that on some occasions the offender may be apprehended and find him or herself subject to the force of the law. The programmes push at the boundaries of acceptable speech for the sake of making something new and hence of producing change, or as I put it, of making a movement of women, while this audacity is tempered by the existence in the background of laws which put limits on the giving of offence.

'Needs and norms' (Bourdieu 1984)

Bourdieu's writing allows us to re-cast symbolic violence as a process which both forms and re-forms subjects in order that they can be brought into line with the needs of the dominant field. In this case our concern is with repro-duction of a feminine habitus through a particular (post-feminist) spatial and temporal framing of female individualisation, the body, and the world of cultural objects. The victim of the make-over television programme pre-sents her class habitus (including home, family, friends and neighbours, and social milieu) for analysis and critique by the experts. That is, although the victim is individualised, he or she is also understood immediately as embodying a social category of persons. These bodies on show display an 'incorporated history', they are familiar to the audience in these terms, they 'give themselves away'. The programmes comprise a series of encounters where experts, or, in Bourdieu terms, cultural intermediaries, impart guid-ance and advice to individuals, ostensibly as a means of self-improvement. The experts guide the victims through various activities, from shopping, cooking and interacting with people, to flirting and going on dates. A key (entertainment) feature of the programmes (and one which most invites a Foucauldian analysis) involves observing the victims by means of hidden video cameras, as ethnographic technique (i.e. so that they can be seen *au naturel*). Usually the victims are given the chance to report back on their progress by making their own video diaries. These comments made to cam-era appear to be moments where the victims voice their misgivings about the whole process of being made-over and also comment on the perceived injustices of being subjected to ritualistic humiliation. In other words this might be a point of possible tension in the programmes, where *pace* Butler, there would be opportunities for an incipient politics of re-signification, where the cruel words could be twisted around, and become a point for mobilis-ing a counter-movement of women which took back the insults and used these to formulate an oppositional body politics. There are few signs of this in the programmes, the only occasion where anything near to this occurred was when the (feminist) comedian Jo Brand appeared on a celebrity make-over edi-tion of *What Not To Wear*. However her self-deprecating humour, as a large woman, undercut her vocal condemnation of the programme format and the presenters. And so, at every turn in the make-over programmes Bourdieu's notion of compliance with the 'rules of the game' is pervasive. Moreover his entire theoretical world finds ample application in these zones of entertainment, from his account of taste to his understanding of the body to be at the centre of what McNay calls 'modern strategies of social control' (McNay 1999). McNay also reminds us that Bourdieu considers how social inequalities are perpetuated as power relations directed directly at bodies and the 'dispositions of individuals'. He focuses on constraint and injury, on practices of symbolic violence and their effectivity. The 'corporeal inculca-tion' of symbolic violence is, McNay argues, 'exercised with the complicity' of the individual. These programmes would not work if the victim did not come forward and offer herself as someone in need of expert help. On the basis of her own subordinate habitus, the individual will have a 'feel for the game', a 'practical sense for social reality' which means that in the context of the pro-grammes she will instinctively, and unconsciously, know her place in regard to the experts, hence the tears, the gratitude and the deference to those who know so much better than she does, and who are willing to (temporarily) share this knowledge and expertise.

In the programmes *What Not To Wear* and *Would Like To Meet* (and also in *Ten Years Younger*) the habitual knowingness of the body (its tired, over-worked saggingness, its unkempt, poor appearance, its self-deprecating ges-tures) is confronted with the demand of the dominant field that the participant copies, or partakes in a kind of mimesis, so that the habitus might be modified to conform with the requirement of good taste. If, as Butler suggests, the habitus is the space for the generation of social belief in the obviousness of dominant social reality, then the cajoling, reprimand-ing and encouragement of the presenters and make-over experts provides clear insight into the operations of the field as it attempts to alter the habi-tus, within carefully specified limits, and while also inculcating the realism of the unachievable (Butler 1999b). As we have already seen, Butler sug-gests that the habitus and the field move towards congruence with each other, in that the habitus is already inclined to submit to social authority. She queries this over-dominative model marked out by the way in which the field invariably procures the submission of the habitus. There is '(t)he ideal of adaptation as the presiding norm of his theory of sociality' (Butler 1999b: 118). Butler ultimately pursues a more Foucauldian approach to social power, as I have already suggested, but she, like Bourdieu, is a theo-rist of constraint, and they share a good deal in common in their dissections of how normativity is inexorably and relentlessly achieved across the social universe. This conceptual world provided by Bourdieu has great value, up to a point. For example field and habitus allow me to suggest re-configuration by cultural means of the relations between class and gender in contemporary

Britain. They help to explain how processes of social re-alignment and a 'movement of women' takes shape forcefully within the space of relaxation and enjoyment provided by media and entertainment. But there are difficulties in relying on field theory and the concept of the habitus across the various institutional and non-institutional spaces that are all involved in the production of programmes like these. Can we talk about, for example the field of television which the experts and presenters represent and the specific class habitus of the presenters that is mobilised in the content of the programmes? It is easy to get lost in a proliferation of fields, from the field of the economy, to that of television, to that of the state which stands in a particular relation to the media, to that of consumer culture which exists outside these other fields but which plays a shadow role in the programmes, as does the field of magazines. Other fields of media including the global media field also become involved, for example, the press and the internet, as well as the field of publishing. A more substantial analysis would need to track the relations of dependency between and across these sites, as well as the different forms of habitus which exist in their midst.

The limits of a Bourdieusian analysis become apparent, when being beholden to his concepts seems to become an obstacle to understanding the flows of power, and the dense network of social relations which traverse this whole terrain, from the bodies of the participants in the programmes, to the employment of cultural intermediaries who are their instructors, to the global corporations which oversee the tie-ins and spin-offs from a highly successful format. What works at ground level, with the programmes themselves begins to spin out of control when the whole world of the make-over genre is to be analysed. We can see how the habitus of the cultural intermediaries (their styles of talking, their embodied social practices) must remain separate (hence unachievable) from that of the victims and participants. There is no suggestion that the victims will ever truly belong to the same social group as their improvers. This is made clear in a multiplicity of small ways, such as the consoling words and concluding comments on the part of the experts who retain an ever critical and sceptical eye. They also maintain monopoly over technical or professional vocabularies, they demonstrate their familiarity with a whole other world still out of reach of those who have now been made-over (often by name-dropping or referring to exclusive shops, neighbourhoods, restaurants or art events). Among themselves they surmise that, once they, the experts, have departed, the victim is bound to return to her bad old ways. This display of an upper middle-class habitus, in sharp contrast to that of the victims allows us to see how in the programmes there is an attempt to transform the female working-class and lower middle-class habitus by means of shaming, instruction and the momentary celebrity glamour of being on television. The faulty habitus is to be brought into line so as to conform with, as Bourdieu would say, the 'needs and norms' of the new labour market (or field of economy) and with the consumer culture. To sum up, we could say that Bourdieu's schema offers a potential model for bringing together a micrological analysis of the programmes themselves with a macro-sociological analysis of the wider field of social relations and institutional practices. However the concepts of field and habitus begin to buckle under the weight of a methodology that would examine the intersections and flows between and across so many fields and so many habituses, at which point one can begin to see again the value of a more open-ended and fluid approach to the discursive operations of power which is not reliant on these schematic terms.

'Panic mingled with revolt' (Bourdieu 1984)

Nevertheless Bourdieu's concepts of cultural capital and cultural interme-diaries also provide fine tools for understanding these programmes as a genre. In front of the camera, the cultural intermediaries, flaunt, or play up, often flamboyantly, their own middle, or upper middle-class backgrounds by bringing these to bear in the way in which they present the programmes, almost to the point of parody. This works in entertainment terms since, after all, everyone knows the British are obsessed with class, and it makes for good television. These class locations are flagged up through their distinc-tive corporeal styles. Often the women are upper middle-class and 'loud' in voice and appearance as they impart aspects of the cultural capital which they have accrued effortlessly. The best example of this are the two older women who presented the cooking programme *The Two Fat Ladies* and of course the voluptuous Nigella Lawson who references the writing of Henry James while presenting the Channel 4 programme *Nigella Bites* (Brunsdon 2005). The knowledge possessed by these women about good taste comes naturally because it is simply part of how they have been brought up. There is 'distance from necessity', there is nothing too urgent, too over-enthusiastic, too *arriviste* about their expertise. They have had all the time in the world to learn about the kinds of things not taught at school and not on the aca-demic curriculum. They simply know this stuff, they know how to put together an outfit without even thinking about it, they know which colours work, they know how to throw a wonderful dinner party and make it look as though there was no labour and no anxiety and no planning involved. They also know what 'not to wear'. They signal various degrees of disgust or repulsion, or extreme bodily displeasure at those who do not possess such good taste. The two women who present *What Not To Wear* are well-connected, young and of upper-middle-class background (boarding school, mix with royalty, etc). Their body language in the programmes indicates a leisurely approach to life and work, they sprawl over the sofa as they watch the video clips of the victims anxiously trying to choose an outfit, and they laugh and giggle at their mistakes. It is not without irony that we now see so many upper middle-class women trying to earn their own living by drawing from their own store of cultural capital, by in effect flogging it on the market-place of populist television. (It is surely a bit like selling off the family silver.) Brunsdon has made a similar point about upper middle-class women now going out to work on the basis of providing instruction about how to look after the home (Brunsdon 2005). Presumably there are those who might suggest that such programmes could be seen as democratising, in the sense that there is some re-distribution of cultural capital going on in them, with BBC television, in a post-modern Reithian mode, performing an educative function for the good of the nation, by kindly providing instruction on areas of everyday life not covered in the school curriculum. There is also within this mode of programming, an unexpected intersection with the governmental world of public policy, spanning cooking and parenting programmes as well as the make-over slots (see note 1). Bourdieu would however surely reply, to those who saw this kind of genre as breaking down the division between high and low culture, and giving, in this case women, the chance to learn about colour, texture, and the various aesthetic codes of fashion, as fallacious, on the grounds that as we have already seen, this pedagogy is mostly about the re-drafting of boundaries, particularly those of class and status which are now more decisively feminised, alongside the overseeing of change for women, which is deemed necessary, but also in need of careful management. In every way the attitudes of the experts conform to Bourdieu's account of the social role of cultural intermediaries which is to inculcate deference, gratitude and cultural goodwill to existing social hierarchies (Bourdieu 1984).

Taking Bourdieu's analysis into account and adding my own comments above about gender changes and a 'movement of women' we could suggest that the two women who present *What Not To Wear* (Trinny and Susannah) now find themselves in the workplace, since they, like most women today, will no longer rely on marriage or a male partner to look after them financially over a lifetime (in post-feminist times this is recognised as a high risk strategy). A career is a better investment. Therefore, upper middle-class young women will be competing against their extremely well-educated, middle-class counterparts in the labour market. The new cultural intermediaries are no longer so predominantly 'gentlemen and scholars', as Bourdieu described, and between whom there is and was also a realm of class conflict and competition for jobs. They are now likely to be 'society girls' and 'educated girls', with the former imparting advice and guidance, sometimes with a sneer and always with casual elegance, and in unhurried ways, while the latter, are more sensible, urgent, more direct, and more professional, with their training as life coaches and degrees in psychology, made more visible. Here too there is a realm of conflict and competition for highly sought-after jobs in the lifestyle as well as life-training and personal coaching field. These are over-crowded spheres, where young women will congregate, thus also confirming Bourdieu's comments about the changing world of journalism, since fashion experts and life-coaches presenting television programmes cannot be described as journalists although they will refer to themselves as broadcasters (Bourdieu 1998). Thus there is also re-designation and change within the world of middle-class women's employment, here too there is movement and sharp competition. Forms of feminised class conflict reverberate through the social hierarchy, from the top to the bottom. There is an urgent need for more sociological studies of these processes, looking in detail at what sort of young women get which jobs, and asking questions about the grounds given for selection. For example, what were the career pathways which led Trinny and Susannah to *What Not To Wear* or Gok Wan to *How to Look Naked* or Nicky Hambleton-Jones to *Ten Years Younger*? There is a great deal of work to be done in the terrain of employment as cultural intermediaries, but alongside this it would be an equally important sociological exercise to consider the programmes themselves, and to track, compare and analyse the role of insult and wounding comments or looks in these programmes. My own notes reveal phrases such as 'what a dreary voice' 'look at how she walks', 'she shouldn't put ketchup on her chips', 'she looks like a mousy librarian', 'her trousers are far too long', 'that jumper looks like something her granny crocheted, it would be better on a table', 'she hasn't washed her clothes', 'your hair looks like an overgrown poodle' 'your teeth are yellow, have you been eating grass?' and 'Oh My God … she looks like a German lesbian'. This last insult was considered so hilarious that it was trailed as a promotion for the programme across the junctions of BBC TV for almost two weeks before it was broadcast. There is cruelty and viciousness often reminiscent of 1950s boarding school stories where the nasty snobbish girls ridicule the poor scholarship girl for her appearance, manners, upbringing, accent and shabbily dressed parents. Programmes like *Would Like To Meet* and *What Not To Wear* are self-vindicating on the basis that the victims are young adults, they are willing participants and submit themselves to being made-over with great enthusiasm. This is popular entertainment that uses irony to suggest that the injurious words and gestures are not meant to be taken literally. However this does not mean that there is no humiliation. Participants frequently dissolve into tears and there is 'panic mingled with revolt' as they are put through their paces, unlearning what is considered unacceptable and unattractive about them. Moments of revolt are only short-lived and confined to brief outbursts of late night anger, as the participants invariably submit the following morning to the authority of those who know better. Overall this process of re-education within the zones of popular entertainment marks out some of the sociological contours of change for women in contemporary Britain. The analysis I have presented so far emphasises the power of the field (or of forces of social domination), to re-direct the habitus of working-class or lower middle-class women, so as to pro-duce a 'movement of women' who show themselves willing to undergo change, so that they more confidently and efficiently take up their places in the emergent labour markets which need their participation, and which will also then provide them with disposable incomes so that they can consume more products and services over a lifetime.

I am aware that I leave several strands hanging. Television scholars would surely point to the more complex production of meanings within these texts, such that there might, on occasion, be a victory by the participants over the presenters when the good taste proffered by the girls is ultimately refused. Sometimes the ordinariness and the unkempt image of the victim retains a resilience, dignity, self-respect and obstinacy, despite and against the efforts of the experts. There is often a kind of tussle between the presenters and the vic-tim for the approval of the assumed audience. But the cultural logic of the programmes is for the victims to concede to change as a good thing, since the benefits invariably outweigh the pain and humiliation. Nor is there a great deal of scope for those who wish to remain shabby and unmade-over mount-ing a challenge to the dominant ethos of self-improvement. Drawing on Butler again, we might argue that the repetition across these formats, of insulting and injurious terms directed to women, might be suggestive of much deeper social anxieties precisely about the status of women in contemporary Britain as unstable, detached from the old moorings of class, ethnicity, marriage, mother-hood and appropriate gender and sexual identity. With their own money in their pockets, who knows what might happen? If the renewed celebration of marriage culture and all of its traditional trimmings including hen nights and stag parties mark out the contours of a consumer-led strategy for ensuring that young women retain a commitment to heterosexual norms and if the new sex-ual contract on offer to them, of work, leisure and degrees of sexual freedom, also seeks to pre-empt dangerous forms of re-politicisation, then this validation of old-fashioned and pre-feminist bitchiness and bullying played out along the lines of class and status is surely another such attempt to ensure that orderli-ness prevails in a context of change and movement?

I want to conclude this account of a highly scripted 'movement of women' with a short discussion of the place of race, ethnicity and sexual identity within these programmes. There are several black and Asian women present-ing programmes like these across the channels. But we might well ask, are eth-nic minority women participants treated with the same contempt as their white counterparts? And where gay men are so prominent as experts in these programmes, how is lesbian identity interwoven with these processes of class re-arrangement? One answer to this lies in social approval being granted across the lines of sex and race, on the basis of the desire of the victim, for improvement and willingness on her part to conform to normative ideals of glamour and good looks which in turn consolidate a re-assuring, usually lower middle-class heterosexual identity. In *What Not To Wear* Trinny and Susannah are disparaging about a woman cab driver who is too 'masculine' and who is 'hiding her fab figure', but to date they do not appear to have offered their services to lesbian participants. And so far I have not come across a pro-gramme where the experts openly laugh at, or make disparaging comments about, black or Asian women, the tone is somehow softened when the sub-ject of the make-over is black. This surely introduces dynamics for further analysis, most importantly for an ethnographic study of the production values and the script-writing process. How are decisions made about how the pre-senters interact with black or Asian participants? How do black women pre-senters (e.g. Mica Paris) respond to black or Asian victims? I would suggest that the programmes rely on an embodied history of class antagonism between white British women, a history which is known to the white audi-ence, since it is integral to 'national culture', from the writing of Virginia Woolf and her derogatory comments about the servants, to the diaries and writings of working-class women themselves. The programmes re-instate parts of these familiar vocabularies with the proviso that the insult is no longer meant to hurt. The historical repertoires of traditional English class hatred are brought back to life in the denigratory comments about the image, appear-ance, voice and accent of white working-class people. These wounding words are still there buried in the habitus of middle-class life, even though they have been dormant. But black people have been understood as racialised subjects rather than class subjects historically, and so they have not been included in this particular vocabulary of symbolic violence. Insults directed at them are invariably racialised. Thus the harsh words of Trinny or Susannah directed at an Asian woman could only be construed as racial insults, in effect they would be cast in terms that were racially abusive. So far no working-class black woman has stripped down to her knickers and pants and looked at herself with shame in the full length mirror as Trinny and Susannah poke or grope at her breasts which are invariably in need of a good bra. Somehow that would be too awkward for the format to deal with. In fact when black or Asian woman do appear they usually find themselves the recipients of more admi-ration and praise than their white counterparts. We can deduce that race and ethnicity introduce difficulties in a genre that relies on a re-instatement of tra-ditional forms of class conflict and hierarchy being established between white women. It could be suggested that there is an assumption underlying these programmes, which in effect allows them to take the form they do, that white women have somehow reached a state of equality. Apart from the pay gap between men and women, they are no longer discriminated against and hence women can be expected to become more like men in the workplace, that is, become more competitive, more individualistic in outlook, less concerned with caring for others, more concerned with the care of the self. So the programmes encourage working-class women to pull up their socks, under the guidance of their social superiors, and 'get out there'. And because there have been improvements, because 'ordinary' white women have gained advantages in recent years, because they have become more equal than before, this input to better themselves, does not, it seems, have the old sting of class condescension. The almost philanthropic mission on the part of Trinny and Susannah to improve the national stock of white womanhood stops short however at the challenge of improving black or Asian British womanhood. Even at a common-sense level, such assumptions about equality cannot be made about black or Asian woman, they remain vastly under-represented in the workforce, black women remain largely employed in gender-segregated areas such as care work, while Asian woman, depending on their class location, are understood to be less individualised than their white counterparts, and are seen as embedded in kinship or community systems. These factors present difficulties for formats like these make-over programmes when it comes to humiliation or denigration, and so as a solution, the victims find themselves treated with more respect, or with less overt cruelty. In the case of one non-white woman hairdresser called Geneve, who appeared in *What Not To Wear*, she so overwhelmed the team with her 'vibrant' personality that she almost silenced the presenters, and was one of the very few participants who did not like the new look and reverted to her old style. Despite this difficulty presented by issues around race and ethnicity, the terms of these programmes are not directly exclusive of black and Asian woman but are actually racially inclusive, they provide an open call to womanhood, across the boundaries of race, to identify with this self-improving ethos. Many of the experts and presenters are black or Asian, the 'problems' only arise at the interface of enaging with the corporeality of the non-white woman's body and its failings. And thus, to dissect and understand the dynamics of race and ethnicity within these programmes, we would need to observe the editorial codes and conventions in place as scripts are being written and victims are being selected and then briefed. There is then, a good deal more work to be done on 'mundane texts' such as these (Rose 1999b).

We might also ponder the narrowing of bodily norms and the strict limits on what constitutes acceptable sexual identity on the part of young women as a counter to earlier feminist and lesbian arguments, and as a means of further excluding or repudiating those who find no comfort, indeed only pain, in the prescribed femininity as defined by Trinny and Susannah. But let me return to Bourdieu. My claim here is that his writing allows an understanding of how social re-arrangement along gender lines takes place and actually happens, within media and popular culture by means of a reprimanding of the habitus of mostly white working-class and lower middle-class women so that their movement *en masse* into the world of work, and their increasing prominence as wage-earning citizens, is managed in such a way that it complies with the new requirements of individualised subjectivity in employment, consumer culture and sexuality. We might say that through these addresses to the female body, the category of womanhood itself is being 'nationally' overhauled so that it is brought into line with the biopolitical demands of the new global economy.

Notes

1   In an article in the business pages of the *Guardian* titled 'Dressing to impress' (29 May 2007: 13) Rachel Williams reports on a government scheme designed to help poor single mothers get back into work. The scheme, which also receives European Social Funds, is jointly run by Jobcentre Plus and an independent training provider called Inspire2Independence. It offers women make-overs so that the job-seekers gain self-esteem and learn the requisite skills of grooming and self-presentation. One task involves, in a setting similar to the TV format for *What Not To Wear*, the women being given £30 and an hour in a shopping mall, with the task of finding the right kind of outfit for an interview. 'The shopping trip was part of a two-week course designed to get long-term lone parents back into work … The course … began in 2004 … and has attracted about 1000 participants … The £30 clothing budget–given to participants in vouchers only after their choices have been approved-comes from … New Deal funding …'. One participant is quoted as saying 'People are opening doors for me now because I'm all dressed up in my suit with my new hair … My kids have noticed it too. They've been saying , 'mum, you're smiling more'. This article tells us something immediate about social policy taking the lead from television and entertainment, and it confirms Couldry's point about media meta-capital and the changing relations between the state and the media (Couldry 2003).
2   See Brundson (2005), see also Moseley and Read (2002), Hollows (2003), Tasker and Negra (2007).
3   Details about these programmes can be found at www.bbc.co.uk/lifetsyle/tv_and_ radio/what not to wear/styleguide and also www.bbc.co.uk/relationships/ singles_and_ dating/
4   See Channel 4 websites e.g. www.channel4.com/life/microsites/0-9/10yy/episodes and also http://www.mavericktv.co.uk
5   This *faux* intimacy is even more emphatic in *Ten Years Younger* and in *How To Look Good Naked*. The male presenter rakes through the woman's underwear drawers in an attempt to encourage her to throw away practical items and invest in more glamorous and attractive bras, knickers, tights and suspenders. He also says things like 'Don't worry ladies, if you have troublesome hips and thighs, I will help you feel good about getting your kit off in front of a roomful of people'.
6   In the series of *What Not to Wear* produced after Trinny and Susannah had left the BBC, one of the new presenters is the black woman musician Mica Paris. Her style is less abrasive and hostile and without the English upper middle class sneering of Trinny and Susannah.

7   See *Trinny and Susannah Undress the Nation,* ITV1.
8   We must refer here to recent legislation in the UK which makes hate speech a criminal offence, including homophobic speech. However this of course does not in itself reduce or stop the uttering of racial slurs and other forms of verbal violence, see www.guardian.co.uk/comment is free/peter tachell. Accessed_ 9/10/2007
9   As the quotation at the start of this chapter shows, the law can be and is prevailed upon to act against injurious speech. However this pathway to justice is not one which is advocated by Butler in her sustained discussion of hate speech (Butler 1997b).

6

CONCLUSION: INSIDE AND OUTSIDE THE FEMINIST ACADEMY

In the feminist classroom

The focus in this book has been on the forces that have been at work in recent years to make feminism something unpalatable and non-transmissable, a social movement of which there is little likelihood of it being revived or renewed. I have pursued this pathway through analysis of popular culture and its intersections with public debate. I have made a good deal of use of words like disarticulate, or disconnect, or of feminism as being undone. I have not meant to suggest that feminism was some sort of fixed thing, a rallying point back in the mists of time, around which so many women gathered in agreement. Quite the opposite was the case, and indeed I have argued that the kind of conjuring up of some fearful and horrifying feminist past in media and popular culture, is something that only existed in the fantasies of misogynist journalists and politicians, usually with reference to activities like the Greenham Common peace camp of the early 1990s. For example Auberon Waugh tellingly described the women in the camp as 'smelling of fish paste and bad oysters' (Stallybrass and White 1986: 23). Nor has it been my intention to imply that the women's movement would have continued and grown in some sort of linear or progressive way, had it not been for concerted actions on the part of those committed to its undoing. So it is not a matter of forwards and then backwards. And I am not implying that feminism is now quite extinguished, that there is nothing left of it. My suggestion is that within a wider context where it seems that feminist ideals have been adopted, or taken on board by various organisations and public bodies, this implementation has been the occasion also for a process of discouraging and also disavowing the further extension of, renewal of, or regeneration of feminism, in whatever shape or form, especially to a younger population of women whose interests now appear to be well looked after by a range of interest groups, including government. So I am interrogating a terrain of practices taking place within political culture and popular culture. I have not engaged in depth with the many forms of feminism that have existed from the 1970s onwards, I have not examined the expansion of feminism in the academy, and the huge growth of feminist academic journals and the enthusiasm of feminist scholars to write for these journals. Nor have I reflected on the energetic feminist internet activity of the last few years, or on, for example, the more recent developments coming out of the *riotgrrrl* subcultures of the 1990s. If I was arguing that feminism had entirely faded away, then the enthusiasm on the part of younger women to attend feminist academic conferences and public talks would surely prove me wrong. Nor is this book a lament for what could have been. Instead it has been an attempt to make an intervention which crosses the borders of a range of academic disciplines, gender studies, sociology, cultural and media studies, with the aim of both animating further debate about the future of feminism inside and outside the academy, and of provoking further rounds of argument.

In this final chapter I interrogate and challenge various forms of what we might call affirmative feminism, I do this by focusing on four topics. First a terrain which makes claims to be at the forefront of feminist success in policy, i.e. gender mainstreaming; second the celebratory third wave (I query the use of waves in the writing of feminist histories); third, as a counter-point to this, the affirmative sexual politics of the feminist philosopher Rosi Braidotti; and fourth I return to the feminist classroom and raise some questions about women's studies, about post-colonialist pedagogy, about teaching in the context of globalisation, and about some of the new or unexpected demands being made of feminist academics as the universities become sites for so-called knowledge transfer, and more generally come to be connected with the world of global enterprise. When each year in my own lecture theatre I am faced with almost 200 young women (and some young men) of whom less than a handful share my own UK nationality and who have come to take a Masters course (or are PhD students) from countries including Japan and China, Korea and Malaysia, Canada and the US, Botswana, Panama, Chile, Argentina, Poland, Hungary, Albania, Uruguay, Brazil, India, Bulgaria, Greece, Scandinavia, Germany, Italy and Spain, and having, over the years, seen that these young women are not from an international élite, but instead from middle-class (often struggling lower middle-class) homes, it is clear that these are young women who are destined for a new international labour market, they are coming to study in London to help them get a good job. And for them there is a perception that feminist pedagogy in sociology and cultural studies is somehow relevant to their lives, even though very few would actually call themselves feminists. And so in this final chapter I am pondering not just the passage for these young women in and out of the feminist academy, but also the postcolonial politics that are played out through these encounters.

Gender mainstreaming and its critics

If there is a single current of feminist thought which runs counter to the arguments presented in this book, it is gender mainstreaming. This concept, at least in the UK, is connected with the work of Sylvia Walby who, over the course of a number of recent articles and edited collections, presents this as a kind of new, modernised, form of feminist practice. There is in her writing, a certain degree of programmatic emphasis, as well as various claims being made about the impact and significance of this turn to the mainstream. Let me imagine that Walby would say the feminist undoing proposed by myself is a wholly cultural or a symbolic thing, meanwhile in the practical world of women's issues, there have been remarkable developments. Walby works between the world of the university and that of large and small political institutions and public agencies, from small NGOs around the world, to the World Bank, the UN and most specifically the EU. Her writing is directed towards this kind of broad constituency, she converses with a field of people working in a professional capacity on issues that concern women. Walby's writing on the topic of gender mainstreaming also shifts in the last five years, and she now engages more fully with diversity and difference (Walby 2002, 2005a, 2005b). The strongest case for gender mainstreaming is made in one key article, where she suggests that there is a shift away from autonomous feminist activity to involvement with the state and with civil society, at the same time there is a decline in socialist-feminism and in radical separatist feminism, and instead a good deal of feminist activity is subsumed within a kind of re-worked equal rights feminism which is compatible with new forms of liberal democracy (Walby 2002). This model can be seen at work in the UK, in New Labour's incorporation of feminist demands, and also in the mainstreaming equality agenda now taken on board by the UN, by other global institutions, and in particular the EU. Where feminism was once rather rowdy and activist (or at least this is the inference that can be drawn) it has now matured. It has embraced human rights discourse, and human rights discourse in turn has fully incorporated women's demands for equality, not just in the individualist sense but also to include women's collective economic and social rights.

Walby emphasises the coalitions and alliances that have supplanted, it seems, the tendency for feminism to splinter into antagonistic factions. The state, in the form of government (including local government) departments, has responded to many of the issues around domestic violence that were originally associated with the more independent and self-help ethos. There are, claims Walby, simply more and more professional women occupying key positions across the offices of the state who will see to it that women's rights are given priority. This demonstrates how gender mainstreaming has become a 'political programme for feminism in a global era' and a 'global movement' (Walby 2002: 538) One clear sign of 'feminist success' has been the way in which the EU has adopted gender mainstreaming as an official policy in line with its 'strategic engagement with globalisation'. There are, she claims, many opportunities now for a new feminist politics to emerge, and women can be said to be undertaking a shift themselves from the domestic to the public realm. Walby presents a slow progress model, based largely on the idea of women now employed in occupations which allow them to offer professional expertise and to form advocacy networks across important sites of policy, legislation and political decision-making. Walby suggests that what feminism may have lost in terms of public visibility as a protest movement, is more than compensated for by more hidden activities taking place behind the scenes. She emphasises not just the professional top-down technocratic advocacy on behalf of women's issues on the national and global stage, but also the wide range of different feminisms that have emerged from different geographical locations in the last 20 years. Gender mainstreaming in this more open form embodies what feminism is today. But in this suggestion there is something like a self-authorisation process going on, and also a claim being made that this strain of feminism carries some kind of official weight. In 'Gender Mainstreaming: Productive Tensions in Theory and Practice' Walby (2005a) states that this process entails the 'reinventing, restructuring and rebranding of feminism' through both promoting gender equality and also ensuring that existing social policies are made more effective through being expected to address gender issues. And in 'Introduction: Comparative Gender Mainstreaming in a Global Era' Walby claims that this is a 'new form of gendered political and policy practice … an international phenomenon … originating in development politics and adopted by the UN at the 1995 conference on women in Beijing and taken up by the European Union (EU) and its member states' (Walby 2005b: 453). Walby looks to the EU, where the definition of gender mainstreaming is the '(re)organisation, improvement, development and evaluation of policy processes, so that a gender equality perspective is incorporated in all policies at all levels at all stages, by the actors normally involved in policy-making'. There is a need for 'equal participation of women and men in political and public life' with 'education … a key target for gender equality'. In her recent articles Walby addresses the difficulties and complexities in responding to the issues raised in feminist theory around the always existing intersections of gender inequities with those of race and class, age, disability, and faith. She is also more attentive recently to debates about the limits of the expert or advocacy model and the importance of gender mainstreaming as a process of democratisation so that marginalised women 'get to have a voice'. Walby argues that in many respects there is a 'duality of expertise and participatory democratic working in this gender mainstreaming that is complementary rather than contradictory'. She refers to Woodward who argues for a 'velvet triangle' of 'feminist bureaucrats, trusted academics and organised voices in the women's movement … for the development of gender mainstreaming in the EU' (Walby 2005) Finally Walby emphasises the role gender mainstreaming has to play on the international stage, as a flexible and culture-sensitive way of unfolding a women's rights programme which is compatible with most existing human rights vocabularies.

If this is then a respectable version of feminism, 'made-over' for approval by global governance, there are some who dispute such a move. Frey et al. (2006) for example, question the way in which terms of dualistic gender difference remain unproblematic, which means that gender mainstreaming keeps intact notions of feminine and masculine capacity, and can then easily be deployed to improve efficiency in the new global economy. Frey et al. write '"Gender Mainstreaming" is increasingly interpreted as a neo-liberal reorganisation strategy in order to optimize "gender specific human resources" … gender equity has mutated into smart management of assumed differences' (Frey et al. 2006: 1–3). That is, women and younger women in particular produce added value by virtue of their particular skills and competencies, which are now, in the age of the service sector, more in demand than in the past. Gender mainstreaming can then be thought of as a non-conflictual accommodating kind of programme or schema which follows a path which has some equalising potential, but which in essence can be absorbed and taken on board by the structures and institutions of capitalism. When, earlier in this book I have talked about 'feminism taken into account', it is this strain of feminism which permits offices of government to claim that women's interests are indeed being looked after. The vocabulary of gender mainstreaming is 'modern', managerial and professional, a programmatic approach, with all kinds of tools for evaluation and assessment of outcomes which can be rolled as marks of good practice within corporate as well as state and public sector institutions. As Hark has pointed out, the very use of the word 'gender' in place of 'women' can have this effect of non-combative, social respectability (Hark 2005). Walby implies, incorrectly, that it is a new thing for feminists to be working inside the offices of the state. She fails to acknowledge the fact that within socialist-feminism, from the mid-1970s onwards, there was always a productive and critical relationship with the state, at local and national levels. The whole tradition of working with the 'Ideological State Apparatuses' in Althusser's terms, was a key feature of Marxist feminist writing, including the work of Michèle Barratt, Elizabeth Wilson, Lynn Segal and Mary McIntosh, none of whom adhered to the kind of autonomous or separatist feminism which Walby implies characterised the women's movement from the mid-1970s. These feminists were effective in their interventions, changing the vocabularies which defined practices within the large social institutions, while also working for more radical change at the same time. Walby is inattentive to the significance and the theoretical underpinnings of Marxist-feminism and its analysis of the state in the last 20 or 30 years. Instead she endorses a kind of mature feminist professionalism working comfortably inside the institutions of the state. But how can she be so sure that the feminist professionals in whom she suggests we must have trust, remain so trustworthy? Inside the New Labour government under Tony Blair's leadership, women who had earlier professed a commitment to women's issues were steadfastly silent and fearful since they were easily assured by the leadership that feminism was a 'turn off' to the electorate. Feminism was endlessly vilified, the Women's Unit shut down, and a swaggering macho style of government (as the diaries of Alistair Campbell show) met with little or no opposition (Campbell 2007). Gender mainstreaming in effect replaces feminism. Walby herself refers to the feminist past as a time of anger and unruliness, times change, she implies, and this is now how feminists can have an impact in a less dramatic fashion. But without also showing how feminist gains are and can be undone, without tackling how the move into political and public life, along the lines that Walby describes, is actually being endlessly contested and discouraged, and without looking at how terms like work-life balance tend to reinstate hierarchical gender norms in the heterosexual household, the values and the agenda associated with gender mainstreaming are reduced to the level of incorporation of principles and the implementation of a limited repertoire of policies whose effectivenss is doubtful. Gender mainstreaming in the UK is then a technocratic-managerial strategy which when combined with the claim that feminist activism of a past era is no longer relevant, becomes a substitute, part of the prevailing logic of feminism undone.

There is however the mundane point which is that there are possibilities for jobs and employment for young women graduates within the field of gender mainstreaming. Outside the academy, this is the dominant and available language for those who wish to earn a living within the field of women's issues, in the UK and particularly within EU-funded programmes. We need to acknowledge that the theoretical vocabularies of gender studies might well be incompatible within the requirements of a working environment given over to improving the chances of, for example, unqualified teenage mothers living in run-down council estates. There will also be many women working within gender mainstreaming who are having to translate this vocabulary to fit with their own policy agenda. And the same is the case in the feminist academy, we also have to be willing to sometimes speak two languages at once. In the grant application process and in our interface with government, we also must deploy an official vocabulary that often goes against the grain of the work to be undertaken. Working almost wholly within the field of EU-funded social projects for girls and women, Frey et al. (2006) make an effort to bring to bear the terms of gender theory into their gender mainstreaming practice. They critique the norms of gender training courses provided to companies and public sector organisations, not just because they often rely on essentialist feminine ideals (hard working, reliable, etc.) to promote the employment of women as a good deal for employees, but also because such courses often seek to re-assure employers that this is not old-school angry feminism by providing a gender team of a male and female, to allay such fears. They also suggest that these training courses could productively introduce ideas drawn from critical gender studies, 'using gender to undo gender' by means of a 'reflective gender practice'. However this is perhaps unlikely since the cost and time constraints inside corporate organisations limits what could be achieved here, especially since theories of gender and performativity do not lend themselves to short and snappy explication. Perhaps only in the context of lifelong-learning pro-grammes and adult education does this kind of practice-based initiative seem realistic. While Walby's position is too one-sided in its assumptions about the success of gender mainstreaming, there does nevertheless seem to be a need for a wider debate about the practices and implementation of gender main-streaming which would acknowledge the difficulties of operating in a policy-context where this is the official vocabulary, and must be deployed and used on a daily basis to attract funding and to create jobs. There are undoubtedly realms of disagreement between gender mainstreamers of a modernising and neo-liberal ilk, and the more leftist, radical social democratic gender main-streaming feminists working within the EU field of social projects. However in this latter area, pragmatics and an affirmative stance appear to prevail, and apart from Frey et al, there has been little open debate about the constraints of the requirement of gender mainstreaming as a technocratic way of dealing with women's issues, nor has there been a dialogue with the insights from recent work in feminist, queer or post-colonialist feminist theory. While Walby stands out as affirmative in her embracing of a model of feminist progress and professionalisation, those who are inside this same world and who might dispute this version are not so visible.

The third wavers

A critical debate about the limitations of what we might call the waves model of feminism is also long overdue. Not only does this feed into a linear narrative of generationally-led progress, taking the form of visible and coherent 'waves', permitting or pointing to occasional changes of direction, and moments of crisis, it also stifles the writing of the kind of complex historical geneaology of feminisms, which would challenge these often journalistic histories which unfailingly have beginnings and endings, and which remain suspicious of the-ory and tied to simplistic ideas and Western-dominated kinship metaphors about mothers and daughters. Even in activist and campaigning spheres the idea of waves of feminism is a hindrance to discussions about change and the impact of new concepts and ideas to existing practices. For these reasons I approach the topic of the third wave with caution and use the term only on the basis of this being a self-description of often web-based activism and writing. And my focus in the pages that follow on the third wave is for the reasons of its affirmative stance. In the edited collection *All About the Girl* (Harris 2004) Baumgardner and Richards present a commentary on their polemical book *Manifesta: Young Women, Feminism and the Future*. In the article they argue that 'it is a progression of feminism that younger 'third wave' women (and men) are embracing girlieness as well as power' (Baumgardner and Richards 2004: 59). The demand they make is for it to be legitimate for feminism to have a particular style of femininity folded into it, and as such for femininity to become a cause for celebration, not a mark of subordination, enjoyment of feminine products moreover isn't shorthand for 'we've been duped'. So the desire is to feel able to wear as much make-up as they like, and to wear sexy underwear, without feeling the disapprobation of this older generation of women whose underwear choices, it is assumed, were more sober. Indeed they say that they re-claim the word 'girlie' as though in an act of re-signification, much like that of 'queer' by gay and lesbian people, or in the way that black men and women in hip-hop jargon, use the term 'nigga'. In fact this both misunderstands and trivialises the value of the political strategy of re-signification, reducing it to a kind of provocation or simply an irritation, in this case directed to an older and seemingly more staid generation. And those feminists who did indeed object to 'girlieness' can hardly be compared to racists violently deploying the word nigger against black people. Baumgardner and Richards suggest that the previous generation had to repress their feminine qualities and desires, to prove that they could do serious jobs as well as their male counterparts, they 'fought so hard for all women not to be reduced to a "girl"'. The authors also connect the earlier feminist critique of consumerism with socialist tendencies, but younger women, they say, have 'grown up with access to the "good" parts of capitalism' and thus do not have the same need to critique it. This polemical commentary tells us little about what social or political forces this third wave of younger feminists is actually organising itself against apart from an older generation of feminists. 'The barrier to individuality and individual expression was no longer "the patriarchy" but feminism' (Baumgardner and Richards 2004: 65).

This is an anti-feminist argument, casting elders as implicitly unattractive and embittered. There is barely a word about inequality, or suffering or the racism black women experience or about the many ways in which gender hierarchies are sustained. Nor is this account self-reflexive about the limits of its seemingly almost all white and US-Anglo focus, only that 'there is proof of its appeal and power around the world and in many disparate communities'. There is a refrain repeated which is that 'girl is good' and that feminism should not mean having to abandon that terrain of enjoyable activities such as 'knitting and canning vegetables or decorating'. So in effect this *Manifesta* is about the right or the entitlement to claim back femininity for an assertive form of women's or girl-power, 'girls today … possess both a freedom and a fierceness' (ibid: 67). This pro-capitalist femininity-focused repertoire plays directly into the hands of corporate consumer culture eager to tap into this market on the basis of young women's rising incomes. This is a polemic about affirmation, that young women have more or less gained all the freedom they need, and that it is their feminist elders who need to learn something from them about being 'strong, smart and bold'. Baumgartern and Richards include under their heading of third wave, the more leftist and radical young women associated with the *riotgrrl* subculture (Kathleen Hanna for example) but overall their notion of third wave actually fits much better with the celebratory commercial values associated with the Spice Girls. The limits of this kind of polemical defence of girlieness is apparent when opened out into the world of wider social issues, of policy-making and of understanding changes in capitalism, and how these effect women. So it is not just a question of it being inimical with recent directions in feminist theory, it is also ill-equipped to deal with war, with militarism, with 'resurgent patriarchy' with questions of cultural difference, with race and ethnicity, and notably with the instrumentalisation of feminism on the global political stage. If it is the case that the polemical third wave writing is sketchy and fragmentary and sometimes belonging more in the domain of pamphlets and websites, there have been nevertheless some attempts to pull this kind of writing into a more systematic shape. In a recent article Stephanie Genz makes a positive claim for third wave feminism to be a kind of feminist version of the third way or *Neue Mitte* in UK, USA and German politics (Genz 2006). This is, within the frame of most feminist thinking, a contentious proposal. Genz argues that post-feminist individualism and the embracing of neo-conservative values by younger women who identify with this third wave of feminism, is part and parcel of that wind of change in the US and in Western Europe which politically goes beyond left and right and which endorses many of the principles of neo-liberalism, especially the celebration of human capital (in work) and the market economy. Genz claims this to be 'exciting' and she appears to be approving of the language of the third way as spoken by Blair and on occasion by the former German Chancellor Schroeder whose various comments on the new third way she describes as 'astute'. Genz sees post-feminism, including its backlash dimensions against other forms of feminism associated with the left, as a logical accompaniment to the third way. She then connects this more plural, flexible, consumer-oriented brand of feminism with the networking activities of younger third wave 'girlies'. This is a young women's neo-liberal feminism which is fluid, individualised and consumer-focused which, astoundingly, given the leftist radicalism which runs through all of Butler's work, Genz then associates directly with the kind of feminism endorsed by Butler. Indeed she claims that third wave young women's feminism can be linked with 'academic post-structuralism' as well as with the increasing social 'importance of consumption'. Both post-feminism and third wave activities involve, she claims 'micro-political forms of gendered agency' though what these actually involve is not spelt out (ibid: 346).

Braidotti's affirmative feminism

The idea of affirmative feminism as articulated by third wave young women, is largely untheorised, with the exception of Genz who makes some attempt to invoke the work of Butler to advance her own argument in favour of playful individualisation. There is a more significant strand of affirmative feminist theory which is quite at odds with the female agency position advocated by the third wavers, (who have no concern with the question of subjectivity and what it means to challenge the assumed unity of the subject) and yet which is also concerned with activity, activism and innovation. Braidotti is perhaps the best-known feminist philosopher of affirmation, and in her recent book she also expresses her misgivings about gender mainstreaming, and postfeminism, saying that

> gender mainstreaming turned out to be an anti-feminist mechanism that increased differences in status, access and entitlement among women. Post-feminist neo-liberalism is pro-capitalist and hence it considers financial success in the world as the sole indicator of status of women ... social democratic principles of solidarity are misconstrued as old-fashioned welfare support, and dismissed accordingly. ... The pernicious part of this syndrome is that it fosters a new sense of isolation among women and hence new forms of vulnerability. (Braidotti 2006: 45)

This critique of post-feminism, which I would endorse, does not, however, lead Braidotti to adopt the kind of narrative of loss which has under-pinned my own account, since in her writing she develops a Deleuzian-influenced feminism which is joyful and affirmative and which focuses on the creation of differences and of singularities in regard to the many possibilities of 'becoming woman'. With a starting point which would warn against giving too much weight to the inexorable and all-consuming power of capital, and instead, concentrating on the cracks and fissures, and possible points of rup-ture, Braidotti's vocabulary is very different from the vocabulary I have employed throughout this book, which takes its lead from Stuart Hall's cul-tural theory, Butler's gender theory, the work of Spivak, as well as earlier fem-inist psychoanalytical writing. The Deleuzian turn takes a different course and the notion of affirmation which Braidotti employs is far removed from the simplistic concept of agency so often used in feminist media studies and also in the polemical work of the third wave feminists. Deleuze challenges the idea of a single humanist subject (the subject is not one) whose agency emerges as an act of volition, who is a kind of doer behind her deeds, and he also refutes the more fragmented psycho-analytical subject who is nevertheless held together through being positioned within oedipal relations. Deleuze also stakes out a space which is different from Foucault's emphasis on processes of subjectification, to focus instead on bodies and flows of affect, on singularities and on productivities which are disembodied and which are not the outcome of a unitary subject undertaking specified actions. Deleuzians take from Spinoza a kind of joyful affirmative desire to live which connects humans with non-humans and which take the form of multiple becomings and which permits a radical politics of 'life itself' to emerge. Braidotti has provided many detailed responses to the work of Deleuze and Guattari (Braidotti 1994, 2002, 2006, see also Colebrook 2002b). There is not the space here to fully engage with this work, except to ask some rather sociological questions of it, which relate to the question of the status of feminism inside and outside the academy. One such question would be how Braidotti can account for the realms of feminist creativity and 'becoming', which charts the gap between the women who remain resolutely outside feminism (those who in the past would have been called 'ordinary women') and those who move into the space of activity and political inventiveness. Frequently she seems to attribute to the non-feminist female population that which applies really only to feminists or feminist-influenced young women (e.g. artists, writers, intellectuals, subcultural participants). This discounts the significance of the forces which deter such becomings, and it does not offer any reflection on the socio-historical factors which have, in the past, for example in the late 1960s, permitted an escape for white middle-class young women so that they could take part in the production of feminism. Thus when Braidotti examines new modes of becoming, and when she reflects on cultural practices which mark out fluid, mutant and nomadic sexualities, my point would be that such phenomena are the inventions of those who are already located within, or at least are moving towards, a space of affirmative feminism, and maybe what she is actually referring to are new energetic and rhizomatic forms of political activism which take a largely cultural form. But even in the Birmingham work of the 1970s on youth subcultures, there was an attempt, through the use of Marxist categories, to explain the precise socio-economic factors which facilitated transitions into 'spaces of resistance' (Hall and Jefferson 1976). Braidotti's affirmative feminism stands in sharp contrast with young women's ambivalence to, and dis-identification with feminism, even inside the gender studies classroom. For example Scharff has noted the low status that gender studies has within the new status-conscious postgraduate population, and she suggests that the successful embracing of femininity nowadays relies on the vocal repudiation of feminism, which adds a further dimension to my own argument that feminism is, on an everyday basis 'taken into account' (Scharff 2008).

Braidotti, like an artist or novelist, brings new worlds into being through the sheer power of her writing and reasoning. Along with Donna Haraway she is a feminist inventor of worlds, an experimentalist who does what Deleuze and Irigaray inspire her to do, which is to break decisively with the binaries of male and female and to inaugurate a feminism based on the critique of rigid heterosexual difference and the creation of new sexualities. She argues for a departure from girlhood *per se*, suggesting that it is the task of feminism to create new kinds of female feminist subjects (maybe non-girls) who are minoritarian, who are not frightened by the idea of leaving traditional femininity, as defined by women's and girls magazines behind. Such a departure is not so unimaginable since lurking beneath the surface (of what I would call the 'post-feminist masquerade') is the proximity of monstrosity, the mask so easily slips, and other side of perfection (total failure) is always within sight, this provides the kind of crack or rupture which Braidotti would take as an opening for transformation (Braidotti 2000). Braidotti aims at liberating the subject from the prison cell of binary gender assignation. She does this by abandoning gender in favour of forces and flows, bodies and desires, and she focuses on the transformative potential which is also a feature of life itself, and which although capitalism is endlessly trying to capture and harness it, for its own purposes, nevertheless this potential for transformation takes shape in marginal practices and in the cultural activities of oppressed social groups. Affirmative politics takes off, as it were, from women's desires to 'posit themselves' as female subjects, this positing is then transposed in an explicitly feminist direction through the desire for being which stakes out a distance from the institutions of femininity, and instead works through the archive of phallogocentric images and texts to arrive at a new and undesignated location which Braidotti calls the virtual feminine. This is indeed a place of proliferating activities, comprising 'subjects endowed with multiple sexualities', this is a nomadic approach which creates a space for existence outside of phallogocentric thinking. Braidotti describes these new nomads as youthful gangs, not quite young women but instead newly undesignated subjects who have found the means of exiting from the grip of male and female spaces of identity. While again it could be argued that there is something of the mythic in this particular concept of nomadic and ungendered gangs, it corresponds with what Deleuze calls a radical political process of becoming-women, a kind of inventive process of moving to being beyond gender, it requires an act of imagination, an envisaging of other states of being like those we might find in feminist science fiction or, for example, in classic lesbian feminist avant-garde films of the late 1970s like Ulrike Ottinger's *Bildnis einer Trinkerin* (1979) or her *Madame X: ein absolute Herrscherin* (1978). This expansive activity is not carried out as a matter of sheer volition, or individual bravery or heroism but instead is a kind of immanent force or power, inherent within marginalised and oppressed peoples, and as Braidotti comments, is already lurking there, in the malfunctioning within the landscapes of subjectivity made available by capitalist political economy. These spaces or cracks provide the triggers for learning to 'reinvent yourself and ... desire the self as a process of transformation'. Braidotti is aware that such a process risks coming close to normative incitements to re-invent oneself according to the intensified logic of the consumer culture, but this affirmative feminism is predicated on the palpable desire for alternatives, and the desire for change, often by means of new figurations, for example a 'different erotic imaginary' one which is perhaps more 'cruel', presumably because it is not tied to the sentimental tropes of romantic heterosexuality, and which brings into being different forms of affect and relations (Braidotti 2003). The transformative feminist politics as invoked by Braidotti mounts a challenge to and escape from the rigidities and dissatisfactions of heterosexual culture. Butler sees some overlap in many of these themes in Braidotti's work, with her own work. For example, she argues that butch desire is unanchored from its seeming referent within masculinity, it defines a masculinity which is quite other than that associated with heterosexual men, and in this respect it is the outcome of the power or potential of desire which is not scripted within phallogocentrism (Butler 2004, also Halberstam 2005).

Butler finds a common interest in the Spinozaist affirmation of life, which for her becomes imperative at that point at which survival itself is threatened, while for Braidotti this moment (which she describes as the 'second last drink', the last one being presumably the one that kills you) does not have quite the gravity that it has for Butler. Braidotti is more open to death, more 'cruel' perhaps in her response to mortality. Where Butler gasps for life, and mourns deaths which are the result of war and global injustices, Braidotti looks to the new politics of mortality for possible spaces for transformation, and perhaps also brings death into the land of the living, part of the exhilaration effect of the multiple becomings of the bodies of which the human is just one. This would put Braidotti at odds with my own account of young women's disorders, for example in regard to self-harming practices, she would perhaps pay more attention to the cultural productivities which emerge from landscapes of pain. She would look perhaps to subcultures or to traditions of black women singing the blues, or even to the actual music of Amy Winehouse, rather than to the question of who lives and who dies. What both Butler and Braidotti share in common is an interest in an 'activism that does not rely upon or implies the possibility of a liberal ontology of the subject' (Butler 2004). Butler suggests that within a field of suffering and marginalisation and oppression Braidotti looks for 'points of rupture which are ripe for transformation' and that Braidotti's work 'exemplifies ... the event of change'. This echoes the points I made above, and it shows the feminist politics of affirmation to be about innovation in theory, about inventing concepts which are useful and which somehow measure up to the multiple becomings which are taking place in ways that capitalism cannot quite contain. Most often Braidotti is referring to feminist female subjects and what they as 'bodies' can do, what changes they can effect, what potential there is within this kind of nomadic philosophy which is aimed at inventing and experimenting with multiple becomings. She is addressing those within the orbit of feminist theory whose passion for change she wishes to unleash in particular directions which are other than those already laid out within existing feminist theory. She is impatient with those feminists too concerned with dissecting capitalist domination and control and who seem to have no interest in potentialities for transformation and with those spaces of rupture within contemporary culture which she so acutely pinpoints, where normative subjectivities find themselves in crisis. Braidotti addresses breaks in the system, and she tunes into art and cultural phenomena which take this breakdown as a starting point. She sees these potentialities in music like that of Laurie Anderson or in the writing and persona of Kathy Acker. Often it seems she is addressing young women, already feminists, and literally, through the sheer energy and force of her writing and her eclectic and exuberant range of cultural as well as philosophical references she is tempting, teasing, and seducing them into embracing a Deleuzian politics of becoming. Braidotti's exuberant, joyful, exciting writing has, arguably, its own performative effect and her re-configuring of what it is to be a woman is decisively non-victim based, non-essentialist, de-gendered, desiring and productive, brimming with potential as to what this new kind of body (beyond girlhood) can do. Braidotti takes a stance against leftist pessimism and her work pushes her readers towards new, rather than established forms of radical activism. This is based neither on political parties nor on clearly defined new social movements but is instead roaming, nomadic and rhizomatic. I have already outlined some of my reservations about this call-to-arms, exciting as it is. Of course it is important to lift feminism out of a corner which is marked by pain, suffering and victimhood and which as a result so easily leads to a feminist culture of individual injury and entitlement as Wendy Brown (1995) has shown. Brown argues that, especially with the decline of a radical collective politics which once looked for more profound social transformation, feminism now runs the danger of becoming a force for the redressing of grievances and for compensation for injuries. And this can lead, in some areas of women's and gender studies, to an ethos of injury or victimhood. But, as a counter to this, there are nevertheless problems with Braidotti's affirmative sexual politics. She does not examine the inroads made by the new right in institutions and in culture, nor does she consider the impact of this on young people including young women, so for example she does not engage with the overt hostility on the part of many young women to feminism, within the liberal university, indeed within the feminist classroom.

The feminist classroom as 'contact zone'

The challenge posed by Braidotti's writing is to invent some feminist newness, and by this means to contribute to a process of becoming other, and to the growth of a new minoritarian politics. Braidotti does not quite answer the question of what kind of feminist productions, carried out by what kind of people, actually qualify as inventive, save for the works she refers to. Let us assume that it entails a kind of leap across some fence and onto the other side, where one is among like-minded creative and radical people, and where there are vibrant signs of change and of transformation which are somehow productive, which embody the process of de-gendering and of radical escapist mutations, where there are many events and encounters, where there are in the academy, possibilities for 'unworking' and for countering the 'total subsumption by capital' as it 'penetrates every aspect of our lives' (O'Sullivan 2007: 241). As a response to Braidotti's work, I offer a series of open-ended reflections on areas of feminist pedagogy in the context of the global university which do not as yet seem to have been an object of critical scrutiny. These observations do not fit with a narrative of feminist loss and anti-feminist individualisation, but neither do they directly confirm a new politics of becoming, what they do is mark out a genuinely new space, drawing on Bhabha, a 'third space' fraught with uncertainty and potential (Bhabha 1994).

The environment of my own teaching situation in London prompts me to suggest this at least as a field of change and difference for young women. It is something new and unexpected to me to be teaching young women from across the world, who are then thrown together with each other and with myself as teacher, along with all my other colleagues, in what is an intensive year of Masters level study. This is a potential site of feminist affirmation, insofar as the students who take my own course choose it as an option and know they will spend time reading feminist and post-colonial theory. Feminist affirmation here comprises approval for the curriculum. But the possibilities opened up in the course of this feminist pedagogy are not necessarily connected with a critique of the international division of labour and of the chances for work and employment in the large corporations or in global institutions. Some might say these possibilities for life and becoming mark out a narrow opportunity structure for middle-class daughters, or as Spivak would say, the chance for upward social mobility for those young women who are able to grasp onto new privileges, leaving behind them a de-populated lower middle-class no longer able to provide teachers in areas of poverty and illiteracy (Spivak 1998). This would be to cast this 'movement of young women' as a process of educational migration undertaken for the sake or economic betterment as dictated by the requirements of the new global economy, what Spivak calls 'diaspora as class line, even if not perceptible from the metropolis' (Spivak 2000: 350). I want to offer now some reflections on this kind of classroom, where I encounter young women from so many different countries, the great majority of whom as enthusiastic about writing essays on Homi Bhabha and Gayatri Spivak and the racial stereotype, as they are keen to spend time on Butler's queer theory. Very few have come across or been taught this work before. Many have a first degree in either (conventional) humanities or in (quantitative) social science, or business studies and marketing. What is going on here? What does it mean for me to call it a 'third space'? The educational institutions I am thinking about are in London, a global city of migration, attracting people of different age, sex, and class as well as nationality (although again Spivak warns this metropolitan domination ignores the 'hybridised spaces of a Third World, so-called colonial city', Spivak 2000: 352), Actually my concern is with a small female fraction of this flow, whose legal status as students is a matter of Home Office jurisdiction, unless they are from EU countries. I suggest this feminised educational milieu as a third space because it is so full of ambivalence and uncertainty, it seems to tell us something about futurity or the 'to come'. These classrooms echo with a sense of potential, and a female desire to 'participate'. Others might dismiss this as a new global female middle-class fraction, but to do so is to miss the tension, anxiety, and sheer uncertainty of a life to come. Of course I cannot fully make sociological sense of this multitudinous flow of young women, I can only argue that it is important to pay it attention. Where are they heading? I would like to think about this pedagogic third space as a 'contact zone' (Pratt 1992). Pratt writing about the colonial expeditions undertaken by people like the famous botanist Humboldt and by the many early travellers and explorers, including those who headed to South America, describes contact zones as 'social spaces where disparate cultures meet, clash and grapple with each other, often as highly asymmetrical relations of domination and subordination' (Pratt 1992: 4). A contact zone is therefore a place marked by transparent differences of power, a space where the coloniser enters into a local or indigenous knowledge ecology (e.g. plant life, the natural world) with the aim of appropriating and bringing home this body of wealth of knowledge, to be put to profitable use by the early industrialists of the 18th and 19th centuries. Pratt makes the point that the natural scientists who became explorers undertook their travels in the spirit of anti-conquest, they were almost 'innocent explorers' whose activities however eventually worked to consolidate and naturalise 'European domination'. There was, argues Pratt, great complexity inside these 'contact zones', as the auto-ethnographies of the travellers revealed. Pratt describes how these habitats, where indigenous people shared their knowledge and expertise with the travellers, permitted the expansion of Europe on the basis of the development potential provided by the materials and the plant life that could be studied under these natural conditions. There was, she suggests, reciprocity and a great deal of interaction within these contact zones, there was surveillance and learning but not within an overtly coercive set of relationships.

Teaching feminist theory and cultural studies in a London university might seem far removed from the contact zones examined by Pratt, but the term allows me to begin to analyse issues about pedagogy in what seems like a 'hospitable' cosmopolitan setting. Where there is a prevailing ethos of radical multi-culturalism and classroom democracy, and where the learning process is understood to be more than just the transmission of knowledge, questions about background and place of origin, about expectations and desires, and about the interface of experience in the university and also in the metropolitan city are all part of the pedagogic encounter. In what Spivak calls the 'teaching machine', knowledge and power are of course deeply entangled, and if the pedagogic process which she might also see disparagingly as 'gender training' is also a subject-producing practice, we need to interrogate in more detail the official educational discourses which apply specifically to the university as it plays a new role in the global economy through what is known as overseas recruitment. If up to nine out of ten of the mostly female students on the MA courses I myself teach are from outside the UK, this in itself tells us something important about the role of education and the institution of the university, for young women in the global economy, as well as the existence of London as a kind of hub in the midst of a network of movements of young women. We are reminded of the great narratives of modern literature, the imperial city, the heart of the old empire, the urban space which is familiar to so many through the work of Dickens or Virginia Woolf and how this has now become a kind of educational 'contact zone' to which young women from many countries gravitate. There is always something more to this journey to London, than the gaining of a degree. These students provide a vital source of income for the institutions of higher education. Is this a far cry from the days of the Commonwealth Scholars coming to the UK as part of the long narrative of civilising the empire, so that, as Spivak would say, there could be the 'production of a colonial subject in order to administer a settled colony'? (Spivak 1998). We know that many such figures have also historically turned such an assignation around, remaining in the UK, for example like Stuart Hall as a post-colonial radical intellectual, or in Spivak's case in the US as a 'Resident Alien'(2002). The question is how might we being to understand this contemporary movement of young women? This would entail an ethnography of the feminist post-colonial classroom informed by awareness of the relations of power and knowledge which underpin the very existence of, as well as the transmission of, the feminist curriculum (for a rich discussion of Western feminism as pedagogy in the context of East European university systems see Cerwonka 2008). An analysis of the contact zone inside the global educational institutions would also need to reflect on the economic value attached to the gaining of qualifications. What do these qualifications lead to? How does the eventual income of the young woman who has graduated from an institution actually function? Does it bring about greater 'independence' and status and if so to what socio-political effect? Perhaps a new diasporic life can be envisaged through the process of educational migration. What the global economy makes available, women's micro-strategies can possibly subvert for purposes other than becoming the modern-day equivalent of Spivak's colonial administrator. Coming to study marks out the possibility of a different life-course, one no longer wholly shaped by, or determined by marriage and motherhood. For the young women in my own classrooms, who are mostly aged between 25 and 35, marriage is not the issue and the students look, with ambivalence, to the feminist teacher for some kind of confirmation of this as a possibility.

Kincaid's Lucy

Gayatri Spivak is one of the few feminist academics writing about such routes and encounters in recent years. her work is littered with references to the interweaving of class and race and gender in this form of post-colonial pedagogy. While these various pedagogies have been subject to attempts to de-colonise and de-westernise knowledge, the curriculum, despite Spivak's attempts, remains reliant largely on scholarship emerging from universities from wealthy countries of the West. These classrooms are then sites of complex interactions, where the deeper life-biographies of the vast flow of young people (mostly young women) through the doors of the university, year in year out, must remain largely unknown to the likes of myself as teacher. Some areas of the course content regularly become a source of passionate investment, key texts, usually works of feminist or post-colonial theory, have seemingly magical capacities to move their readers. This might be a banal point, but it also conveys the affective power of the educational field to act as a counterdiscourse, counter that is to the dominant social norms that seek to instil an uncritical relation to the world of business and to the role of education in 'knowledge transfer'. This academic milieu has become in recent years a 'space of flows', a vital important 'hub' within the new knowledge economy, a place of networking and of producing new generations of female labour power for global capitalism (Castells 1996). This dimension of the university, more closely than before, intersects with the new international division of labour, has not been the subject of specifically feminist attention. Spivak's response would surely be sceptical and guarded against any inflated claims being made about the potential for radicalisation on the basis of educational migration to the cosmopolitan classroom. She would insist we interrogate the social processes which permit a small fraction of a middle class to travel to the metropolitan cities and gain a university degree in prestigious institutions, and become by these means upwardly mobile, and she would also ask at whose expense is this possible, and what is at stake in this journey? Spivak consistently brings her readers back to the geographical space of the subaltern, especially the subaltern women, and to questions of pedagogy, especially basic literacy and the importance of being able to write. She would point to the deficit of teachers and educators in rural India, and also to the still rigid pedagogy based on rote-learning which means that girls in the three years they might have of education are unable to write a message for example, or anything about their lives. She reminds us that the skills of writing, skills which have historically produced slave narratives and 'women's secret writing', are invaluable for the recording of hidden lives and for the production of records in overlooked and impoverished spaces of the world. Spivak has also challenged those who focus unduly on the Western city as the point of arrival for the new tides of migration, including Derrida's emphasis on hospitality, Balibar's notion of the migrant as the new proletariat and Hardt and Negri's focus on the multitude as a flowing movements of peoples who are not wholly accounted for in terms of class or nation or race. Spivak rightly wants to counter the fading to invisibility of the place of departure that occurs when such attention is given to arrival points.

As supplier of this new global labour power, of 'mass intellectuality', the university is indeed suddenly more tightly embedded with capital than before. Academia now occupies a prominent place in the training of the new international workforce. Writers such as Virno and Lazzarato refer to the role of communications (in our parlance surely media and communications and cultural studies) in the new global economy. This is the key site for productivity, to the extent that capital frequently lags behind the interface of subjects who co-produce (perhaps in the classroom) the kinds of 'big ideas' and 'solutions' that are vital to the knowledge economy. The radical politics which emerges from this recent work combines the diversity of the multitude (along the lines of the multi-nationalities found in my own classroom) with the possibilities which migration has for developing a kind of enhanced understanding, awareness and potential for critique, and alongside this the inability of Capital to totally control and keep tabs on the 'immaterial labour' in its emotional as well as intellectual dimensions. Once again not only can we translate this model directly into the space of the classrooms that I have described, but we must forcefully add to this the significance of gender. Global capital needs well-qualified young women, and where the universities and the humanities and social sciences were once places for a gentleman's education, in culture, civilisation and national identity, this function is transformed dramatically in recent years (Readings 1996). In a transnational world, and a global economy, the university becomes the foot-servant of neo-liberal values. (Readings accuses cultural studies of complicity in this regard.) Across this debate about the new role of the university no mention is made of gender as imperative to this form of capitalist re-structuring for the international division of labour (Readings 1996, Rossiter 2007, Lazzarato 1996, Virno 2004).

There is indeed something like feminist affirmation institutionally made available to the minority-other as she finds her way into the classroom of feminist cultural studies. This begs the question of what is 'outside the teaching machine' and what are the borders of the feminist academy? Let us think back for a moment to that commitment in cultural studies through figures like Williams, Hoggart and Hall, to 'adult education', to non-traditional routes into the university system, or to 'evening classes' or extra-mural study. In this context a wide range of subjects, of which cultural studies is but one, developed a critical counter-curriculum from the late 1960s onwards. If female educational migration bears some relation to the long tradition of evening classes then, against Spivak, we might argue that the future labour power of these young women might be understood as not wholly and inevitably in the service of 'economic restructuring for exploitation' (Spivak 1998). This may be hard to agree with when the students say they hope to work for *Marie-Claire* magazine, or in fashion PR, or as a journalist for Al-Jazeera, but these job opportunities also need to be critically reflected on rather than simply dismissed. The world of work is after all very different from those jobs and careers found in welfare democracies like the UK in the 1970s. Hardt and Negri, Virno and Lazzarato all argue against a fatalist leftist account of the decline of politics, and the death of radicalism, and the triumph of neo-liberalism. They see politics now as taking new forms and shapes (as Braidotti also proposes) which are as yet relatively unformed, but somehow present and forward-looking. They imagine this new kind of politics emerging from the whole world of everyday life, which is now subsumed by work, or by the making of livings (no longer located in workplaces but co-extensive now with the field of the social, with life itself). And so, instead of writing off the potential for radical politics *per se*, on the part of those graduates who, let us say, earn a living working in a global fashion company, we might say that we need to reflect on and analyse the small counter-cultures existing within the disciplinary regimes of working life. Spaces of critique can emerge. And as education segues into working life, shaping some of the new professional values and ideas, in the form of critique, the two enter into a much deeper relation with each other. Spivak again reminds us of the liberation pedagogy of Paolo Friere, and she asserts that teaching and pedagogy could now, given so many other battles lost, be construed as a social movement for radical change (although she also hesitates since the curriculum nowadays is so weighted towards business and enterprise). Spivak also recalls a moment in the novel *Lucy* by Jamaica Kincaid that touches on many of the themes in this chapter (Spivak 2000). Lucy's mother, to Lucy's distress, indeed trauma, in that it inaugurates a process of not just falling out of love with her mother as a young girl, but of beginning to hate her in such a way as to make her incapable herself of ever loving another person, refuses Lucy that which is the rightful privilege of her sons. In an episode which recalls a similar one, much earlier by George Elliot in *Mill on the Floss*, when the rather dim son Tom gets the education which Maggie is not allowed, the mother dismisses the possibilities of an education for her daughter while looking favourably to her son's future prospects through a good education overseas. I am not suggesting that gender inequality in education is now over-turned. Spivak repeatedly warns us against the Trojan horses of Western governments that nowadays might bear the gift of 'education for girls'. But still, just as Lucy eventually, and by means of migrating as an au pair, gets to her evening classes after days spent looking after children, and then eventually gets to the point that she thinks she can become a writer, we might say that it is perhaps possible to imagine a new feminist politics from within the dictates and the requirements of this new global economy where young women are being strongly urged and mobilised into moving backwards and forwards, to and fro, as educational migrants and also as au pairs and domestic workers, according to class location. These processes, from the point of departure to that of arrival produce a new gender map and emergent geo-politics of work, labour and of life itself. Pedagogy and learning have become vital spaces of encounter, and new kinds of contact zones where histories, including gender histories, which have otherwise been subject to enforced forgetting have perhaps a small chance now of being written.

BIBLIOGRAPHY

Adkins, L. (2000) 'Objects of Innovation: Post-occupational Reflexivity and Re-traditionalizations of Gender' in S. Ahmed, J. Kilby, C. Lury, M. McNeil, B. Skeggs (eds), *Transformations*, pp. 259–272. Routledge, London.

Adkins, L. (2002) *Revisions: Gender and Sexuality in Late Modernity*. Open University Press, Buckingham.

Allen, K. (2008) 'Young Women and the Performing Arts: Creative Education, New Labour and the Remaking of Class and Gender', PhD Thesis, Goldsmiths College, University of London.

Arnot, M. David, M. and Weiner, G. (1999) *Closing the Gender Gap*. Polity Press, Cambridge.

Barlow, T., Dong, U., Ramamurthy P., Thomas, L., and Weinbaum A. (2005) 'The Modern Girl Around the World': A Research Agenda and Preliminary Findings', in *Gender and History*, 17 (2): 245–294.

Bartky, S. L. (1990) *Femininity and Domination: Studies in the Phenomenology of Oppression*. Routledge, London.

Bauman, Z. (2002a) *Liquid Modernity*. Polity Press, Cambridge.

Bauman, Z. (2000b) *The Individualized Society*. Polity Press, Cambridge.

Baumgardner, J. and Richards, A. (2004) 'Feminism and Femininity: Or How We Learned to Stop Worrying and Love the Thong' in A. Harris and M. Fine (eds), *All About the Girl*, pp. 59–69. Routledge, London.

Beck, U. (1992) *Risk Society: Towards a New Modernity*. Sage, London.

Beck, U. and Beck-Gernscheim, E. (1995) *The Normal Chaos of Love*. Polity Press, Cambridge.

Beck, U. and Beck-Gernscheim, E (2001) *Individualization*. Sage, London.

Beck U., Giddens, A. and Lash, S. (1994) *Reflexive Modernization: Politics, Tradition and Aesthetics in the Modern Social Order*. Polity Press, Cambridge.

Bennett, T. and Woollacott, J. (1987) *Bond and Beyond: The Political Career of a Popular Hero*. Macmillan, Basingstoke.

Blackman, L. (2004) 'Self-help, Media Cultures and the Production of Female Psychopathology', *European Journal of Cultural Studies,* 7 (2): 219–236.

Blackwood, S. and Adebola, Y. (1997) 'Black vs Black: The Women Who Hate Their Own', *Pride*, March: 20–23.

Bourdieu, P. (1984) *Distinction: A Social Critique of the Judgement of Taste*, trans. R. Nice. Routledge, London.

Bourdieu, P. (1996) *On Television*, trans. P.P. Ferguson. The New Press, New York.

Braidotti, R. (1994) *Nomadic Subjects: Embodiment and Sexual Difference in Contemporary Feminist Theory*. Columbia University Press, New York.

Braidotti, R. (2000) 'Teratologies' in I. Buchanan and C. Colebrook (eds), *Deleuze and Feminism*. Edinburgh University Press, Edinburgh.

Braidotti, R. (2002) *Metamorphoses: Towards a Materialist Theory of Becoming.* Polity Press, Cambridge.

Braidotti, R. (2003) 'Becoming Woman: Or Sexual Difference Revisited', *Theory, Culture & Society*, 20 (3): 43–64.

Braidotti, R. (2006) *Transpositions*. Polity Press, Cambridge.

Breines, W., Cerullo, M. and Stacey, J. (1978) 'Social Biology, Family Studies, and Antifeminist Backlash', *Feminist Studies*, 4: 43–67.

British Medical Association (2000) *Eating Disorders, Body Image and the Media*. BMA, London.

Brown, W. (1995) *States of Injury.* Princeton University Press, Princeton: NJ.

Brown, W. (2000) 'Resisting Left Melancholia' in P. Gilroy, L. Grossberg and A. McRobbie (eds), *Without Guarantees: In Honour of Stuart Hall*, pp. 21–30. Verso, London.

Brown, W. (2005) 'Neoliberalism and the End of Liberal Democracy' in W. Brown, *Edgework: Critical Essays on Knowledge and Politics*, pp. 36–60. Princeton University Press, Princeton: NJ.

Brunsdon, C. (1991) 'Pedagogies of the Feminine: Feminist Teaching and Women's Genres' in *Screen*, 32/4, 364–81.

Brunsdon, C. (1997) *Screen Tastes: Soap Opera to Satellite Dishes*. Routledge, London.

Brunsdon, C. (2003) 'Lifestyling Britain: The 8–9 Slot on British Television', *International Journal of Cultural Studies,* 6 (1): 5–23.

Brunsdon, C. (2005) 'Feminism, Postfeminism, Martha, Martha, and Nigella', *Cinema Journal,* 44 (2): 110–116.

Budgeon, S. (2003) *Choosing a Self*: *Young Women and the Individualisation of* Identity, Praegar Publishing, Westport CT

Budgeon, S. (2001) 'Emergent Feminist(?) Identities: Young Women and the Practice of Micropolitics', *European Journal of Women's Studies*, 8 (1): 7–28.

Butler, J. (1990) *Gender Trouble: Feminism and the Subversion of Identity.* Routledge New York.

Butler, J. (1992) 'Contingent Foundations: Feminism and the Question of "Postmodernism"' in J. Butler and J. W Scott (eds), *Feminists Theorize the Political,* pp. 3–22. Routledge, New York.

Butler, J. (1993) *Bodies That Matter: On the Discursive Limits of 'Sex'*. Routledge, New York.

Butler, J. (1994) 'Gender as Performance: An Interview with Judith Butler' by P. Osborne and L. Segal, *Radical Philosophy,* 67: 32–39.

Butler, J. (1997a) *The Psychic Life of Power*. Stanford University Press, Stanford: CA.

Butler, J. (1997b) *Excitable Speech*: *A Politics of the Performative*. Routledge, New York.

Butler, J. (1999a) *Gender Trouble: Feminism and the Subversion of Identity*, 2nd edn. Routledge, New York.

Butler, J. (1999b) 'Performativity's Social Magic' in R. Shusterman (ed.), *Bourdieu*: *A Critical Reader*, pp. 113–128. Blackwell, Oxford.

Butler, J. (2000a) *Antigone's Claim: Kinship Between Life and Death*. Columbia University Press, New York.

Butler, J. (2000b) 'Agencies of Style for a Liminal Subject' in P. Gilroy, L. Grossberg and A. McRobbie (eds), *Without Guarantees: In Honour of Stuart Hall*, pp. 30–35. Verso, London.

Butler, J. (2004) *Undoing Gender*. Routledge, New York.

Butler, J. (2007) 'Sexual Politics, Torture and Secular Time', Public Lecture, London School of Economics, November, London.

Butler, J. (2008) 'Sexual Politics, Torture and Secular Time', British Journal of Sociology, 59(1): 1–23.

Butler, J., Laclau, E. and Zizëk, S. (2000) Contingency, Hegemony, Universality. Verso, London.

Campbell, A. (2007) The Blair Years: Extracts from the Alistair Campbell Diaries. Random House, London.

Castells, M. (1996) The Rise of the Network Society. Blackwell, Oxford.

de Certeau, M. (1984) The Practice of Everyday Life. University of California Press, Berkeley: CA.

Cerwonka, A. (2008) 'Traveling Feminist Thought: Difference and Transculturation in Central and Eastern European Feminism', Signs A Journal of Women in Culture and Society, 33 (4): 809–832.

Colebrook, C. (2002a) 'From Radical Representations to Corporeal Becomings: The Feminist Philosophy of Lloyd, Grosz and Gatens', Hypatia, 15 (2): 76–93.

Colebrook, C. (2002b) Understanding Deleuze. Allen and Unwin, Crows Nest, New South Wales.

Constantine, S. and Woodall, T. (2002) What Not To Wear. Weidenfeld & Nicolson, London.

Couldry, N. (2003) 'Media Meta-capital: Extending the Range of Bourdieu's Field Theory', Theory and Society, 32 (5): 653–678.

Crompton, R. (2002) 'Employment, Flexible Working, and the Family', British Journal of Sociology, 53 (4): 537–558.

Coward, R. (1984) Female Desire. Paladin, London.

Deleuze, G. (1986) Foucault, trans. S. Hand. University of Minnesota Press, Minneapolis.

The Depression Report (2006) London School of Economics, London.

Devine, F., Savage, M., Crompton, R. and Scott, J. (eds) (2004) Rethinking Class, Identities, Cultures and Lifestyles. Palgrave, Basingstoke.

Doane, MA. (1982) 'Film and the Masquerade: Theorising the Female Spectator', Screen, 23 (3–4): 74–87.

Driscoll, C. (2002) Girls: Feminine Adolescence in Popular Culture and Cultural Theory. Columbia University Press, New York.

Duggan, L. (2003) The Twilight of Equality?: Neoliberalism, Cultural Politics, and the Attack on Democracy. Beacon Press, Boston.

Dyer, R. (1997) White: Essays on Race and Culture. Routledge, London.

Emin, T. (1995) (dir) 'Why I Never Became a Dancer'.

Evans, M. and Thornton, C. (1989) Women and Fashion: A New Look. Quartet, London.

Faludi, S. (1992) Backlash: The Undeclared War Against Women. Vintage, London.

Foucault, M. (1984) in P. Rabinow (ed.), The Foucault Reader. Penguin, London.

Fraser, N. (1997) Justice Interruptus: Critical Reflections on the 'Postsocialist' Condition. Routledge, London.

Frey et al. (2006) 'Gender Manifesto'. Available at www.gender.de

Fuss, D. (1994) 'Fashion and the Homospectatorial Look' in S. Benstock and S. Ferriss (eds), On Fashion, pp. 211–235. Rutgers University Press, New York.

Genz, S. (2006) 'Third Way/ve: The Politics of Post-feminism', Feminist Theory, 7 (3): 333–353.

Giddens, A. (1991) Modernity and Self-identity. Polity Press, Cambridge.

Gill, R. (2003) 'From Sexual Objectification to Sexual Subjectification: The Resexualisation of Women's Bodies in the Media', Feminist Media Studies, 3 (1): 99–106.

Gill, R. (2006) Gender and the Media. Polity Press, Cambridge.

Gilroy, P. (1987) *There Ain't No Black in the Union Jack*. Hutchinson, London.

Gilroy, P. (1993) *The Black Atlantic*. Verso, London.

Gitlin, T. (1995) *The Twilight of Common Dreams: Why America is Wracked by Culture Wars*. Henry Holt and Company, New York.

Griggers, C. (1990) 'A Certain Tension in the Visual/Cultural Field: Helmut Newton, Deborah Turbeville, and the VOGUE Fashion Layout', *differences: A Journal of Feminist Cultural Studies*, 2 (2): 76–104.

Hacking, I. (2006) 'Making Up People', *London Review of Books*, 17 August.

Halberstam, J. (2005) *In a Queer Time and Place: Transgender Bodies, Subcultural Lives*. New York University Press, New York.

Hall, S. and Jefferson, T. (eds) (1976) *Resistance Through Rituals*. Hutchinson, London.

Hall, S. (1988) *The Hard Road to Renewal*. Verso, London.

Hall, S. (2003) 'New Labour's Double-shuffle', *Soundings*, 24: 10–24.

Haraway, D. (1991) *Simians, Cyborgs and Women*. Free Association Books, London.

Hardt, M. and Negri, T. (2000) *Empire*. Harvard University Press, Cambridge: MA.

Hark, S. (2005) 'Blurring Boundaries, Crossing Borders, Traversing Frontiers'. Paper delivered at workshop of the EU-funded research project Disciplinary Barriers Between the Social Sciences and the Humanities. Turko/Åbo, Finland June 9–11.

Harris, A. (2004) *Future Girl*. Routledge, London.

Hebdige, D. (1979) *Subculture: The Meaning of Style*. Methuen, London.

Hoefinger, H. (2005) Professional Girlfriends, unpublished MA Thesis, Clark University, Worcester: MA.

Hollows, J. (2003) 'Feeling Like a Domestic Goddess: Post-feminism and Cooking', *European Journal of Cultural Studies*, 6 (2): 179–202.

Kaplan, C. (1986) '*The Thorn Birds*: Fiction, Fantasy and Femininity', in V. Burgin, J. Donald and C. Kaplan (eds) *Formations of Fantasy*. Routledge, London. pp. 142–167.

Laclau, E. and Mouffe, C. (1985) *Hegemony and Socialist Strategy*. Verso, London.

de Lauretis, T. (1987) *Technologies of Gender: Essays on Theory, Film, and Fiction*. Macmillan, Basingstoke.

Lazzarato, M. (1996) 'Immaterial Labour', trans. P. Colilli and E. Emery in P. Virno and M. Hardt (eds), *Radical Thought in Italy: A Potential Politics*. University of Minnesota Press, Minneapolis.

Lewis, R. (1997) 'Looking Good: The Lesbian Gaze and Fashion Imagery', *Feminist Review*, 55: 92–110.

Lister, R. (2002) 'The Dilemmas of Pendulum Politics: Balancing Paid Work, Care and Citizenship', *Economy and Society*, 31 (4): 520–532.

McNay, L. (1999) 'Gender, Habitus and the Field: Pierre Bourdieu and the Limits of Reflexivity', *Theory, Culture & Society*, 16 (1): 95–117.

McRobbie, A. (1994) *Postmodernism and Popular Culture*. Routledge, London.

McRobbie, A. (1999a) 'All the World's a Stage, Screen or Magazine'in A. McRobbie, *In the Culture Society*, pp. 22–31. Routledge, London.

McRobbie, A. (1999b) 'Feminism v the TV Blondes', Inaugural Lecture, Goldsmiths College, University of London.

McRobbie, A. (2000a) 'Feminism and the Third Way', *Feminist Review*, 64: 97–112.

McRobbie, A. (2000b) *Feminism and Youth Culture*. Routledge, London.

McRobbie, A. (2002) 'Club to Company', *Cultural Studies*, 16 (4): 516—532.

McRobbie, A. (2003) 'Mothers and Fathers, Who Needs Them?', *Feminist Review*, 75 (1): 129–136.

McRobbie, A. (2005) *The Uses of Cultural Studies*. Sage, London.

McRobbie, A. (2008) 'Pornographic Permutations', in *The Communication Review* 11 (3): 1–11

Mohanty, C. T. (1988) 'Under Western Eyes', in *Feminist Review* no 30 Autumn: 61–88.

Mohanty, C. T. (2002) '"Under Western Eyes" Revisited: Feminist Solidarity Through Anticapitalist Struggles', *Signs: Journal of Women in Culture and Society*, 28 (2): 499–535.

Moseley, R. (2000) 'Makeover Takeover on British Television', *Screen*, 41 (3): 299–314.

Moseley, R. and Read, J. (2002) '"Having it Ally": Popular television Post-feminism', *Feminist Media Studies*, 2 (2): 231–249.

Mouffe, C. (2000) *The Democratic Paradox*. Verso, London.

Mulvey, L. (1975/1989) *Visual and Other Pleasures*. Macmillan, Basingstoke.

Nancy, J-L. (2002*) Le création du la monde ou mondialisation*. Galilée, Paris.

Nixon, S. (2003) *Advertising Cultures*. Sage, London.

Noble, D. (2000) 'Ragga Music: Dis/respecting Black Women and Dis/reputable Sexualities' in B. Hesse (ed.), *Un/settled Multiculturalisms: Diasporas, Entanglements, Transruptions*. Zed Press, London.

Nussbaum, M. (2003a) 'Capabilities as Fundamental Entitlements: Sen and Social Justice', *Feminist Economics*, 9 (2–3): 33–59.

Nussbaum, M. (2003b) 'Women's Education: A Global Challenge', *Signs: Journal of Women in Culture and Society*, 29 (2): 325–355.

Odone, C. (2000) 'If High Flyers Refuse to be Mums', *The New Statesman*, 3 April: 21.

O'Sullivan, S. (2006) 'Academy: The Production of Subjectivity', in De Baere et al. (eds), *Academy*, pp. 238–244 Revolver verlag Frankfurt.

Pateman, C. (1988) *The Sexual Contract*. Stanford University Press, Stanford: CA.

Pearson, A. (2003) *I Don't Know How She Does It*. Vintage, London.

Pratt, M. L. (1992) *Imperial Eyes: Travel Writing and Transculturation*. Routledge, New York.

Probyn, E. (1988/1997) 'New Traditionalism and Post-feminism', in C. Brunsdon, J. D'Acci and L. Spigel (eds), *Feminist Television Criticism: A Reader*, pp. 126–139. Clarendon Press, Oxford.

Probyn, E. (2000) *Carnal Appetites: Foodsexidentities*. Routledge, New York.

Rabine, L. W. (1994) 'A Woman's Two Bodies: Fashion Magazines, Consumerism, and Feminism' in S. Benstock and S. Ferriss (eds), *On Fashion*, pp. 59–76. Rutgers University Press, New York.

Readings, B. (1996) *The University in Ruins*. Harvard University Press, Cambridge: MA.

Riviére, J. (1929/1986) 'Womanliness as a Masquerade', in V. Burgin, J. Donald and C. Kaplan (eds), *Formations of Fantasy*, pp. 35–44. Methuen, London.

Rose, N. (1999a) *Powers of Freedom*. Cambridge University Press, Cambridge.

Rose, N. (1999b) 'Inventiveness in Politics', *Economy and Society*, 28 (3): 467–493.

Rose, T. (1994) *Black Noise: Rap Music and Black Culture in Contemporary America*. Wesleyan University Press, Hanover and London.

Rossiter, N. (2006) *Organised Networks: Media Theory, Creative Labour, New Institutions*. NAi Publication's, Rotterdam.

Safia Mirza, H. (1992) *Young, Female and Black*. Routledge, London.

Scharff, C. (2008) 'Perspectives on Feminist (dis-)identification in the German and British Contexts: A Performative Approach', forthcoming, *Feminist Review*.

Skeggs, B. (1997) *Formations of Class and Gender*. Sage, London.

Skeggs, B. (2004) *Class, Self, Culture*. Routledge, London.

Silverman, K. (1994) 'Fragments of a Fashionable Discourse' in S. Benstock and S. Ferriss (eds), On Fashion, pp. 183–197. Rutgers University Press, New York.

Smith, A-M. (1998) *Laclau and Mouffe: The Radical Democratic Imaginary*. Routledge, London.

Spivak, G. C. (1988) *In Other Worlds: Essays in Cultural Politics*. Routledge, New York.

Spivak, G. C. (1993) *Outside in the Teaching Machine*. Routledge, New York.

Spivak, G. C. (1998) 'Foucault and Najibullah' in K. L. Komer and R. Shideler (eds), *Lyrical Symbols and Narrative Transformations: Essays in Honour of Ralph Freedman*, pp. 218–235. Camden House, Columbia: SC.

Spivak, G. C. (1999) *A Critique of Postcolonial Reason*. Harvard University Press. Cambridge: MA.

Spivak, G. C. (2000) 'Thinking Cultural Questions in "Pure" Literary Terms' in P. Gilroy, L. Grossberg and A. McRobbie (eds), *Without Guarantees: In Honour of Stuart Hall*, pp. 335–358. Verso, London.

Spivak, C. G. (2002) 'Resident Alien?' in D. T. Goldberg and A. Quayson (eds), *Relocating Postcolonialism*, pp. 47–65. Blackwell, Oxford.

Spivak, C. G. (2005) 'What Is Gender? Where is Europe? Walking with Balibar', The Fifth Ursula Hirschmann Annual Lecture on Gender and Europe, European University Institute, 21 April, Florence.

Springer, K. (2002) 'Third Wave Black Feminism?', *Signs: Journal of Women in Culture and Society*, 27 (4): 1059–1082.

Stacey, J. (1986) 'Are Feminists Afraid to Leave the Home?' in J. Mitchell and A. Oakley (eds), *What is Feminism?*, pp. 219–248. Blackwell, Oxford.

Stallybrass, P. and White, A. (1986) *The Politics and Poetics of Transgression*. Methuen, London.

Stuart, A. (1990) 'Feminism: Dead or Alive?' in J. Rutherford (ed.), *Identity: Community Culture, Difference*. Lawrence & Wishart, London.

Tasker, Y. and Negra, D. (eds) (2007) *Interrogating Post-feminism*. Duke University Press, Chapel Hill: NC.

Trinh, T. M. (1989) *Woman, Native, Other*. Indiana University Press, Bloomington.

Virno, P. (2004) *A Grammar of the Multitude*, trans. I. Bertoletti, J. Cascaito and A. Casson. Semiotext(e), New York.

Walby, S. (1997) *Gender Transformations*. Routledge, London.

Walby, S. (1999) 'Introduction' in S. Walby (ed.), *New Agendas for Women*. Macmillan, Basingstoke.

Walby, S. (2002) 'Feminism in a Global Age', *Economy and Society*, 31 (4): 533–557.

Walby, S. (2005a) 'Gender Mainstreaming: Productive Tensions in Theory and Practice', *Social Politics: International Studies in Gender, State & Society*, 12 (3): 321–343.

Walby, S. (2005b) 'Introduction: Comparative Gender Mainstreaming in a Global Era', *International Feminist Journal of Politics*, 7 (4): 453–470.

Walkerdine, W., Lucey, H. and Melody, J. (2001) *Growing up Girl: Psychosocial Explorations of Gender and Class*. Palgrave, Basingstoke.

Walsh, H. (2004) *Brass*. Canongate, Edinburgh.

Walter, N. (1998) *The New Feminism*. Virago, London.

Ware, V. (1992) *Beyond the Pale: White Women, Racism and History*. Verso, London.

Weldon, F. (1997) *Big Women*. Flamingo, London.

Williams, F. (2002) 'The Presence of Feminism in the Future of Welfare', *Economy and Society*, 31 (4): 502–533.

Williams, L. R. (2005) *The Erotic Thriller in Contemporary Cinema*. Edinburgh University Press, Edinburgh.

Williamson, J. (1978) *Decoding Advertisements*. Marion Boyars, London.

Williamson, J. (1986) *Consuming Passions: The Dynamics of Popular Culture*. Marion Boyars, London.

Wittel, A. (2001) 'Toward A Network Sociality', *Theory, Culture & Society*, 18 (6): 51–76.

Wolf, N. (1991) *The Beauty Myth*. Vintage, London.

Young, L. (2000) 'How Do We Look? Unfixing the Singular Black (Female) Subject' in P. Gilroy, L. Grossberg and A. McRobbie (eds), *Without Guarantees: In Honour of Stuart Hall*, pp. 416–431. Verso, London.

INDEX